HOW
BUSINESS
WORKS

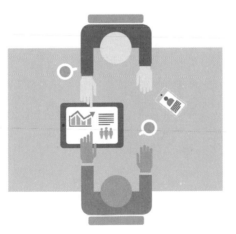

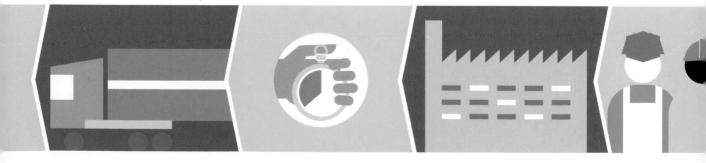

HOW BUSINESS WORKS

A GRAPHIC GUIDE TO BUSINESS SUCCESS

DK Penguin Random House

Senior editor	Georgina Palffy
Project art editor	Saffron Stocker
Editors	Anna Fischel, Alison Sturgeon, Suhel Ahmed, Hannah Bowen, Joanna Edwards, Alex Beeden
Designers	Natalie Clay, Stephen Bere, Phil Gamble, Vanessa Hamilton, Jemma Westing
US senior editor	Margaret Parrish
US editor	Christine Heilman
Managing editors	Stephanie Farrow, Gareth Jones
Senior managing art editor	Lee Griffiths
Publisher	Liz Wheeler
Deputy art director	Karen Self
Publishing director	Jonathan Metcalf
Art director	Phil Ormerod
Senior jacket designer	Mark Cavanagh
Jacket assistant	Claire Gell
Jacket design manager	Sophia MTT
Pre-production producers	Ben Marcus, Nikoleta Parasaki
Producer	Christine Ni

First American edition 2015

Published in the United States by
DK Publishing, 345 Hudson Street
New York, New York 10014

A Penguin Random House Company

15 16 17 18 19 10 9 8 7 6 5 4 3 2 1
001—196402—Mar/2015

Published in Great Britain by Dorling Kindersley Limited

A catalog record for this book is
available from the Library of Congress.

ISBN: 978-1-4654-2979-7

DK books are available at special discounts when purchased in
bulk for sales promotions, premiums, fund-raising, or educational use.
For details, contact: DK Publishing Special Markets, 345 Hudson Street,
New York, New York 10014 or SpecialSales@dk.com.

Printed in China

A WORLD OF IDEAS:
SEE ALL THERE IS TO KNOW
www.dk.com

Contents

HOW SALES AND MARKETING WORKS 176

HOW OPERATIONS AND PRODUCTION WORK 268

Contributors

Dr. Julian Sims (consultant editor) entered academia after a successful career in industry in the US and UK. He is a lecturer in the Department of Management at Birkbeck, University of London, UK; a Chartered Accountant (CPA Aus); and a Chartered Information Technology Practitioner (CITP). His work is widely published in academic journals.

Philippa Anderson is a business writer and communications consultant, who has advised multinationals including 3M, Anglo American, and Coca-Cola. She collaborated with Lord Browne, former CEO of BP, on his memoir, *Beyond Business*, and was a contributor to DK's *The Business Book*.

Alexandra Black studied business communications before writing for financial newspaper group Nikkei Inc. in Japan. While in Tokyo, she was an editor at the Risk Analysis division of investment bank JP Morgan. Now based in Cambridge, UK, she covers subjects as varied as business, technology, and fashion. She was a contributor to DK's *The Business Book*.

Joe Stanley-Smith is a reporter at the *International Tax Review* in London, UK, where he specializes in indirect tax and tax disputes. He graduated in journalism with a business specialty from Kingston University, UK, and has previously worked in social media and local news.

Paul McDougall (US/Canada writer) is Deputy Technology Editor for the *International Business Times*. He has written for *Scientific American*, *InformationWeek*, *SHAPE* magazine, and others. A native of Toronto, Canada, he currently resides in New York City.

Introduction

The term "business" refers to an organization or commercial enterprise engaged in producing and trading goods and services for money. We can trace the origins of business to the very foundations of human society. When *Homo sapiens* evolved, mankind left behind the nomadic hunter-gatherer lifestyle to become farmers. This allowed for specialization of work, where individuals would become skilled at specific tasks to serve a particular community need. Over time, this enabled more complex goods and services to be produced and traded, in order to provide for all members of society. Thus, human society has been engaging in "business" for thousands of years.

Today the world of business is inescapable—businesses are no longer just local providers of goods and services, but extend to vast corporate enterprises operating on a global scale. For governments to function and economies to flourish, a successful and thriving business sector is essential. Whether businesses are small or large, public or private, for-profit or nonprofit, they each play a key role in supporting the global economy, and together they form the backbone of the modern world. Business underpins every aspect of the world we live in today, and understanding how it works is the key to understanding society.

This book explains the complex world of business in a simple and graphic way. It examines every aspect of how a business works, including forming a company, raising capital, product development and marketing, management strategies, tracking revenue, financial reporting, and legal, social, and environmental responsibilities. Through visual explanations as well as real-life examples to make even the most complex concept immediately accessible, *How Business Works* offers a clear understanding of what business is all about and how business, in its many forms, shapes modern society.

HOW
COMPANIES
WORK

Business ownership ❯ Start-ups
Buying and selling business ❯ Who's who
Corporate structure ❯ Human resources

Business ownership

Every type of business has to choose an ownership structure. Although there are variations globally, most countries offer similar types of legal entities, from a single-person private enterprise to a massive organization trading on a stock exchange. There are three key considerations: how big the venture is expected to grow; the complexity of financial recording, management, and reporting that the proprietor is willing to take on; and the amount of liability the owner is willing to accept.

Small and simple

❯ A sole proprietorship or partnership is simple to set up and requires little capital.

❯ One or more owners conduct business as a legal entity.

❯ Owners are personally liable for business debts. *(See pp.14–15.)*

Private companies

❯ More complex to set up and run, a private company is a legal entity separate from its owner or owners.

❯ The company structure means the owners are not usually personally liable for business debts.

❯ Private companies are owned by shareholders, often the company's managers. *See pp.16–19.*

Public companies

❯ Companies that go public are large businesses, and they have many legal and financial reporting obligations.

❯ The general public and other institutions can buy shares in public companies.

❯ The public company structure is good for a major capital injection, allowing the business to expand. *See pp.16–19.*

7%
of global economic activity **is accounted for by the world's 100 largest companies**

NAMING A COMPANY

Do's

❯ **Use a domain suggestion tool** to search for available internet domain names and work back from there.

❯ **Be descriptive** so potential customers instantly grasp the nature of the business.

❯ **Say the name out loud**—it may come across differently from the written word. The goal is that people can search and find it, especially online, just from hearing it.

❯ **Keep it short** and simple and avoid puns.

Don'ts

❯ **Include your name**—if the venture fails, your name will be associated with it.

❯ **Ape competition**, because if your name is unique, you have a better chance of topping search-engine results. If your name is similar to that of competitors, customers can't distinguish.

❯ **Spend time** thinking of a name until your product and brand is finalized. Get the product right first and the name will follow naturally.

Multinationals

❯ For both growth and flexibility, multinationals have operations in various countries.

❯ Multinationals can save money by setting up operations in countries where costs are cheaper.

❯ Foreign branches can adapt to the local market and also find new markets. *See pp.20–21.*

Franchises

❯ In this model, a business (the franchisor) authorizes a franchisee to set up a branch under its name, in return for a fee.

❯ The franchisor needs less capital than it otherwise would to develop a business.

❯ The franchisee takes on a known, successful business model and name, so minimizing risk. *See pp.22–23.*

Nonprofit sector

❯ Common nonprofit organizations include charities and trade associations.

❯ Their organizational structure is similar to that of a company.

❯ They may generate substantial sums of money, but plow it back into beneficial causes rather than distributing profits. *See pp.24–25.*

Sole proprietorships and partnerships

The simplest business structures are those formed by one person as a sole proprietor, or by two or more people as a partnership, for commercial activity. Many cost little to set up and some are easy to run.

How it works

Many businesses start out as the most basic unit—either a sole proprietor or a partnership. A sole proprietor is an individual who is the only owner of the business. This structure is easy to set up and there are no extra taxes to pay, unlike with a company. Instead, the sole proprietor files a personal tax return. There is risk attached, though. A sole proprietor has unlimited liability, so if the business fails, the owner must personally pay debts. Partnerships have more than one owner, and each can be held liable for the whole debt of the business in case of failure.

Pros and cons

Both sole proprietorships and partnership structures are excellent for anyone starting out or running a small business—as long as the business stays out of debt: owners are personally liable for business debts.

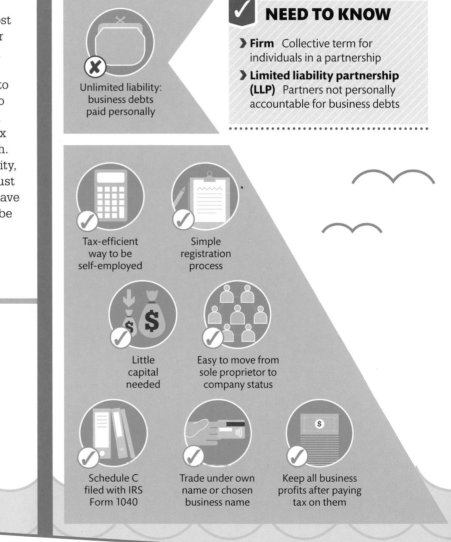

Unlimited liability: business debts paid personally

NEED TO KNOW

> **Firm** Collective term for individuals in a partnership
> **Limited liability partnership (LLP)** Partners not personally accountable for business debts

Tax-efficient way to be self-employed

Simple registration process

Little capital needed

Easy to move from sole proprietor to company status

Schedule C filed with IRS Form 1040

Trade under own name or chosen business name

Keep all business profits after paying tax on them

Sole proprietorship
Working alone requires only simple administration and relatively few start-up costs.

FROM INDIVIDUAL TO MULTINATIONAL

Sole proprietorships and partnerships may grow into global names.

❯ **Richard Branson** Sole proprietorship that expanded into Virgin empire

❯ **Steve Jobs and Steve Wozniak** Partnership that created Apple brand

❯ **Bill Hewlett and David Packard** Partners who founded HP technology

❯ **John D. Rockefeller, William Rockefeller, Henry Flagler, Jabez A. Bostwick, Samuel Andrews, Stephen Harkness** Partnership that grew into Standard Oil corporation

66%
of EU private sector jobs **are in** small **or** medium-size enterprises

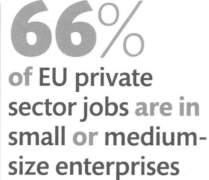

WHEN TO MOVE TO COMPANY STATUS

If the need for capital increases (and potential debts grow), forming a company may be beneficial. *See pp.16–17.*

Profit and control of the business shared

Allows for specialization by each partner

Option to set up a limited liability partnership

Furnish Schedule K-1 (IRS Form 1065) to partners

More partners mean more capital and expansion

New partners bring new business skills

If partner leaves, new partnership needed

Each partner pays tax on own portion of profit

Partnership

Like sole proprietors, partners file only personal tax returns and are liable for business debts.

Corporations

A corporation is a business entity considered distinct from its employees and shareholders. The primary purpose of forming a corporation is for shareholders to avoid personal liability.

How it works

A corporate structure protects management and workers in the case of litigation or other claims. It is, however, a more complex structure and subject to greater regulation than the simpler business entities of sole proprietorships and partnerships. A corporation is owned by one or more stockholders, and is managed by a board of directors and run by the company's officers, who are appointed by the board of directors. The company retains any profit made and may distribute it to the stockholders in the form of dividends. Corporate and securities laws regulate the sale of shares. Legally, the stockholders cannot be held liable for the company's actions and debts.

Types of incorporation

Anyone who operates a business may incorporate by registering articles of incorporation. General incorporation (C Corporation) is the most common structure. An S Corporation, created through IRS tax election, provides limited liability; it is favored by small businesses because it combines the advantages of sole proprietorship, partnership, and the corporate forms of business structure. Nonprofits can also incorporate.

Publicly traded company

A publicly traded company is usually a large business—such as a technology company—with stock traded on a stock exchange, such as NASDAQ.

✓ NEED TO KNOW

> **Stockholder** An individual, group, or organization that owns shares in a company
> **Doing business as (DBA)** Operational rather than company name
> **Professional corporation (PC)** Corporate form used for primarily for doctors, lawyers, and similar professional service providers

Public characteristics

> Issues securities through an Initial Public Offering (IPO)
> Can sell future equity stakes
> Has greater access to financing
> Must meet reporting requirements set out by Securities and Exchange Commission (SEC)
> Reduced control for initial owners

LIMITED LIABILITY COMPANIES IN THE US

A limited liability company (LLC) is a hybrid between a corporation and a partnership. The upside of an LLC is that it offers many of the advantages of a corporation, but is cheaper to create and maintain. Taxation rules vary, depending on the Articles of Organization of the LLC. Laws also differ from state to state. A limited liability company is an "LLC," not an "Inc." or "Corp."

Corporation

Corporations operate as legally and financially independent entities. They may be publicly traded or privately held.

CANADIAN COMPANIES

Businesses in Canada can be sole proprietorships, partnerships, or corporations. A business can also be run as a cooperative, a business that is owned and controlled by its members. Canadian companies must register in the province or territory in which they are domiciled.

Privately held

In a privately held company, a limited group of private stock owners controls the company. These companies do not offer shares to the general public on stock exchanges.

56.5%
of UK limited companies have employees; the remaining 43.5% are single-member companies (SMCs)

Private characteristics

❯ May issue stock and have shareholders. Shares, however, do not trade on public exchanges

❯ Management is not required to file disclosure statements with the SEC

❯ Dependant on private funding

Private and public companies

While the owner-shareholders of a private company may buy and sell their shares privately (usually with director approval), any investor in the financial market can trade the shares of a public company.

How it works

Although most of the world's companies are set up as private, public companies are seen as more prestigious and profitable. For business ventures requiring large amounts of capital, a public company offers greater opportunity for raising funds, since shares can be sold to public investors to generate cash. Private companies must rely on private investors or use the capital investment of their owners. Public companies are subject to more stringent legal controls than private ones, and are expected to disclose financial details.

27 million
the number of companies in the US, fewer than 1% of which are public

FAMOUS PRIVATE COMPANIES

> **Mars** Confectionery and pet food; third-largest private US company

> **Rolex** Swiss-based English company making status-symbol watches

> **LEGO®** Danish company producing household-name toy bricks

> **Hearst Corporation** Mass media multinational based in New York City

> **IKEA** Swedish retailer registered in Netherlands selling flat-pack furniture

> **PwC** Largest professional services network

Differences between private and public companies

Private company directors have to weigh up the potential capital increase of floating on the stock exchange against the legal red tape aimed at protecting public shareholders.

Private

Directors
Usually control all of the shares.

Reporting
In the US, no disclosure is required outside the company; in the UK, it is mandatory to file accounts at Companies House.

Shareholders and management
Shareholders are often actively involved in management so decisions can be made quickly.

Financing
Company must rely on private investment, which is often harder to attract because there are fewer financial details available.

Valuation
Value of the company is more likely to fluctuate; it is more difficult to assess because there are fewer available financial details.

Size
Number of shareholders is limited, usually to fewer than 2,000.

$55 billion

the amount raised on 141 IPOs at the NYSE in 2013

Public

Directors
Not necessarily shareholders.

Reporting
Companies have a legal obligation to disclose accounts and submit regular financial reports.

Shareholders and management
Clear boundary is drawn between the role of shareholders and management; may lead to a conflict of interest.

Financing
Can tap financial markets to raise capital by selling stock or bonds.

Valuation
Value of the company is easier to assess, from the trading price of shares and financial statements.

Size
Number of shareholders is unlimited.

GOING PUBLIC

There are legal requirements at each stage of converting a company from private to public, such as voting in a board of directors and deciding on a new name.

Choose board members
Usually at least three directors to allow future board decisions to be made with only two members present (representing a majority)

Inform staff
Must notify in writing anyone with an interest (including employees and proposed board members) that company intends to go public

Vote for conversion
Board meeting held to vote in favor of changing company's Articles of Incorporation (specifying private or public company)

Register company
Documents setting out board resolutions sent to Secretary of State, who issues certificate declaring the company is public

Make public announcement
Press releases issued, events for business held, and emails sent to inform contacts of change

✓ NEED TO KNOW

> **Unquoted/unlisted company** Another term for a private company

> **Initial public offering (IPO)** Stock-market launch

> **Secondary stock offering** Second-round sale of shares to raise more capital

> **Ticker symbols** Unique code assigned to publicly traded companies and used by stock exchanges

Multinationals

A multinational corporation has business operations in more than one country. It usually starts as a national company and sets up subsidiary (branch) companies abroad for production and sales.

How it works

Multinationals have several goals: to increase revenue by finding new markets; to streamline operations and production by taking advantage of global locations with lower labor and/or transport costs; and to adapt to local cultural/market differences. A company may achieve such goals by outsourcing (using external suppliers) or offshoring (relocating functions). Companies may also insource (move operations in-house) to rightsource (find a good balance).

Case study: mapping a multinational

Sportswear company Nike has successfully spread around the globe from its corporate base in the US. It has manufacturing functions where technical expertise maximizes efficiency and keeps costs down; distribution hubs in strategic locations; marketing and retail departments in countries where it is establishing local markets; and call centers where they are cost-effective.

GLOBAL VS. MULTINATIONAL

A global company has facilities in different countries but operates as a single corporate culture with common processes. A multinational has facilities in different countries but each functions as its own entity, adapting locally, with little communication between geographic divisions.

Global

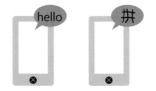

Apple is an example of a global company—the product is essentially the same except for a language change.

Multinational

McDonald's is a multinational—the product changes to suit the market. For example, it serves a shrimp burger in Japan and chicken rice porridge in Malaysia.

United Kingdom
London

One of many country HQs in major European cities, the London office serves the UK market. Nike also has a product creation center in Italy.

 Regional HQ Management and core admin functions

 Marketing UK campaigns and merchandising

United States
Beaverton, Oregon

Senior management are located at the company's corporate base, or "campus", its center for decision-making on global strategy, design, and marketing, and core functions.

 World HQ Management, finance, legal, IT, and admin

 Global marketing Branding and marketing

 R and D Sport research lab and design facilities

 Retail Online sales and stores across North America

Memphis, Tennessee

 Distribution Hi-tech hub in location with good links

The Netherlands
Hilversum

Based in a central location, a European headquarters supports operations across Western, Central, and Eastern Europe, and is close to the company's European distribution center in Belgium.

 European HQ Management, finance, legal, IT, and admin

 Design HQ for global soccer apparel business

 Retail Online sales and stores across Europe

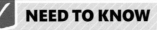

✓ NEED TO KNOW

❱ **Transnational corporation**
Similar to a multinational but does not identify itself with any particular parent nation

❱ **Platform corporation**
Multinationals that do not manufacture, but outsource products they have designed

China
Shanghai

The company's second-largest and fastest-growing market, China is also a major manufacturing base due to local expertise and low production costs.

 Chinese HQ Operations and core support functions

 Manufacturing Sportswear factories and innovation hubs

 Marketing Campaigns for the Chinese market

 Retail Continually expanding retail network for sports brand

Japan
Tokyo

Most manufacturing is based in the Asia-Pacific region, benefiting from expertise and lower wages. Regional offices in 13 countries also support production and retail.

 Regional HQ Core operations and marketing

Manufacturing Sites in several countries

Brazil
São Paulo

Operations, marketing, and distribution for the Central and South American market are based in Brazil, with offices and retail outlets in all major countries.

 Central and South American HQ Operational center

 Distribution Hub for retail stores across the continent

India
Bangalore

Call centers draw on a supply of English-speakers on lower wages.

 Customer support Complaints and returns

Franchises

The franchise is a business model in which an independent entity—the franchisee—is entitled to set up a branch of an established brand. There are advantages for both parties.

How it works

Rather than developing an original business idea, the franchisee pays for the right to represent an existing, successful brand in a particular location. The size of a franchise can vary from a single unit—one outlet only—to an area development in which the franchisee takes on the option to represent the brand through several branches in a city or region. The franchiser can develop the business with modest capital outlay while the franchisee takes on a proven business model and brand name, so everyone reaps the benefits.

> ## "I put the hamburger on the assembly line."
> Ray Kroc, founder of McDonald's

✓ NEED TO KNOW

❯ **Franchise disclosure documents (FDD)** Pre-agreement information

❯ **Microfranchising** Support and training for small-scale businesses in the developing world

❯ **International Franchise Association (IFA)** The oldest and largest franchise organization

Three types of franchise

The franchiser's level of control varies from managing the contracts for the entire supply chain to input on every detail down to the last French fry. In a product franchise, the franchiser lends its trademark and brand but not an entire business system.

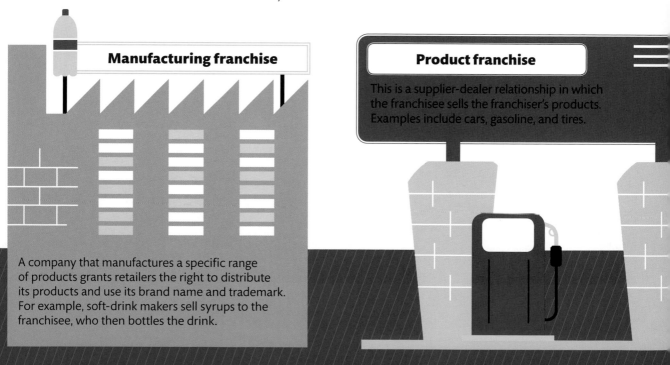

Manufacturing franchise

A company that manufactures a specific range of products grants retailers the right to distribute its products and use its brand name and trademark. For example, soft-drink makers sell syrups to the franchisee, who then bottles the drink.

Product franchise

This is a supplier-dealer relationship in which the franchisee sells the franchiser's products. Examples include cars, gasoline, and tires.

TOP 10

Fastest-growing franchises worldwide

1. **Subway** fast-food sandwich outlets
2. **McDonald's** fast-food outlets
3. **KFC** fast-food outlets
4. **Burger King** fast-food outlets
5. **7-Eleven** convenience stores
6. **Pizza Hut** restaurants
7. **GNC** health and beauty products
8. **Wyndham Hotel Group** hotels
9. **Dunkin' Donuts** bakery/coffee shops
10. **Dia** grocery stores

CASE STUDY

Business-format franchise: fast-food outlets

The business-format franchise, in which a franchisee takes on a whole blueprint for running a business as well as the product itself, was pioneered in the US in the late 1940s.

Fast-food outlets were a new concept at the time and were generating great demand. To increase the rate of expansion, these original fast-food entrepreneurs developed a franchise system under which the franchisee was contractually obliged to run the outlet according to strict guidelines.

A limited and uniform menu was the key to the success of these franchises. The consistency of the menu, service, and surroundings helped to establish a strong brand identity, since customers were assured that the product and experience would be the same anywhere in the country.

McDonald's is the most successful example, collecting an estimated 11.5 percent royalty fee from its 31,000 franchises worldwide.

Business-format franchise

The most common type, this has high input from the franchiser including brand name and trademark, training, store identity, marketing plan, and company culture. The franchisee buys supplies from the franchiser and pays fees and royalties. Fast-food outlets are typical business-format franchises.

Not-for-profit

Some organizations are run not for the benefit of shareholders, but for the benefit of their members or an external community or charity. Unlike conventional businesses, profit is not the goal.

How it works

Organizations that do not intend to generate profit for their shareholders, are self-governing, and committed to a common cause come under the broad umbrella of not-primarily-for profit, not-for-profit, and nonprofit entities. On this spectrum, cooperatives may disburse profits to members, but charities are strictly nonprofit. Although their goals differ, not-for-profits have a similar type of company status and structure to businesses.

9.2%
of all wages and salaries paid in the US come from the not-for-profit sector

The not-for-profit universe

There are many forms of not-for-profit organization (NPO). Joel L. Fleishman, Professor of Public Policy and Law at Duke University, has characterized the not-for-profit sector as a universe that embraces all NPOs, whatever their mission.

Cooperative
Owned by members; can benefit from profit; clear ethos of pursuing common economic, social, or cultural goals; one member, one vote

Private foundation
Similar to a charity but funded by one source, not the public; generates revenue from investments; makes grants to other charitable bodies

Fraternal organization
Based on common interests or beliefs such as social or academic interest or a benevolent cause; Freemasons and college fraternities are both examples

THRIVING SECTOR

Despite being NPOs, many cooperatives and mutuals have a sizable annual turnover (gross revenue transacted).

❯ **Japan** Zen Noh cooperative: $53 billion
❯ **France** Crédit Agricole Group of cooperatives and mutuals: $32 billion

❯ **US** Nationwide Mutual Assurance: $23 billion
❯ **Germany** Edeka Zentrale AG cooperative: $16 billion
❯ **UK** Co-operative Group: $16 billion
❯ **Spain** Mondragon cooperative: $14 billion

✓ NEED TO KNOW

❯ **Philanthropic sector** Alternative umbrella term for the not-for-profit sector or universe

❯ **501(c) corporation** An IRS-recognized nonprofit; one of several types of nonprofits, organized for purposes specifically designated in the Internal Revenue Code

❯ **Associated charity** An organization related to a main charity that takes on a particular aspect of the charity's work

❯ **Payouts** 5 percent of assets that private foundations must pay out each year; no such requirements exist for public charities

NOT-FOR-PROFIT STRUCTURE

Chairman coordinates work of the directors.

Board of directors are usually unpaid; may also be called the board of trustees.

Committees formed by board members carry out specific tasks such as fundraising.

Administration staff often include a proportion of voluntary workers.

Nongovernmental organization (NGO)
Funded by government or by international donor agencies such as the World Health Organization (WHO); operate independently

Mutual
Raises funds from members (usually customers); often takes the form of financial institutions; profits reinvested in the mutual or to sustain or grow the organization

Chamber of commerce
Chambers from various regions gather to promote trade, investment, and cooperation; usually funded by subscriptions from local businesses

Charity
Must be registered as a charity; tax exempt; all resources must be devoted to the charity's stated charitable activities; may be organized as a trust, corporation, or association

Social enterprise
May sell goods or services to fund community projects; any surplus revenue reinvested in the enterprise for the community

Start-ups

A start-up is a new business in the early stages of development and operation, during which an entrepreneur or founding group comes up with an idea for a product or service, researches it, develops a business plan, raises funds, and launches with the goal of rapid growth. Registering intellectual property (IP)—a unique creation, not just an idea—to protect it is an important stage of the start-up process. Protection includes trademarks, patents, and copyright.

The early days

Before a company is fully developed, with a working business model, it is known as a start-up. The start-up evolves from an entrepreneur, or group of entrepreneurs, with an idea or invention. It can take a few years to turn the initial concept or prototype into a viable, profitable venture, so the start-up founder tries to attract support and financial backing to achieve rapid growth. During this phase, which can take anything from a few months to several years, the business changes quickly.

476,000
new businesses are started every month in the US

✓ NEED TO KNOW

Internal start-ups Start-ups that originate from inside a large organization

Patent trolls Companies or individuals who buy up the patents of failed start-ups and attempt to collect licensing fees from potential infringers of the patent

INTELLECTUAL PROPERTY (IP) VALUE

The term "start-up" became commonplace during the dot.com boom of the late 1990s, when thousands of entrepreneurs with web-based products and services found funding, many on the strength of their intellectual property alone. Giants Google and Amazon both started up at that time. Since then, technology businesses have become one of the most talked-about start-up types. Their value is often based 100 percent on intellectual property.

TM
©
®

The big idea

Consider the IP
- Register IP.
- Find a name.
- Buy a domain.
- Research the market.

Launch
- Win? Lose?
- Research indicates that, in most Western countries, 80–90 percent of start-ups fail.

Choose a start-up type?
- With a social conscience?
- Primed to grow big?
- To fit lifestyle?

See pp.30–31.

Prepare to launch
- Plan a marketing campaign.
- Run a test launch and refine message and offer.

See pp.196–197.

Make a business plan
- Explain how the business will make money.
- Describe the unique aspects of the business.
- Set out how much money the business will need and how much it will make.

See pp.32–33.

Find funding
- Invest savings
- Ask friends and family.
- Take out a bank loan.
- Seek venture capital.
- Try crowdfunding.

See pp.34–37.

Seek help
- Join a business accelerator.
- Enter a business incubator.
- Go it alone.
- Find an investor.

See pp.38–39.

40%
the sales growth achieved by online start-ups in France, in 2011–2012

Start-ups from concept to launch

A new business can be described as a start-up in the early phases of its launch, when an entrepreneur comes up with the idea for a product or service, and develops the concept into something that will sell.

How it works

The idea is just the start. Next comes the process of expanding the concept into a viable business. Specialized help may be needed in some areas—hiring a website and logo designer, for example, and an accountant to advise on the best structure and financial setup. What the business and product or service are called can make or break the start-up, so it is worth spending some time doing online research to make sure no one else is using an intended name, especially in a negative context. Location is another consideration with significant cost implications. It may be possible to create a virtual office and work from home. Finding premises is an extra stage, but the goal at start-up is to keep costs low.

START

Come up with a good idea
Develop a product, or an idea for a product.

Register IP
For an invention or innovation, register your intellectual property (IP).

Set up an online presence
Register the domain name and set up web hosting.

Decide on a name
Check to determine whether your proposed name is available; check that the domain name is available; search online for competitors with similar names.

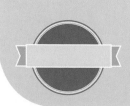

Create a look
Design a logo and visual identity for the business.

Make a website
Build a website. Research search engine optimization (SEO) words to use on it (*see pp.230–231*).

START-UP STRUCTURE

Business	Pros	Cons
Sole proprietorship	Low cost, easy to set up, minimum of financial reporting	May be seen to lack credibility; challenge to raise capital
Partnership	More input, more potential to raise funding	Harder to dissolve in case of failure; partners liable for debts
Limited company	Low risk of personal liability; tax benefits; dividends can supplement wages	More financial reporting necessary; more paperwork
Limited liability partnership	Personal liability of partners is limited to the amount they invest in the business	Must file annual accounts; can be dissolved once a partner leaves

75%
of all US start-ups failed between 2004 and 2010

Research market
Study your proposed target market and potential competitors, and evaluate the viability of the idea.

Decide structure
Choose a business structure that suits your initial needs, but also allows flexibility for growth.

Obtain backing funds
Consider a business incubator if the business requires large-scale support.

Devise a plan
Draw up a plan (see pp.32–33), including your goals, mission statement, and key financial information.

Set up finances
Include an accounting and cash-flow system, sales tax if applicable, and bank account.

Start marketing
Plan a marketing campaign. Run a test and make any refinements to the message or strategy.

LAUNCH

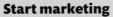

Types of start-up

Entrepreneurs go into businesses for many reasons. Some start-up decisions are based on personal ethos and conviction, while others are founded firmly on the desire to make money.

How it works

Not all start-ups fit the same mold. Although they often follow a similar process in their initial evolution, they are as varied in type as the personalities behind them. Start-ups can broadly be divided into those that are aimed from the outset to be large ventures within a corporate environment, and those intended to work on a more personal scale to suit the lives and passions of individuals.

Lifestyle

Motivation
Working is a passion

Example
Ex-athlete starts fitness coaching business

Type of funding
Self, friends, peers, bank loan

Social start-ups

Motivation
Making a difference

Example
Malaria blood-test kit for smartphone

Type of funding
Community, charity, government, donation

173%
the projected revenue increase over three years for mobile gaming start-ups

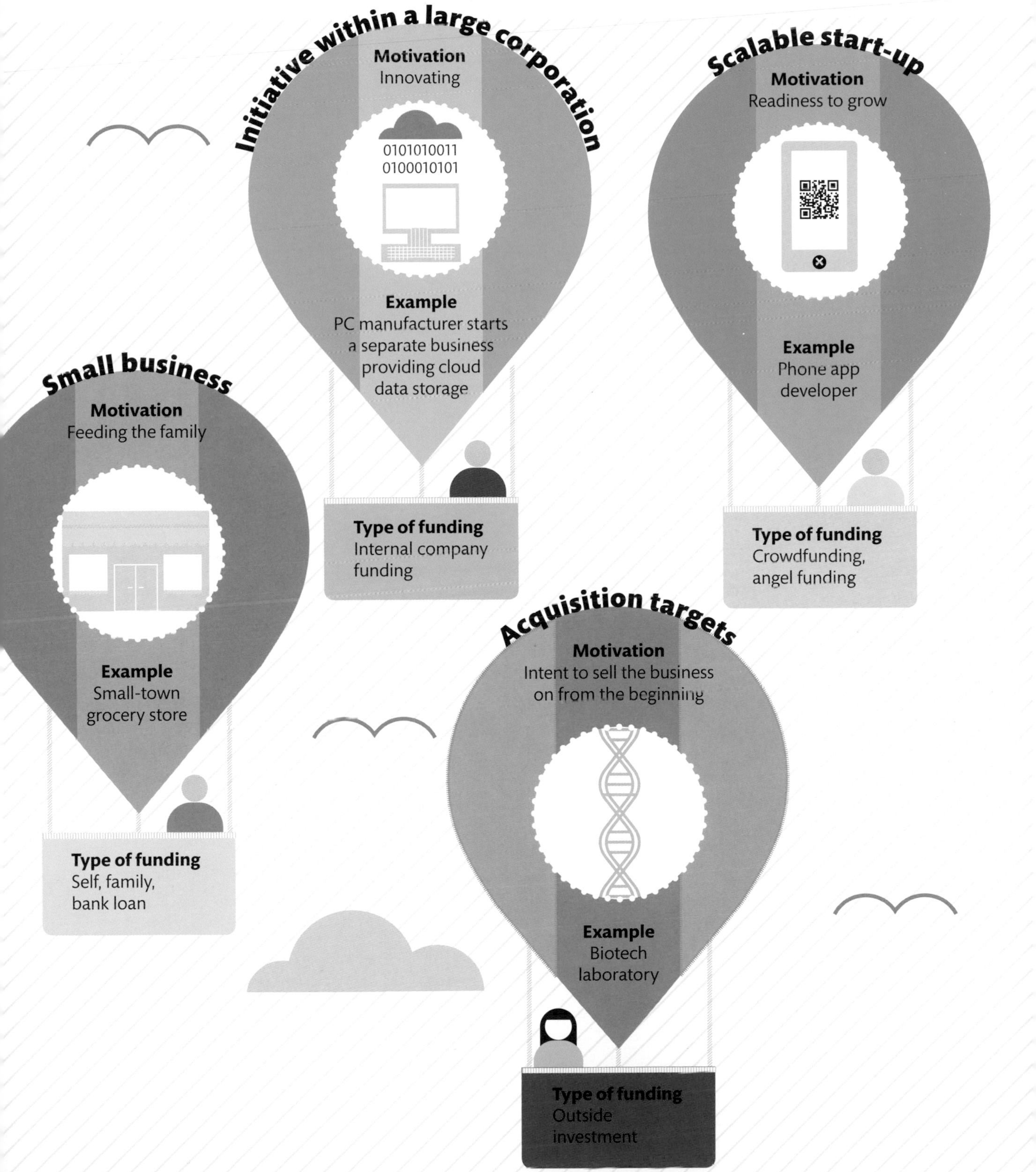

Initiative within a large corporation

Motivation
Innovating

0101010011
0100010101

Example
PC manufacturer starts
a separate business
providing cloud
data storage

Type of funding
Internal company
funding

Scalable start-up

Motivation
Readiness to grow

Example
Phone app
developer

Type of funding
Crowdfunding,
angel funding

Small business

Motivation
Feeding the family

Example
Small-town
grocery store

Type of funding
Self, family,
bank loan

Acquisition targets

Motivation
Intent to sell the business
on from the beginning

Example
Biotech
laboratory

Type of funding
Outside
investment

Business plans

Writing a business plan is one of the most important steps in developing a start-up. The plan sets out the new business's goals, market analysis, and projected income and profit.

How it works

Before a start-up entrepreneur can write a business plan, they need to have done enough research to identify a clear opportunity in the market for the product or service, and to define how the proposed new business will be uniquely positioned to capture that market, given the services or products offered. An outline of existing finances and an accurate projection of sales and profit are essential components, especially if seeking external funding.

Key elements

Preparing a business plan can take several weeks, and it is worth doing thoroughly. It is a vital document for securing funding, so the financial forecast must be both realistic and accurate. If showing it to others, pare the executive summary down to two pages, write it in plain English, and explain any technical terms.

Start-ups in the US are 2.5x more likely to go into business if they have a written plan

Executive summary

Fill in this section last, bearing in mind that it may be the only part a busy person reads:

> **Business summary** Company structure, name, product or service, and customer profile
> **Business goals** Three objectives over one, three, and five years
> **Financial summary** Expected sales and costs, and funding
> **Elevator pitch** Two-minute talk to sell your idea to a customer

Business background

Provide details of each person in the business:

> **Experience** Relevant work carried out to date
> **Qualifications** Credentials, such as diploma in horticulture for a gardening service
> **Training** Past and future, including business skills such as assertiveness

Products and services

Describe what the business is going to sell:

> **Product or service** With a picture if product is new
> **Range** If more than one, such as garden design and maintenance
> **How it is different** What makes the product or service stand out from the crowd?

The market

Set out specific details of your potential market:

> **Typical customer** Businesses or individuals and their profile; local, national, or international
> **Market research** What the local market is for similar products or services

Marketing strategy

Choose about three of these methods:

> **Word of mouth**
> **Advertising**
> **Business literature**
> **Direct marketing**
> **Social media**
> **Website**

TOP FIVE REASONS TO WRITE A PLAN

> **The process** Working through each element ensures nothing is forgotten.

> **Costing** The only way to find out whether the business is viable is to work out details of costs and sales.

> **Funding** A good business plan improves chances of getting a loan.

> **Areas of expertise** Making a business plan clarifies where outside help is needed—for instance, in bookkeeping or marketing.

> **Getting to know the competition** Conducting market research is the best way to give a business an edge.

✓ NEED TO KNOW

> **SWOT analysis** Stands for Strengths, Weaknesses, Opportunities, and Threats

> **Unique selling point (USP)** The feature that makes a product different from the competition

Competitor analysis

Show how the business idea compares with the competition:

> **Table of competitors** Who and where they are, what they sell and for how much, how good they are

> **SWOT analysis** Including how to remedy any weaknesses and combat known threats, such as a garden center opening nearby

> **USP** The unique selling point of the product or service

See Need to Know box, above.

Operations and logistics

Describe from start to finish how the business will run day to day:

> **Supply and delivery** How the goods or service will get from A to B

> **Equipment** Details of transportation, office items, and premises

> **Payment, legal, and insurance** How customers will pay and how that translates into salaries; compliance with the law

Costs and pricing strategy

Work out how much the product or service costs and its sale price:

> **Cost** How much each unit or batch costs to make and deliver

> **Price** How much each unit or batch will sell for

> **Profit margin** The difference between cost and price per unit

Financial forecasts

Predict sales and costs over the year, allowing for seasonal fluctuation, such as spring demand for lawn services:

> **Sales calculations** For each month, the expected number of sales

> **Costs calculations** The costs of the predicted sales each month

> **Cash-flow forecast** The money coming in and out of the business

See How Finance Works, pp.98–175.

Back-up plan

Make a Plan B in case something goes unexpectedly wrong:

> **Short-term changes** Cutting costs or boosting sales immediately

> **Longer-term changes** Shifts such as working online, not on premises

> **Closure** Lessons learned and skills acquired if the business closes

Raising money

Almost every new enterprise needs funding to get it going, and to keep afloat until it turns a profit. Financial help is at hand from a variety of sources, suitable at different stages of start-up growth.

How it works

Capital for new enterprises comes from two main sources: lenders and investors. Lenders, such as banks, provide debt capital in the form of a loan that is returned with interest. Investors, such as business angels and venture capitalists (VCs), provide equity capital in the form of a share in the business that may include a proportionate share of control and rewards. Both types of funding can be corporate—from a company—or more quirky and alternative, such as crowdfunding.

Types of start-up funding

Corporate, traditional, and substantial funding comes largely from banks and VCs, while smaller sums come from more personal sources.

Lenders
Debt capital most often takes the form of loans paid back with interest.

Term loan Paid back regularly over a set period of time

> **Bank** Offers either personal or business loans

> **Government** Offers low-interest start-up loans

> **Credit union** Cooperative that gives members low-interest loans

> **Peer-to-peer (P2P) lending** Unsecured personal loans

> **Friends and family** May give interest-free loans

Bank overdraft or credit card Interest charged monthly if balance not paid in full

> **Bank or credit company** Financial organization that makes loans to commercial ventures

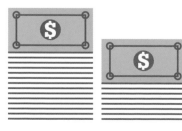

Factoring/invoice discounting Start-up sells unpaid invoices at a discount to a company that collects them at a profit

> **Factors and discounters** Companies that offer advance on unpaid invoices, for a profit

✓ NEED TO KNOW

> **P2P lending** Loans made between individuals over internet

> **Crowdfunding** Debt or equity raised via internet platforms

Start-up funding

5–10%
of small and medium-sized enterprises in the UK need no start-up funding

Investors
Equity capital is paid to the start-up in return for a share of the business.

Grants
Financial awards and prizes are provided by public bodies.

Founders, friends, family (FFF) May buy shares in the company rather than lending money

Local, national, global Funded by a local authority, government initiative, or international charity

Crowdfunding Large number of supporters, each contributing a small amount of money, usually online

Business angels Investors who give favorable terms because their focus is on the company's success rather than profit

Venture capitalists (VCs) Companies that provide capital for new businesses in the hope of making a profit

SUPER ANGELS

❯ **What they are** Serious investors in technology start-ups. Facebook was funded by super angels, some of whom are now famous in their own right.

❯ **Who they are** Former Silicon Valley professionals who invest their personal money in new ventures.

❯ **How they differ from ordinary angels and venture capitalists (VCs)** Funding level straddles the two, often reaching millions of dollars as what started out as a hobby becomes a profession.

❯ **Pros and cons** Super-angel investing acts like a magnet to other investors, but individual super angels can rarely provide the full funding of a VC.

Alternative models

Since the start of the economic downturn that started in 2008, several innovative and more personal types of funding, such as crowdfunding and peer-to-peer (P2P) lending, have evolved and blossomed on the internet. All involve the principle of raising small amounts of money from large numbers of individuals who pool their resources to provide the loan or equity needed.

CREDIT ANALYSIS CRITERIA FOR LENDING

Capacity
The borrower's ability to repay the loan is shown by the business plan.

Capital
The borrower's net worth is assessed to check that assets exceed debts.

Character
The lender usually looks for a borrower with a good credit history.

Collateral
The borrower is often expected to pledge an asset that can be sold to pay off the loan if funds are too low to pay the monthly interest or repay the capital at the end of the term.

Conditions
The lender is swayed by the current economic climate as well as by the sum requested.

Life cycle of investment

The key to successful funding is to choose the right type of finance at each stage of a company's early growth. Start-ups usually begin modestly, with self-funding and help from friends, family, and anyone else who is prepared to take a high risk. Crowdfunders and business angels are amateurs willing the entrepreneur to succeed, while venture capitalists become interested when the level of risk goes down and they can expect a healthy profit in return for injecting substantial funds. Public markets such as stock exchanges may step in as sales soar and success looks probable. At all stages, investors will conduct credit analyis to asses a company's ability to repay its debt.

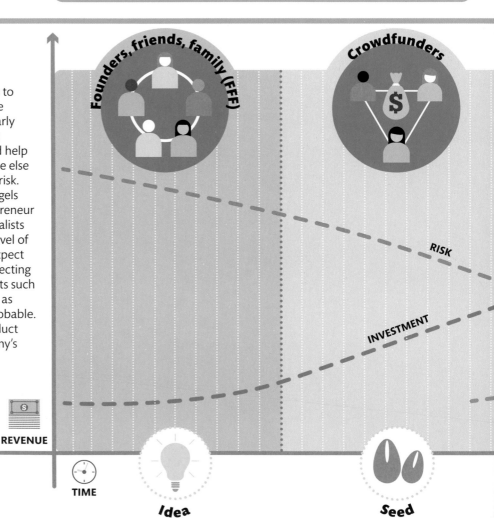

Start-up finance of small and medium-sized enterprises (SMEs)

The chart shows sources of start-up finance of SMEs over a three-year period in the UK, taken from a 2004 survey by Warwick Business School. Most funding comes from individual savings, and least from equity (shares), a type of investment associated more with larger companies.

66% Personal savings	**5%** Home mortgage	
12.5% Friends and family	**5%** No funds used	
10% Bank loan	**1.5%** Equity investment	

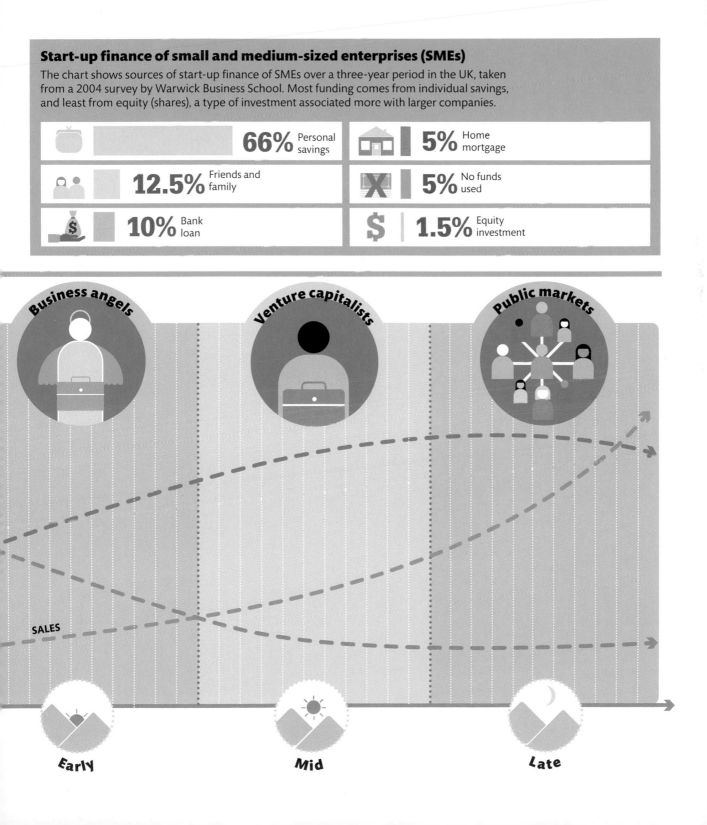

Business angels

Venture capitalists

Public markets

SALES

Early

Mid

Late

Business accelerators and incubators

Starting a new venture can be a long process. Business (also called venture) accelerators and incubators are specialized organizations devoted to developing and supporting start-ups.

How it works

Business accelerators and incubators provide expertise and connections in the formative stages of a business in return for a percentage of ownership. They are two separate types of services. Business accelerators are short-term programs that offer wide-ranging support including mentorship, business advice, and connections to potential sources of financing. Business incubators, on the other hand, provide a supportive environment in which fledgling start-ups can develop, with technical assistance, working space, and networking opportunities.

Business accelerators

Suitable for start-ups that have no or limited financing; short–term, 1–3-month boot camps; clients include web and software developers

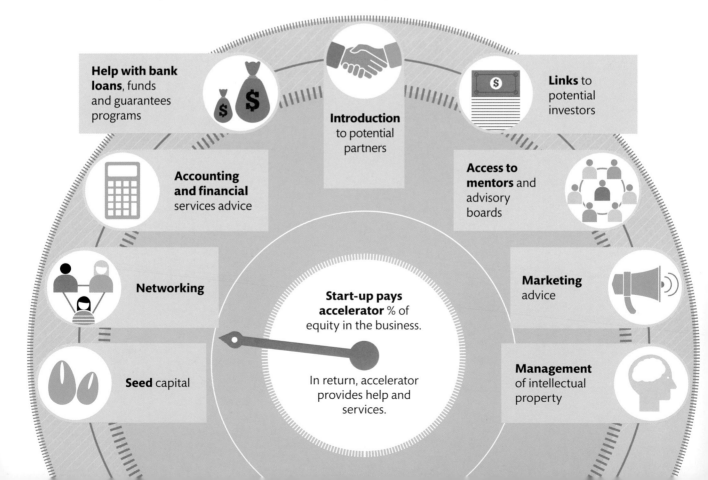

Help with bank loans, funds and guarantees programs

Introduction to potential partners

Links to potential investors

Accounting and financial services advice

Access to mentors and advisory boards

Networking

Marketing advice

Start-up pays accelerator % of equity in the business.

In return, accelerator provides help and services.

Seed capital

Management of intellectual property

Business incubators

Often sponsored by nonprofit organizations and universities; medium-term, 1–5 years; variety of clients, especially science-based

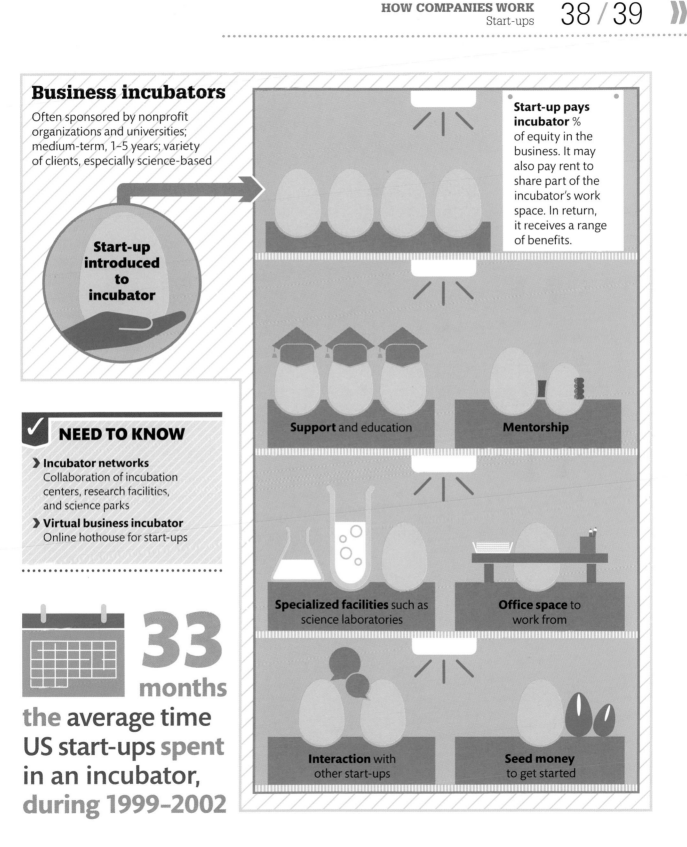

Start-up introduced to incubator

Start-up pays incubator % of equity in the business. It may also pay rent to share part of the incubator's work space. In return, it receives a range of benefits.

Support and education

Mentorship

Specialized facilities such as science laboratories

Office space to work from

Interaction with other start-ups

Seed money to get started

✓ NEED TO KNOW

❯ **Incubator networks**
Collaboration of incubation centers, research facilities, and science parks

❯ **Virtual business incubator**
Online hothouse for start-ups

33 months
the average time US start-ups spent in an incubator, during 1999–2002

Buying and selling business

Both private and public companies regularly change hands—they are bought, sold, and restructured to reflect changing business conditions. These deals all come under the umbrella term of mergers and acquisitions (M and A). Acquisition financing is usually needed to pay for the purchase of another company, often in the form of a loan or venture capital.

How to acquire a company

A company is typically acquired in one of two ways—either by a management team or by another company. When a company is buying, the result can be a merger, in which two companies join forces, an acquisition (outright purchase), or a divestiture, in which part of a company is hived off and sold. Management team purchases are often funded by private equity.

Target company

Management team acquiring

Private equity firms look for companies to buy and then sell their shares when profits have maximized. They fund the management team. *See pp.48–49.*

Buy-out

The existing management team buys out the company they work for.

Buy-in

An external management team buys into the company.

Divestiture

Part of company is split off to form new company; may become acquisition target. *See pp.44–45.*

FOR SALE

$311.5 million

the average size of M and A deals, globally, in 2013

Another company acquiring

Companies may want to expand by joining with another business.

Merger
The company combines with another company. *See pp.42–43.*

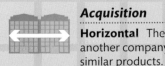

Acquisition
Horizontal The company buys another company that makes similar products.

Vertical The company buys another company that makes different products.
See pp.46–47.

SIZING UP M AND A'S

Measuring a big deal

The corporate world categorizes acquisition deals according to the capitalization size (the value of the company's shares).

Small Under $500 million

Mid-market $500 million to $2 billion

Large $2 billion to $10 billion

Megadeal Above $10 billion

Due diligence

Before any company sale, the potential buyers see a detailed report prepared by lawyers, covering key aspects of the target business.

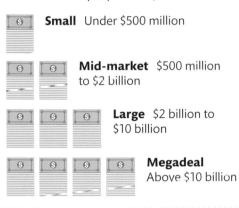

> **Financial** Identifies problem areas that could affect the future value of the company.

> **Legal** Gauges possible legal risks attached to corporate status, assets, securities, intellectual property, and employee reshuffling.

> **Commercial** Includes industry trends, market environment, the company's capabilities, and the competition.

> **Environmental** Uncovers potential liabilities such as land or water contamination and estimates remediation costs.

Mergers and acquisitions

Two of the quickest ways to accelerate expansion are for a business to buy out another—an acquisition—or to amalgamate with another business in a merger.

How it works

Mergers and acquisitions (M and A) is a general term used to describe the ways in which companies are bought, sold, and recombined. In the case of either a merger or an acquisition, two separate legal entities are unified into a single legal entity. While a merger combines two companies on a reasonably equal footing to create a new company, which will make both parties better off, an acquisition is usually a purchase of a smaller company by a larger one. This benefits the company making the purchase but may not necessarily benefit the target company. M and A can be friendly or hostile—agreed to or imposed.

REASONS TO PURSUE M AND A

❯ **Improved economies of scale**
Wider operations streamline production and sales.

❯ **Bigger market share**
Combining the existing markets expands share of the total market.

❯ **Diversification** A different product lineup gives the chance to cross-sell or create more efficient operations if the products are complementary.

Merger

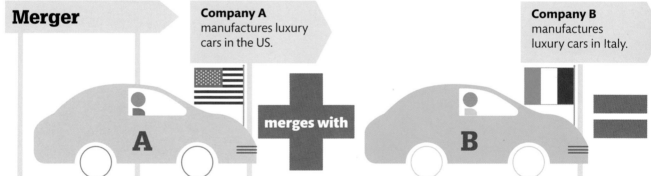

Company A
manufactures luxury cars in the US.

Company B
manufactures luxury cars in Italy.

merges with

Acquisition

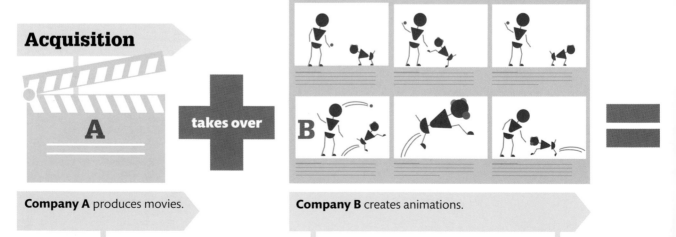

takes over

Company A produces movies.

Company B creates animations.

FRIENDLY AND HOSTILE

- ❯ The target company's board of directors and management agree to be bought out.
- ❯ The acquiring company makes an offer of cash or stock to the target company's board and management.
- ❯ The stock or cash offer is set at a premium level.
- ❯ Because the offer is above actual market level, shareholders usually agree to it.

- ❯ The acquiring company bypasses management and goes straight to the target company's shareholders.
- ❯ The target company's management fight the deal.
- ❯ The buying company convinces shareholders to vote out the management (a proxy fight) or it makes an offer to shareholders to buy shares at an above-market price (a tender offer).

✓ NEED TO KNOW

- ❯ **Pacman strategy** The target company tries to take over the very company attempting the hostile buyout
- ❯ **Swap ratio** An exchange rate between the value of the shares of two companies when merging
- ❯ **Defensive merger** Undertaken to anticipate a merger or takeover attempt that threatens a company
- ❯ **Economies of scale** Benefit to company of M and A expansion

New company A + B now has an expanded market spanning Europe and North America.

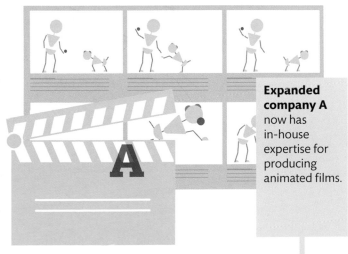

Expanded company A now has in-house expertise for producing animated films.

$112 billion

the record spend by Japanese **companies on overseas mergers and acquisitions, in 2012**

Divestitures

While a merger results in a bigger company, a divestiture reduces the size of a business by breaking it down into smaller components or divisions, which are then sold off or dissolved.

How it works

The typical scenario for a divestiture is a company that is struggling to pay off debt it has taken on to expand into new areas of business that are not yet profitable. To save the rest of the company from the burden of debt, management decides to start a divestiture. Generally, the goal is to shed the least profitable areas of operation, or from the potential buyer's point of view, those which have promise but are not yet profitable. The process of restructuring by divestiture is designed to free the company of divisions with low return, to reduce debt and financing requirements, and to give the shareholders a stronger return. The market price of the parent company's shares often bounces back strongly and its spin-off companies may thrive too.

Divestiture in practice

Smith Industries Inc. is one example of an industrial paint conglomerate that has grown rapidly over the past five years, due to an increase in profits from its expanding sales in China. It diversified into agricultural chemicals, textiles, and biotechnology, and set up a separate division for each. Share prices fell in response to poor financial performance.

Making a decision

Faced with a downturn in business, the company divests the newer business areas that have not yet shown strong returns despite positive signs of growth.

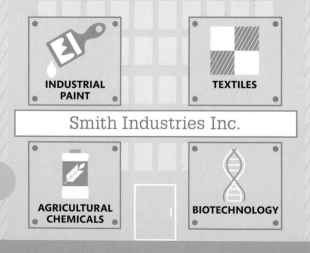

Announcing the sale

Smith Industries Inc. now announces the sale of its three remaining divisions: agricultural chemicals, textiles, and biotechnology.

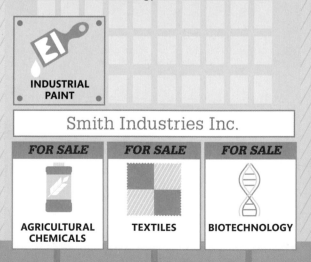

✓ NEED TO KNOW

> **Spin-off** New company formed as the result of a divestiture; also called a hive-off

> **Tracking stock** Special type of shares issued by a parent company for the division or subsidiary they will sell; tracking stock is tied to the performance of the specific division rather than the company as a whole; also known as targeted stock

> **Letter of intent** Letter stating serious intention to do business, often concerning M and A

> **Reverse merger** Not to be confused with a divestiture, this is a quick and cheap method for a private company to go public by buying a shell stock— a public company that is no longer operating because it went bankrupt or was simply closed.

> **Demerger** Term commonly used in the UK for divestiture

52%

the potential rise in a parent company's share price following a divestiture

The shareholders benefit

Shareholders in the original company also receive the same percentage holding in shares from the three new companies.

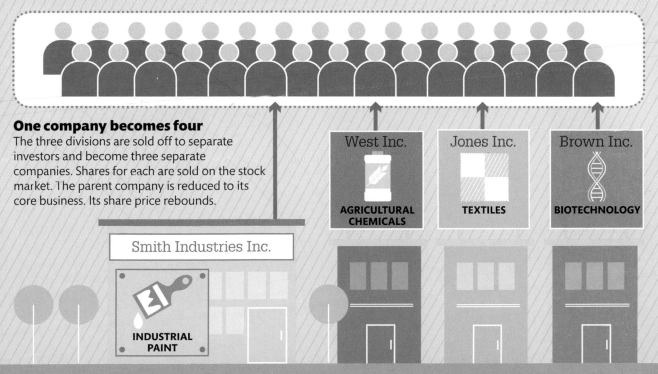

One company becomes four

The three divisions are sold off to separate investors and become three separate companies. Shares for each are sold on the stock market. The parent company is reduced to its core business. Its share price rebounds.

Smith Industries Inc.

INDUSTRIAL PAINT

West Inc.

AGRICULTURAL CHEMICALS

Jones Inc.

TEXTILES

Brown Inc.

BIOTECHNOLOGY

Vertical vs. horizontal integration

Companies that want to expand through a merger or acquisition may decide on a strategy of either horizontal or vertical integration, combining businesses involved in similar or dissimilar activities.

How it works

Companies can choose from several strategies when they merge or are part of an acquisition. Two of the most common are horizontal and vertical integration.

Horizontal deals are always done between competitors that produce similar types of products, such as cars or mobile phones, and often share—or compete for—the same suppliers and clients. As a result of merger or acquisition, the newly formed company can make cost savings in production, distribution, sales, and marketing. Vertical deals are usually between businesses involved in the same industry but at different stages—for example, a computer maker and a component manufacturer. These deals can be upstream (toward the market) or downstream (in the direction of operations and production).

✓ NEED TO KNOW

❭ **Lateral integration** Another term for horizontal integration

❭ **Horizontal monopoly** When a company controls the market after buying up the competition

❭ **Synergy** The potential of merged companies to be more successful as a single entity

Integration models in practice

In these hypothetical examples, a cluster of printers, publishers, and bookstores merge or acquire each other in horizontal or vertical deals that aim to strengthen their market position, take advantage of economies of scale, and exploit synergy.

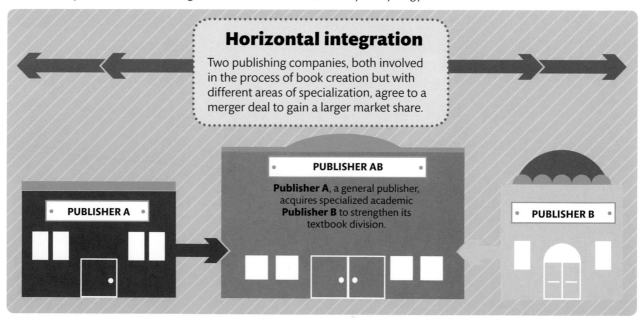

Horizontal integration

Two publishing companies, both involved in the process of book creation but with different areas of specialization, agree to a merger deal to gain a larger market share.

PUBLISHER AB

Publisher A, a general publisher, acquires specialized academic **Publisher B** to strengthen its textbook division.

PUBLISHER A

PUBLISHER B

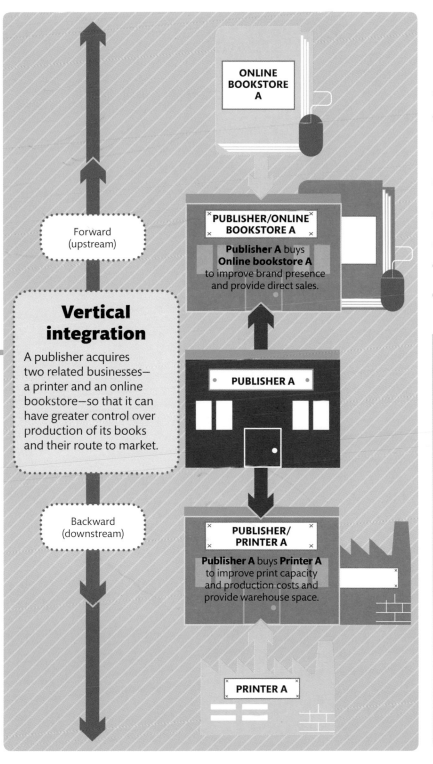

Forward
(upstream)

Vertical integration

A publisher acquires two related businesses—a printer and an online bookstore—so that it can have greater control over production of its books and their route to market.

Backward
(downstream)

ONLINE BOOKSTORE A

PUBLISHER/ONLINE BOOKSTORE A

Publisher A buys **Online bookstore A** to improve brand presence and provide direct sales.

PUBLISHER A

PUBLISHER/ PRINTER A

Publisher A buys **Printer A** to improve print capacity and production costs and provide warehouse space.

PRINTER A

31%
of businesses worldwide planned to expand through a merger or acquisition in the three years from 2014

MERGER AND ACQUISITION TYPES

Conglomerate

Combining two companies with nothing in common: for example, in 1985, tobacco-producer Philip Morris purchased General Foods, a new line of business unconnected to legal wrangles around smoking.

Market extension

Combining two companies that sell the same products but in different markets: for example, in 1996, the Union Pacific Railroad Company acquired the Southern Pacific Rail Corporation to link railroads in adjacent US regions.

Product extension

Combining two companies that sell different but related products in the same market: for example, in 2014, Microsoft bought Nokia's mobile-phone unit to address flagging PC sales and its weakness in the mobile device market.

Management buy-ins and buy-outs

A company's ownership may undergo a change, which can be driven either externally, known as a management buy-in, or internally, known as a management buy-out.

How it works

In a management buy-in (MBI), a group of managers or investors from outside the company raises the funds to buy a majority stake in the company and then takes over its management. This type of action occurs when a company appears to be either undervalued or underperforming. In a typical management buy-out (MBO), the company's existing management team purchases all or part of the company they work for. Despite the name, MBOs are not restricted to managers, and they can include employees from any level of the organization who wish to make the transition from employee to owner.

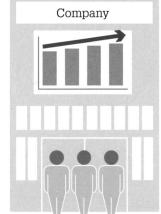

✓ NEED TO KNOW

> **Earnout** A percentage of the purchase price paid to the sellers after acquisition if the business has performed as expected

> **Leveraged buy-out** Acquisition of a company using equity and borrowed money, with company as collateral for loan

Buy-in

Some companies, such as investment banks or venture capitalists, can make sizable profits by purchasing undervalued businesses and transforming them.

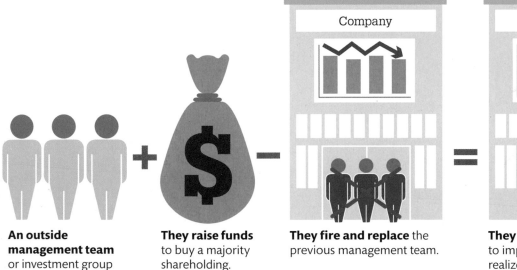

An outside management team or investment group sees that a company is undervalued.

They raise funds to buy a majority shareholding.

They fire and replace the previous management team.

They overhaul the business to improve performance and realize its true value.

BUY-IN MANAGEMENT BUY-OUT (BIMBO)

In this type of transaction, the existing management of a company stages a buy-out, but additional external management is brought in by financers to strengthen the company's leadership and to provide expertise in particular areas that might be lacking in the original team.

Existing management members buy company

Outside management members brought in

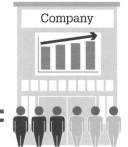
New management team

$22.2 billion

Europe's biggest ever leveraged buy-out—of chemist chain Alliance Boots in 2007

Buy-out

A buy-out allows a large company to sell off a part of the business it no longer wants or helps a small business owner to retire or move on.

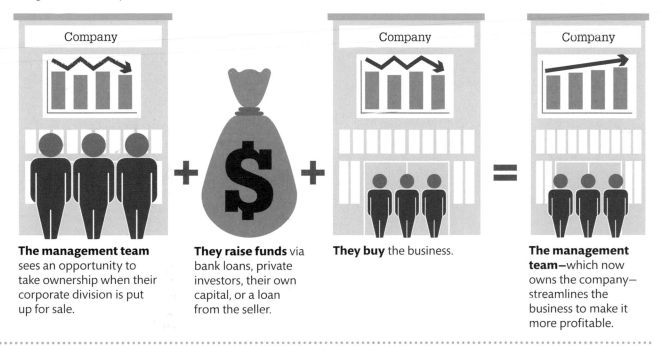

The management team sees an opportunity to take ownership when their corporate division is put up for sale.

They raise funds via bank loans, private investors, their own capital, or a loan from the seller.

They buy the business.

The management team—which now owns the company—streamlines the business to make it more profitable.

Who's who

Determining a company's hierarchy—including how many layers of power it has, and how many staff to appoint at each level—is one of the biggest challenges of modern management. In family-run businesses, positions are usually filled by family members who answer to the head of the family. The emergence of public companies has meant that company ownership is separated from management, so that shareholder interests are prioritized.

Who's who in an organization

Stakeholders and shareholders

Stakeholders are anyone with a vested interest in the company. Shareholders are stakeholders who have bought stock in the company. *See pp.60–63.*

Board of directors

The board of directors makes sure the company is run profitably to provide returns to shareholders. The board votes in a chairman, who is sometimes also the chief executive officer (CEO). *See pp.52–55.*

C-suite executives

The top level operates the company day to day and sets strategy. All titles of top management begin with a "C" for chief. Senior managers are headed by the CEO. *See pp.56–59.*

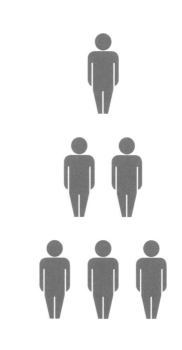

**%**

**of UK employees
believe what senior
managers tell them
about what is happening
in their organization**

Mid-level management

Division and department heads are
usually called directors or managers.
Jobs at this level are often the first to
go when a company downsizes or
restructures. *See pp.56–59.*

Junior management

Supervisors, managers, or team
leaders directly manage groups of
employees carrying out specific tasks.
Examples include a head nurse or
foreman. *See pp.56–59 and pp.74–75.*

Non-management
employees

The lowest ranks of the organization:
skilled and unskilled workers carry out
core tasks needed for the company to
operate. *See pp.56–59 and pp.74–75.*

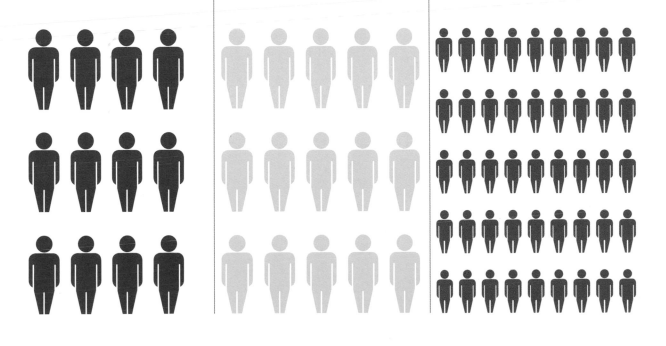

Board of directors

Public companies are required by law to appoint a board of directors to provide oversight.

How it works

All companies must have at least one director. If a company goes public and issues shares, it is legally required to have a board of directors. The board is made up of experienced business advisers who provide independent oversight of the company for shareholders and are mandated by law to govern the company responsibly.

Board members may come from within the company or be independent outsiders, and should cover a range of expertise—such as legal, financial and marketing—or have specialized industry knowledge. Networkers are also highly prized for their ability to build connections with influential figures in the corporate and governmental spheres. From within their ranks, the board elects a chairman, vice-chairman, secretary, and treasurer.

Board of directors

The board of directors of a publicly listed company sits between the company and its shareholders.

REPORTS TO

EVALUATES

Secretary

Appointed by

The board

Responsible for

> Publicly representing the company's policies and leading board meetings

Treasurer

Appointed by

The board

Responsible for

> Presenting yearly accounts

> Leading audit committee

Shareholders

Any person or institution that has bought shares in a publicly listed company is a shareholder. The board works for the shareholders, who effectively own the company.

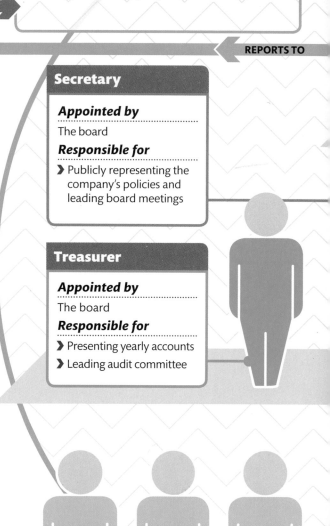

Chairman

Appointed by
The board

Responsible for
> Publicly representing the company's policies
> Leading the board, conducting board meetings
> Determining the composition of the board
> Mentoring and monitoring the CEO or managing director (MD)
> Communicating with shareholders

The average company board in the US has
9.2
directors

Company

Responsible for day-to-day production, sales and marketing operations, and finance. The company reports to the board via its chief executive officer (CEO), who executes the board's decisions.

Vice-chairman

Appointed by
The board

Responsible for
> Standing in for chairman
> Undertaking special projects for chairman
> Assisting chairman in balancing experience, personality, and age of directors on board

REPORTS TO   EVALUATES

CEO

Appointed by
The board

Responsible for
> Performance of the company
> Implementing board strategy
> Leading senior management
> Reporting back to chairman and board

Directors

Appointed by
The board

Responsible for
> Determining strategy
> Monitoring achievement of implemented policies
> Appointing managers
> Accounting for company's activities to shareholders and other stakeholders

 REPORTS TO   EVALUATES

Management

Managers pass the CEO's decisions down to employees.

Balancing the board

The board has three clear areas of responsibility: developing business strategy, advising the company, and overseeing how the firm is run. Selecting the right mix of directors to fulfill these functions is crucial.

Board members may come from inside or outside the company. Those who work for the company (executive or internal directors) have more expertise in running the business, but independent members (non-executive or external directors) are better placed to offer perspective, scrutinize the actions of company executives, and call them to account. When potential conflicts of interest arise between management and shareholders, independent directors can weigh decision-making in favor of acting in the company's best interests.

The ideal balance is a hot topic in corporate governance. In US companies, CEO and chairman roles have traditionally been combined, but following a spate of corporate scandals, the roles are now more often vested in two individuals. In Europe, keeping the roles separate has long been seen as best practice.

✓ NEED TO KNOW

❯ **NEDs** Non-executive directors, also known as independent, external, or outside directors

❯ **Executive directors** Board members who also work for the company—not to be confused with the term executive director when used as a title for the CEO

❯ **Model Business Corporation Act** Developed by the American Bar Association, this model is used as the basis for corporate governance in the US

Board structure variations

Independent board of directors

The board sits between shareholders and company. The CEO is the main channel of communication between board and company, while the chairman is the principal conduit between shareholders and board. This structure gives the board most independence.

CEO as chairman

A setup in which the company's CEO serves as the board's chairman. While this offers less independent scrutiny of finances, strategy, performance, and pay, it avoids duplication of roles. This setup is found in US corporations and in many small- and medium-sized companies in other countries.

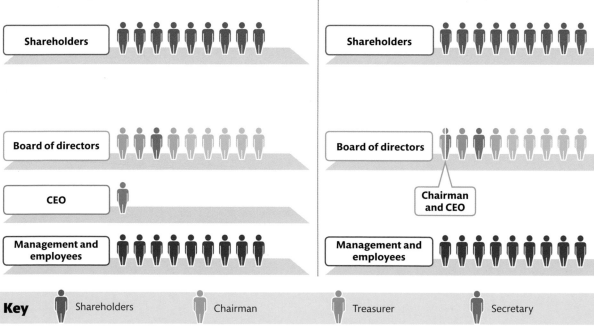

Key — Shareholders — Chairman — Treasurer — Secretary

PROS AND CONS OF CEO AS CHAIRMAN

Pros

- **Strong, central leadership** Decisions hold fewer conflicts.
- **Efficiency** CEO/chairman can implement board decisions swiftly.
- **Expertise** CEO has company and industry knowledge (a CEO may become chairman after retirement).
- **Balance of power** Established hierarchy between CEO/chairman and other directors reduces risk of conflict on the board.

Cons

- **Lack of transparency** Conflicts of interest/corruption are more likely.
- **Reduced objectivity** Board headed by CEO is unable to monitor CEO's work objectively.
- **Higher remuneration** Combined role generally commands higher pay than two separate individuals.
- **Mentoring** Chairman who is also CEO cannot offer independent mentoring and support for the role.

44%

of S&P 500-listed companies had distinct CEO and chairman roles in 2012–up from 21% in 2001

Senior management as directors

A structure in which senior managers also sit on the board. The chief financial officer (CFO) is appointed board treasurer and the chief operations officer (COO) is vice-chairman. In some countries (Germany, for example), employees must be included on the board by law.

Two-tier board

An arrangement that is made up of separate supervisory and executive boards. The supervisory board is composed of outside directors, led by a chairman. The executive board comprises senior managers, including the CEO. The two boards always meet separately.

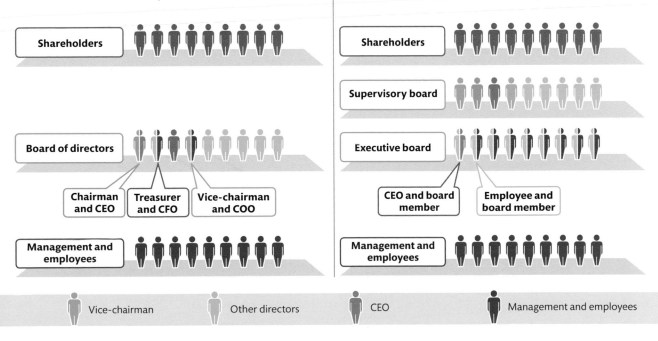

Senior management as directors

Shareholders

Board of directors
- Chairman and CEO
- Treasurer and CFO
- Vice-chairman and COO

Management and employees

Two-tier board

Shareholders

Supervisory board

Executive board
- CEO and board member
- Employee and board member

Management and employees

Vice-chairman | Other directors | CEO | Management and employees

Company hierarchy

Almost every organization has a structured arrangement of levels for members, from the board of directors at the top to junior employees at the bottom. There is a trend toward reducing the number of levels.

How it works

There are five levels in the conventional corporate structure with a line of authority from top to bottom. The chief executive officer (CEO) is the highest-ranking person in the company, reporting to the board of directors and sometimes also sitting on the board. Reporting to the CEO are a number of high-level executives, known as C-level executives—their job titles begin with a "C" and end with an "O." Below the C-level is management, in tiers that differ from company to company, with employees forming the bottom level. As well as skilled and unskilled employees, there may be staff on fixed-term contracts, taken on for the duration of a project or for a set length of time, and casual temporary workers.

C-LEVEL VARIATIONS

The range of C-level positions varies for each company. In addition to the three top posts, there may be:

CAO   Chief Administrative Officer

CIO   Chief Information Officer

CTO   Chief Technology Officer

CPO   Chief Product/Production Officer, responsible for overseeing product development and production

CMO   Chief Marketing Officer, responsible for marketing strategy and business development

C-level positions are evolving, adapting to market conditions and business priorities. New roles are emerging while some traditional roles are disappearing. The role of COO, for example, is less popular in modern organizations. Some of the new roles include:

CPO   Chief Privacy Officer

CSO   Chief Sustainability Officer

CDO   Chief Digital Officer

CKO   Chief Knowledge Officer

CCO   Chief Customer Officer

51%

of CIOs and CTOs say they are pioneering new digital approaches within their business

C-suite executives

These are the most senior jobs in the company, with the CEO at the top, the COO and CFO traditionally on the next level down, and other C-positions below that. In many companies, the C-level positions have equal authority and all report directly to the CEO.

Mid-level management

Responsible for overseeing specific functions in the organization, the most senior managers at this level head up different departments or divisions. These managers are often called directors (not to be confused with the board of directors) or, in the US, vice-presidents. The exact job titles, and the number of mid-level managers, vary depending on the company.

Junior management and other employees

Team leaders, such as supervisors and assistant managers, implement management plans. They also coordinate teams of skilled and unskilled workers in, for example, production, customer service, and sales to carry out the core tasks needed for the company to function efficiently and profitably.

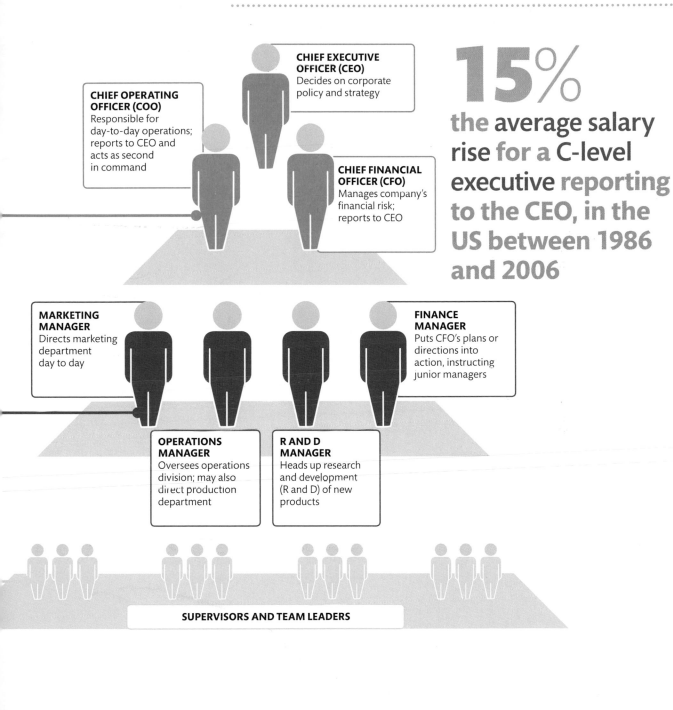

CHIEF EXECUTIVE OFFICER (CEO)
Decides on corporate policy and strategy

CHIEF OPERATING OFFICER (COO)
Responsible for day-to-day operations; reports to CEO and acts as second in command

CHIEF FINANCIAL OFFICER (CFO)
Manages company's financial risk; reports to CEO

15%
the average salary rise for a C-level executive reporting to the CEO, in the US between 1986 and 2006

MARKETING MANAGER
Directs marketing department day to day

FINANCE MANAGER
Puts CFO's plans or directions into action, instructing junior managers

OPERATIONS MANAGER
Oversees operations division; may also direct production department

R AND D MANAGER
Heads up research and development (R and D) of new products

SUPERVISORS AND TEAM LEADERS

NON-MANAGEMENT EMPLOYEES

Flattening hierarchies

The trend in management over the past few decades has been to eliminate layers from company hierarchies, which means they are becoming flatter—in other words, there are not as many levels to go through in order to reach the top.

One example is the role of chief operating officer (COO), which has been disappearing in recent years. Between 2000 and 2012, there was a 10 percent decline in the number of Fortune 500 (an annual list of the top US corporations compiled by *Fortune* magazine) companies with COOs. Only 38 percent of the 500 have a COO position now. CEOs have also eliminated layers of middle management, and in the US there was a 300 percent increase between 1986 and 2003 in the number of division heads reporting directly to the CEO.

Sometimes companies decide restructure the other way round instead—from flat to tall—by eliminating a number of senior management posts and replacing them with a greater number of junior supervisory roles.

Tall vs. flat hierarchies

There are pros and cons for both types of hierarchy, and each company has to find the number of levels, and positions within each level, that suits the nature of its business.

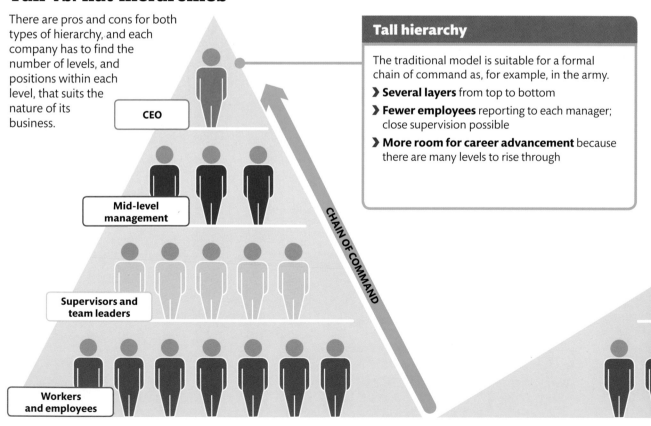

CEO

Mid-level management

Supervisors and team leaders

Workers and employees

CHAIN OF COMMAND

Tall hierarchy

The traditional model is suitable for a formal chain of command as, for example, in the army.

❯ **Several layers** from top to bottom

❯ **Fewer employees** reporting to each manager; close supervision possible

❯ **More room for career advancement** because there are many levels to rise through

CASE STUDY

Restructuring the big three US car manufacturers

The economic crisis of 2008 caused the big three American car-making companies—General Motors (GM), Ford, and Chrysler—to rethink their corporate structures. Market share had fallen and the three companies needed to shed employees and find ways to cut production.

All three took similar action to reorganize the company hierarchy, removing some managerial roles from the mid-management level and installing more team leaders at a lower level in the organization to create a flatter, less top-heavy company hierarchy.

❯ **Before restructuring** Thirty technicians reported to one production supervisor.

❯ **After restructuring** Seventy-five technicians now reported to one production supervisor, through 18 newly created team leader positions.

25%

the decline in the levels of hierarchy between division heads and CEOs in the US, from 1986 to 2003

Flat hierarchy

This looser model is more flexible and suitable for companies that foster creativity.

❯ **Only a few layers** so mid- and low-level management are merged

❯ **Large number of employees** reporting to each manager; close supervision not possible

❯ **More freedom for employees** to make their own decisions

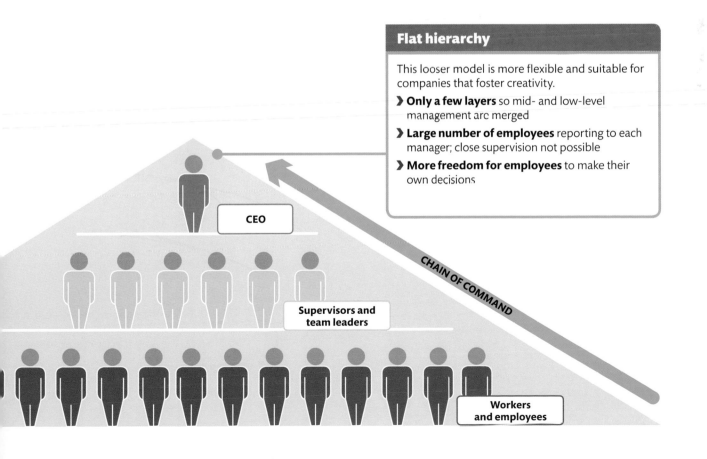

CEO

CHAIN OF COMMAND

Supervisors and team leaders

Workers and employees

Stakeholders

A stakeholder is anyone who is affected by the performance of the company, while shareholders own one or more shares in a company, which makes each of them a part-owner of the company.

How it works

Because shareholders part-own the company, they have the right to vote on how it is managed and to receive a share of its profits. All shareholders are stakeholders, since the performance of the company has a direct impact on the value of the shares they own: when the company does well, the share value rises, and when it performs badly, the share value falls.

However, stakeholders can also be non-shareholders—individuals or groups who have an interest in what the company does or whose financial situation depends on the company. Some stakeholder groups are interested in a company mainly for its ethical treatment of workers, sustainable approach to the environment, and attitude to society. These are known as environmental, social, and governance (ESG) criteria.

Stakeholders' areas of interest

A few stakeholder groups are concerned only with environmental, social, and governance (ESG) factors, while others, such as shareholders and suppliers, may be more interested in the company's financial performance. Most stakeholder groups have at least some interest in both areas, especially since negative publicity for a company can cause share prices to fall.

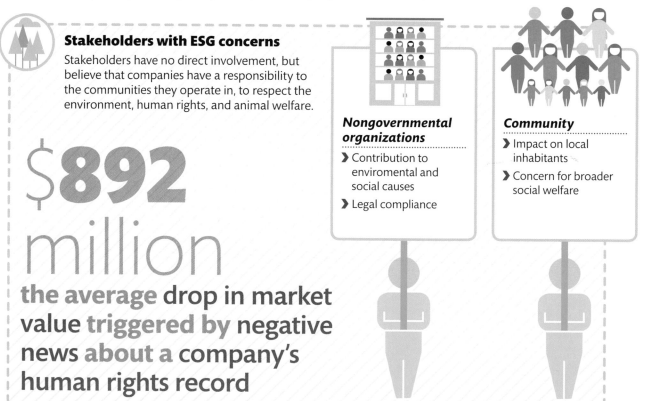

Stakeholders with ESG concerns

Stakeholders have no direct involvement, but believe that companies have a responsibility to the communities they operate in, to respect the environment, human rights, and animal welfare.

$892 million
the average drop in market value triggered by negative news about a company's human rights record

Nongovernmental organizations
❯ Contribution to enviromental and social causes
❯ Legal compliance

Community
❯ Impact on local inhabitants
❯ Concern for broader social welfare

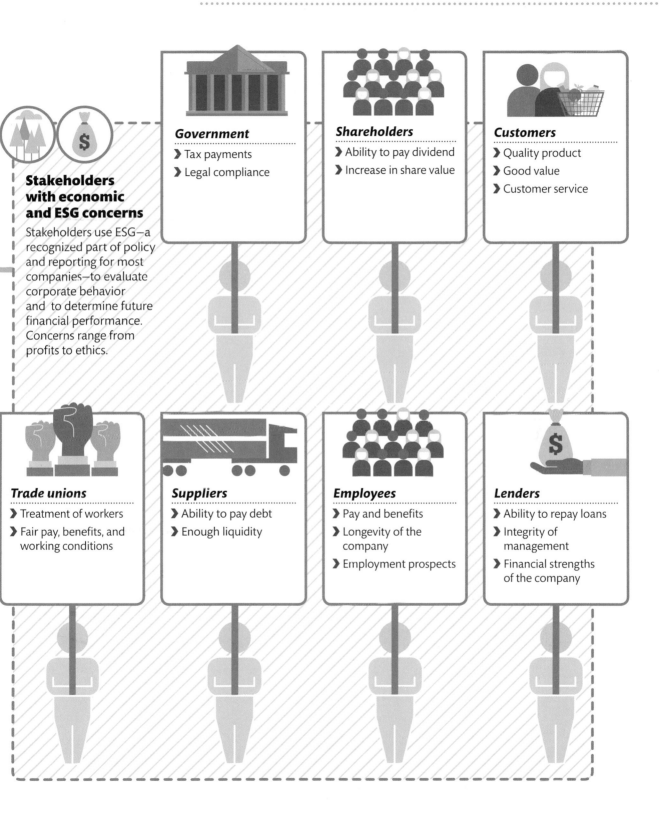

Stakeholders with economic and ESG concerns

Stakeholders use ESG—a recognized part of policy and reporting for most companies—to evaluate corporate behavior and to determine future financial performance. Concerns range from profits to ethics.

Government
❯ Tax payments
❯ Legal compliance

Shareholders
❯ Ability to pay dividend
❯ Increase in share value

Customers
❯ Quality product
❯ Good value
❯ Customer service

Trade unions
❯ Treatment of workers
❯ Fair pay, benefits, and working conditions

Suppliers
❯ Ability to pay debt
❯ Enough liquidity

Employees
❯ Pay and benefits
❯ Longevity of the company
❯ Employment prospects

Lenders
❯ Ability to repay loans
❯ Integrity of management
❯ Financial strengths of the company

Stakeholders in action

Compared with other stakeholders, shareholders have the most interest in the financial performance of a company. They are also forced to take an interest in how seriously the company takes its corporate social responsibility (CSR), whether or not they are socially and environmentally conscious themselves. Several high-profile cases have shown how stakeholder reaction has caused a significant decline in share prices. By using social media, stakeholders can generate a storm of public disapproval, leading to angry consumers and nervous investors.

How stakeholders affect share value

In April 2010, an offshore oil rig owned by British Petroleum (BP) exploded in the Gulf of Mexico. BP attempted to alleviate stakeholder concerns, but stakeholders responded negatively, starting their own social media campaigns to shame the company. Sixty-six days after the oil spill, BP's share value on the New York Stock Exchange had dropped by 52 percent.

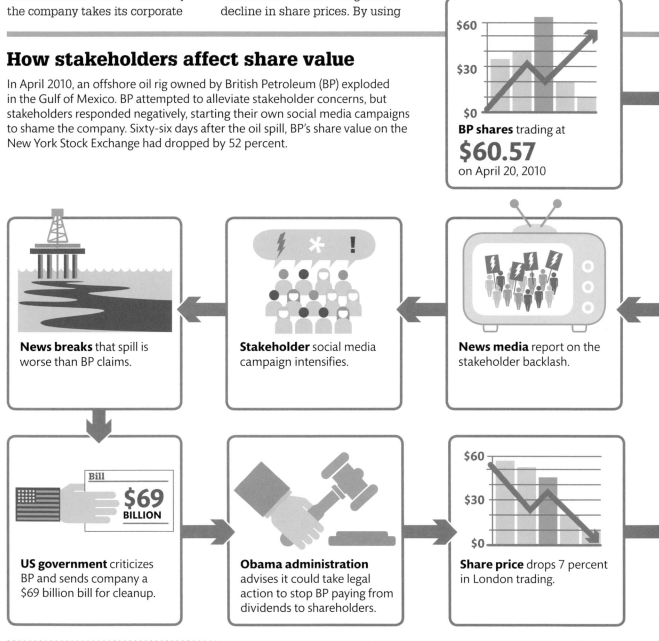

BP shares trading at
$60.57
on April 20, 2010

News breaks that spill is worse than BP claims.

Stakeholder social media campaign intensifies.

News media report on the stakeholder backlash.

US government criticizes BP and sends company a $69 billion bill for cleanup.

Bill
$69
BILLION

Obama administration advises it could take legal action to stop BP paying from dividends to shareholders.

Share price drops 7 percent in London trading.

75% the increase in the number of publicly traded companies* reporting on ESG

* in the Bloomberg database for the period 2008–2011

Oil rig explodes, killing 11 employees and spewing millions of gallons of oil into the Gulf of Mexico.

News media report on the event.

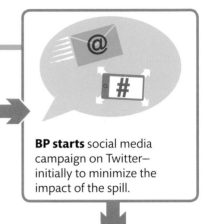

BP starts social media campaign on Twitter— initially to minimize the impact of the spill.

Stakeholders of the BP oil spill

- Inhabitants along the affected coastline
- Local fishermen
- Oil spill cleanup workers
- Environmental activists
- BP employees
- BP shareholders
- Gasoline buyers
- Tourists and tourist businesses
- Media
- Government
- General public

Stakeholders use social media to voice anger and concern over perceived lack of responsibility by BP. Conservationists warn of wildlife devastation. Celebrities offer to help in the cleanup. Stakeholders call for more disclosure from BP.

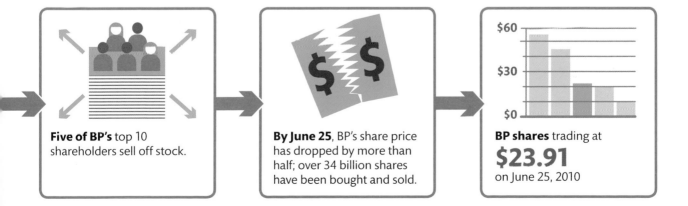

Five of BP's top 10 shareholders sell off stock.

By June 25, BP's share price has dropped by more than half; over 34 billion shares have been bought and sold.

BP shares trading at **$23.91** on June 25, 2010

Business cultures

Every organization has a particular workplace environment, consciously or unconsciously shaped by the personalities, values, and behavior of the people leading it and working in it.

How it works

The organizational culture of every business is different, reflecting the ethos of the company, its workplace habits, and the image the company projects. It is also tied to the type of work that has to be done. In a high-stakes financial trading company, the pace and pressure of the work makes the atmosphere of the corporate environment crackle, whereas in a company relying on creativity for its products, the mood is likely to be more relaxed. The type of incentives offered to management and employees may also affect the workplace, resulting in either a competitive or a collaborative culture, or a mix of both.

Types of corporate cultures

Management experts have tried to explain how organizational cultures work. Charles Handy, a former professor at the London Business School, describes them in terms of four major types: power, task, role, and person.

Role culture

Where a company is based on the structural support of specialized roles. Each role is crucial and will persist even if the person occupying it leaves. Procedures and systems are strictly followed, as in a government department.

Power culture

Driven by a powerful individual at the center of the organization, who is relied on for decision-making and the company's successes. Those closest to the center have most influence. Typical of a family-owned business.

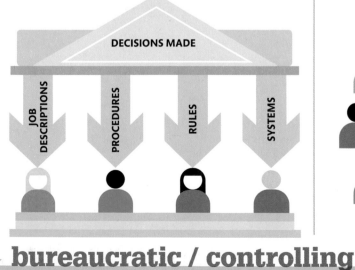

DECISIONS MADE

JOB DESCRIPTIONS • PROCEDURES • RULES • SYSTEMS

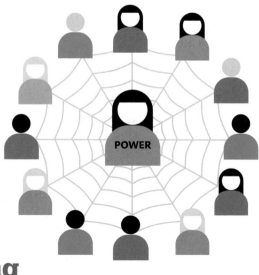

POWER

bureaucratic / controlling

WHAT SHAPES CORPORATE CULTURE?

Many factors reinforce a culture. To bring about change, the workforce needs to be inspired by different motivations, values, and types of role models.

Organization size
Big business, or small company

Company structure
Strict hierarchy, or power shared among many people

Founding values
Includes origination myths and stories

Leaders
Their personality and behavior

Symbols
Titles, dress codes, interior aesthetic

Control systems
Rewards, incentives, performance assessment

86%
of senior managers in global organizations agree that organizational culture is critical to success

Task culture

Project-oriented work where a project's completion is the motivating force. Relies on teamwork and individuals' expertise, but results are more important than personal objectives. Found in technology companies, for example.

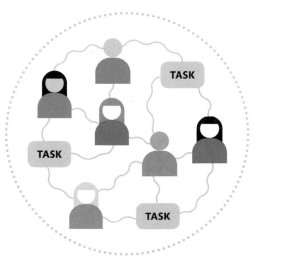

Person culture

Company power and influence is shared among individuals who work semi-autonomously. Individuals count for more than the company, which is made up of people with similar specialist training, such as in an architects' practice.

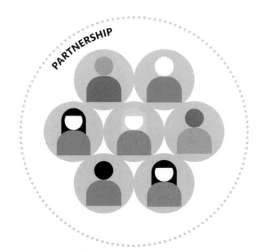

PARTNERSHIP

entrepreneurial / flexible

Corporate structure

A company's structure—the way in which it is organized—can have a major impact on the way it performs. There are several models of corporate structure typically used in the business world, and they continue to evolve. The first consideration is whether power should be centralized at the top, with decision-making in the hands of a few key senior employees, or decentralized, with more power in the hands of staff, and with fewer people to go through for approval.

Choosing a structure

Most start-ups have a centralized structure. More complex structures either evolve or are designed as the company grows, depending on the nature and size of the business, the complexity of the work, any requirement for instant expertise, and the geographical location of parts of the business.

Centralized

Power rests in the hands of a few people, with a long chain of command.

> Power at the top
> Rigid
> Conventional
> Inflexible
> Slow response to change

Functional

Good for strict control and formal relationships, as in the military.
See pp.68–69.

CEO COORDINATES

Divisional

Suits companies with many global offices or product lines.
See pp.70–71.

CEO COORDINATES AND EACH DIVISION RESPONSIBLE FOR GENERATING PROFIT

Matrix

Good for large corporations with complex projects in different locations.
See pp.76–77.

DIVISIONAL AND FUNCTIONAL MANAGERS COORDINATE

78%
of groups reach solutions to simple tasks faster in centralized structures

100%
of groups reach solutions to complex tasks faster in decentralized structures

! WARNING

When change is needed

Signs that a structure is not working include low morale and high staff turnover, no new products being developed, and profit suddenly accelerating or decelerating. Tools to amend poor structure include:

❯ **Business process reengineering (BPR)** Analyzing and redesigning the workflow within a company.

❯ **Altering the reporting line** In a traditional solid-line reporting relationship, one line manager oversees goals and performance. It can be beneficial to switch to the weaker chain of a dotted-line reporting relationship, in which a manager sets some but not all the objectives.

Network

Suits creative and technology companies in which everyone is online. *See pp.72–73.*

CORE COMPANY COLLABORATES WITH VIRTUAL COMMUNITY

Team-based

For companies that rely on innovation and are customer focused. *See pp.74–75.*

STAFF SELF-COORDINATE

Decentralized

Power is spread through the company, and staff make their own decisions.

❯ Power shared
❯ Organic
❯ Experimental
❯ Flexible
❯ Fast response to change

Functional structure

The classic way to organize a company is by dividing it into departments that reflect the main functions of the business, each headed by a director or manager.

How it works

The chain of command is straightforward. The business typically consists of a chief executive officer (CEO) or president at the top, with the various specialist departments or divisions, such as marketing and finance, aligned below.

Each department operates as an independent unit, with its own budget, and reports directly to the CEO, who takes responsibility for the operation of all the departments. A functional structure is the most common type of organization.

Typical departmental hierarchy

The departments operate independently, with the managers reporting to the CEO or president, who has overall command. The sales and marketing department usually takes responsibility for managing product lines.

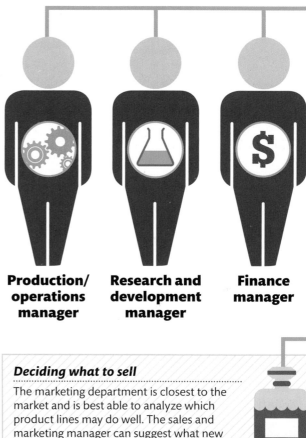

Production/ operations manager

Research and development manager

Finance manager

WARNING

Dangers of silo mentality

Silo mentality describes a scenario in which each department has a different, closed view of its role within the overall scheme and information does not get shared.

1 Sales and marketing decides to launch a special online two-for-one offer.

2 Finance is not briefed and processes the order for one item only.

3 Operations is not briefed and sends customers one item instead of two.

4 Customer services is not briefed and is unprepared for calls from angry shoppers.

Deciding what to sell

The marketing department is closest to the market and is best able to analyze which product lines may do well. The sales and marketing manager can suggest what new products the company could make.

PRODUCT A

CEO

41%
of UK companies say the structure of their organization is a barrier to improving customer experience

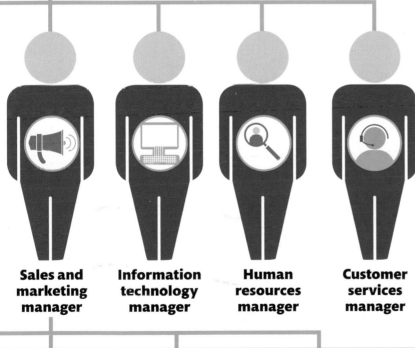

Sales and marketing manager

Information technology manager

Human resources manager

Customer services manager

PRODUCT B

PRODUCT C

PRODUCT D

FUNCTIONAL: PROS AND CONS

Pros
❯ Allows for the development of specialization and expertise
❯ Enables efficient use of resources and potential economies of scale
❯ Offers obvious career path for employees in each department
❯ Simple, efficient structure for manufacturers producing a limited range of goods for sale

Cons
❯ Formal lines of communication; stifles innovation and creativity
❯ Departments fail to coordinate efficiently with one another
❯ Response time on problems and queries between different departments slow
❯ Many decisions referred up to the top, creating a backlog

✓ NEED TO KNOW

❯ **Line relationship** Chain of command down the structure
❯ **Reporting structure** Who reports to whom
❯ **Silo** Pejorative term for a department that works in isolation: a vertical, closed structure like a grain silo

Divisional structure

Some companies arrange their staff into divisions devoted to a specific product or market. Each division is a self-sufficient team employing the personnel for the various functions within it.

How it works

Under the overall control of a CEO or president, several divisions work alongside one another to design, research, produce, and sell a particular product, or to service a specific market. Each division runs its own specialized functions, such as operations and production, sales and marketing, and finance. A company may arrange its divisions according to the types of product it makes, the regions in which it operates, or the customers to whom it sells. Large companies may adopt hybrid structures—by product and geography, for example.

Division by geography

For businesses with products that need to be adapted to local markets, an organization can be structured according to each of the regional markets it serves. These may be domestic or international. Print technology and services company Xerox has successfully adopted this structure (*see case study, right*).

North America
The company's main market

DIVISIONAL: PROS AND CONS

Pros

❭ If one division fails, there is no threat to the rest of the business

❭ Can respond quickly to changes in the market

❭ Focused on customer needs

❭ Performance of each division clearly measurable

Cons

❭ Duplicating resources—for example, each division employing finance personnel

❭ Lack of expertise-sharing between divisions

❭ Career path for staff restricted

❭ Heightened sense of competition among divisions

Division by product

Businesses selling different types of products may pick a structure by which each division handles one category. Fast-food chain McDonald's has been organized by product division.

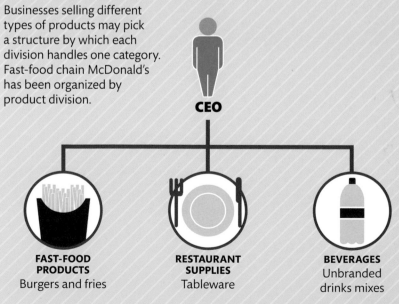

CEO

FAST-FOOD PRODUCTS
Burgers and fries

RESTAURANT SUPPLIES
Tableware

BEVERAGES
Unbranded drinks mixes

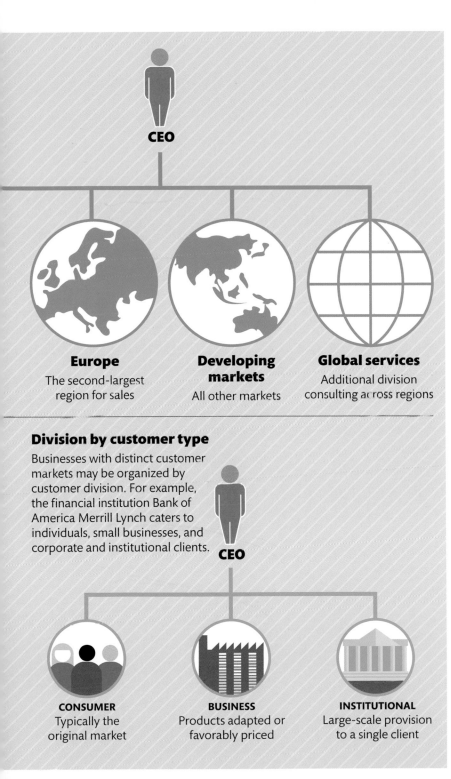

CEO

Europe
The second-largest
region for sales

Developing markets
All other markets

Global services
Additional division
consulting across regions

Division by customer type

Businesses with distinct customer
markets may be organized by
customer division. For example,
the financial institution Bank of
America Merrill Lynch caters to
individuals, small businesses, and
corporate and institutional clients.

CEO

CONSUMER
Typically the
original market

BUSINESS
Products adapted or
favorably priced

INSTITUTIONAL
Large-scale provision
to a single client

Printer technology and services
company Xerox has restructured
several times to align the business
with the main markets that buy its
products. In 1992, Xerox's high-
profile change from a functional
to a new divisional structure, with
nine self-contained divisions each
serving a particular customer type,
hit the headlines. This also allowed
the company to focus on its core
business—digital publishing, color
copying, and printing.

Dividing the company by market
location is another strategy Xerox
has used successfully. In 2006, each
division was organized once again,
geographically, to ensure that those
making the decisions were closest
to the customers in each market.

7%
the increase in
Xerox's share
value when
it announced
its move from
a functional
to a divisional
structure
in 1992

Matrix structure

Unlike a conventional company hierarchy organized either by function or division, a matrix combines the two approaches so that staff work in both functional and divisional units, and report to two bosses.

How it works

A business that uses a matrix setup often begins with the more traditional functional structure. As the business develops, it may make sense to overlay a divisional structure to meet changes in business conditions—for example, if a company is managing several large projects for a client or expands globally and is selling its products in several regions. A matrix grid may start out as temporary—perhaps formed to manage short-term projects—and become permanent.

The two chains of command in a matrix create the grid. Staff report along a vertical line to a functional manager, such as the marketing director, and along a horizontal line to the project manager of a specific business line, brand, project, or region.

FOUR BIG MATRIX ORGANIZATIONS

Each of the following companies has been cited as a model of success for making the matrix structure work:

❯ **Procter & Gamble (P&G)** To help it innovate and respond faster to the market, the consumer-product company is segmented into baby and family care, global beauty, health and grooming, and global fabric and home care.

❯ **IBM** Because it needs to control many global processes, the matrix at the technology and consulting corporation is structured vertically by divisions such as sales and distribution, finance and marketing, and software, and horizontally by country and region.

❯ **Cisco** In 2001, the IT company reorganized to enable committees to make decisions across several different functions and divisions. The idea was to stimulate ideas throughout the organization and quickly implement solutions to problems.

❯ **Starbucks** The coffee-shop chain is arranged by product on one axis of the matrix and business function on the other to ensure that quality and innovation meet customers' expectations and anticipate their desires.

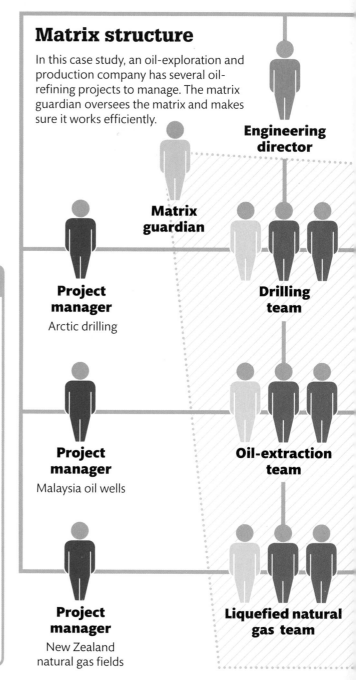

Matrix structure

In this case study, an oil-exploration and production company has several oil-refining projects to manage. The matrix guardian oversees the matrix and makes sure it works efficiently.

Engineering director

Matrix guardian

Project manager
Arctic drilling

Drilling team

Project manager
Malaysia oil wells

Oil-extraction team

Project manager
New Zealand natural gas fields

Liquefied natural gas team

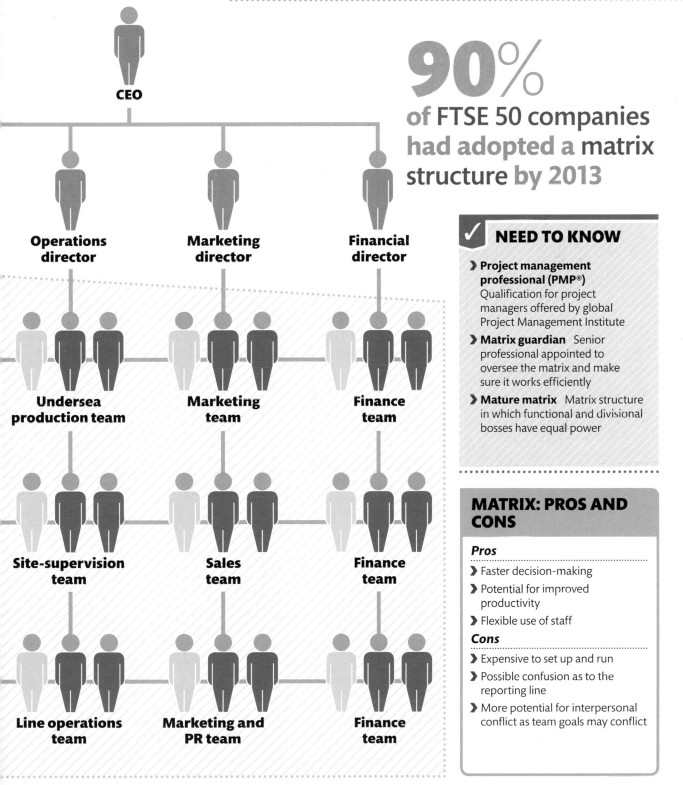

CEO

Operations director

Marketing director

Financial director

Undersea production team

Marketing team

Finance team

Site-supervision team

Sales team

Finance team

Line operations team

Marketing and PR team

Finance team

90% of FTSE 50 companies had adopted a matrix structure by 2013

✓ NEED TO KNOW

> **Project management professional (PMP®)** Qualification for project managers offered by global Project Management Institute

> **Matrix guardian** Senior professional appointed to oversee the matrix and make sure it works efficiently

> **Mature matrix** Matrix structure in which functional and divisional bosses have equal power

MATRIX: PROS AND CONS

Pros
> Faster decision-making
> Potential for improved productivity
> Flexible use of staff

Cons
> Expensive to set up and run
> Possible confusion as to the reporting line
> More potential for interpersonal conflict as team goals may conflict

Network structure

Also called a virtual organization or virtual corporation, a network structure is centered around a streamlined company, with digital connections linking it to external, independent businesses.

How it works

The company at the center of the structure is stripped back to basic functions that are essential to the type of business being operated—research and development, for example, in the case of a technology company. All other functions are outsourced to external specialists.

The various parties can be scattered around the globe and are connected by the internet. Together, they provide all the services needed for the network to function as one entity. This type of business structure is based on the idea of the social media network, and so is known as a network enterprise.

✓ NEED TO KNOW

> **Agile business** Buzzword to describe a networked organization; the opposite of a traditional bureaucracy

> **Decentralized** Organization with a wide span of control and often an upward flow of ideas

Network structure in practice

Network Screen is a small film production company based in Los Angeles, CA, operating from a studio space with two employees—a producer and an assistant. For each project, the producer connects with outsourced talent around the world and everyone collaborates to create the finished film. The producer contracts and pays these external suppliers.

VARIATION: MODULAR STRUCTURE

In a business with a modular structure, parts of a single product are outsourced (it is functions or processes, not products, that are outsourced in a network structure). A modular structure is especially suitable for organizations producing appliances, computers, cars, and mechanical consumer goods. Toyota is an example of a company with a modular structure, managing hundreds of external suppliers to produce its finished vehicles.

Pros

> Potential for round-the-clock work because of global locations

> Can source the best expertise wherever it is in the world

> Low overheads because there are minimal staff in the core company

> Flexible and highly creative environment

Cons

> Extreme reliance on technology—network errors can stop effective performance of the business

> Potential for misunderstandings because there is little face-to-face communication

> Difficult to find common time across time zones for virtual meetings

27%
of networked organizations report higher profit margins than their competitors

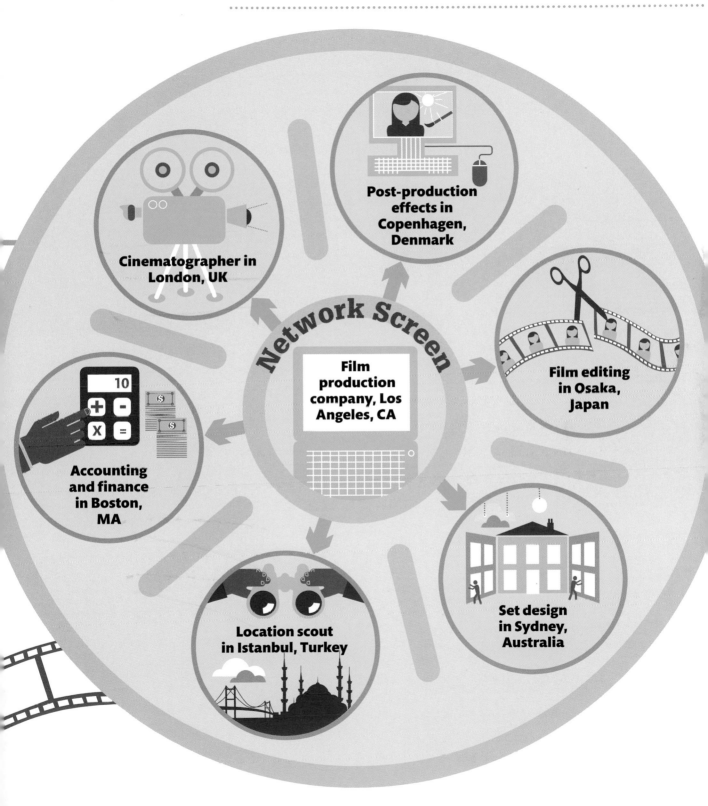

Network Screen

Film production company, Los Angeles, CA

Post-production effects in Copenhagen, Denmark

Cinematographer in London, UK

Film editing in Osaka, Japan

Accounting and finance in Boston, MA

Set design in Sydney, Australia

Location scout in Istanbul, Turkey

Team-based structure

As its name implies, a team-based organization (TBO) is made up entirely of teams. Managers and staff from different departments join to form teams handling specific projects, in the short or long term.

How it works

In a TBO, teams reach decisions through brainstorming and mutual agreement among team members, rather than a senior management member issuing orders from the top down the chain of command as in a traditional organizational structure. Communication is less formal in TBOs, often carried out on social media such as blogs and forums and using software for networking such as Groupware.

One step beyond the team-based structure is a holacracy (*see box, right*), an unconventional type of organization in which there are no managers, and even the CEO relinquishes power, allowing employees to self-govern through regular committee meetings, which they organize themselves.

✓ NEED TO KNOW

> **Cascading** Successful passing of information or objectives down through the workforce

> **Lateral structure** Decentralized structure in which departments work to a common goal

> **Flat lattice** Structure with no chains of command, in which workers choose to follow leaders

Team-based hierarchy

While TBOs still have a CEO, little other hierarchy exists. Team leaders are part of the team rather than in a chain of command. At its best, a team-based model fosters a culture of trust, so individuals take pride in their work and responsibility for carrying out tasks well and on time and budget.

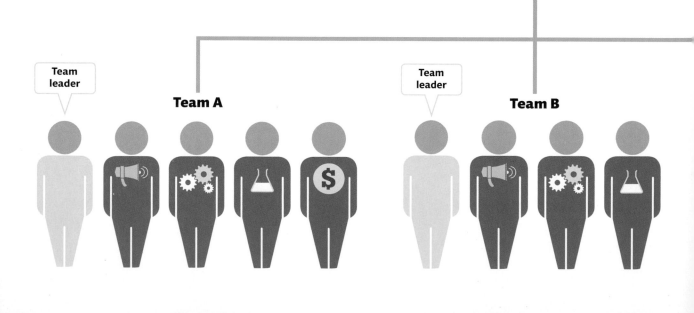

CEO

Team leader

Team A

Team leader

Team B

HOLACRACY–BREAKING BOUNDARIES

Staff are grouped into teams that set their own roles and goals and choose their own leaders. The idea is that if power and responsibility are shared, employees will give their very best. In 2014, the Las Vegas–based online clothing retailer Zappos adopted the model for its 1,500 staff. Holacracy is a trademarked term used by the company that invented this specific management system. It follows the same principle as a flat lattice, but takes the idea one step further by presenting a comprehensive management structure with clear processes for internal operations and governance.

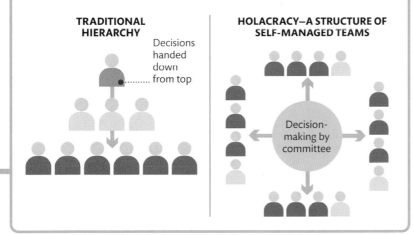

TRADITIONAL HIERARCHY

Decisions handed down from top

HOLACRACY–A STRUCTURE OF SELF-MANAGED TEAMS

Decision-making by committee

200–300%

the productivity increase at US sausage-maker Johnsonville Foods, from 1982 to 1990, by moving to a team-based structure

TEAM-BASED: PROS AND CONS

Pros

❯ Quick decision-making and rapid response to problems and challenges

❯ Reduced overheads because there is no heavy management structure

❯ Open communication because there is no fear of management reaction

Cons

❯ If staff lack expertise, decisions may be flawed

❯ Limited sharing between teams may affect business performance

❯ Decisions by consensus harder to reach

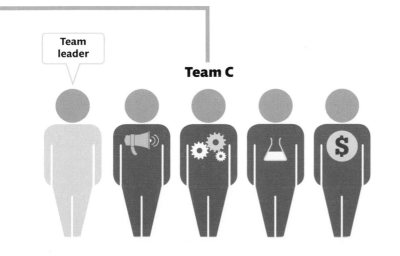

Team leader

Team C

Human resources

The human resources (HR) department is responsible for all policies and processes relating to the people employed by a business. To help the business achieve its goals, HR has to make sure that it employs the right people with the right skills, treats them consistently and fairly, and has a supporting framework to drive and deliver the required level of performance.

HR framework

The starting point for any decision in an organization is its business goals. HR supports the delivery of these goals by ensuring that there is a staffing strategy to support the business plan. Typically, an HR framework sets out a people strategy including the competencies of the people who best suit the organization. This is then implemented in a range of areas, from recruitment and selection to learning and development. HR professionals work closely with business leaders and line managers to design and implement HR systems that back up strategic business goals.

Business goals

Business goals are the driver for every business decision, and HR polices support them.

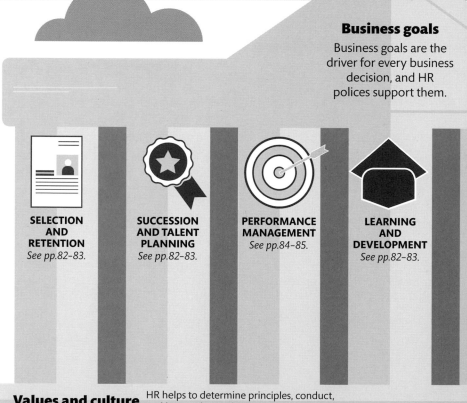

SELECTION AND RETENTION
See pp.82–83.

SUCCESSION AND TALENT PLANNING
See pp.82–83.

PERFORMANCE MANAGEMENT
See pp.84–85.

LEARNING AND DEVELOPMENT
See pp.82–83.

Values and culture HR helps to determine principles, conduct, and how tasks are done in a business.

Organization design HR formulates the structure and formal reporting relationships that define a company's shape.

People and performance HR is responsible for employees' welfare and their contribution to business goals.

3.2 billion
people were in recorded employment globally in 2014

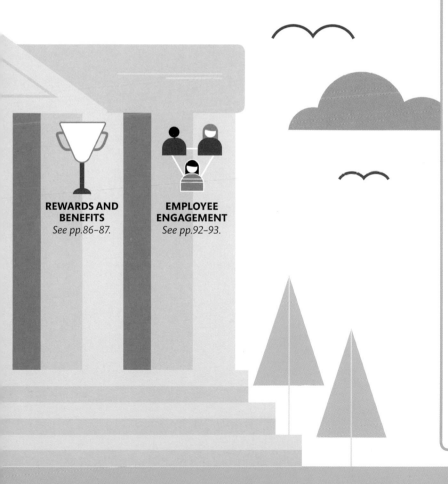

REWARDS AND BENEFITS
See pp.86–87.

EMPLOYEE ENGAGEMENT
See pp.92–93.

ESSENTIAL PEOPLE SKILLS

As well as recruiting effectively and ensuring that employees deliver, HR plays a role in nurturing essential people skills across the organization.

Relating to others

❯ Some people are natural leaders, but most leaders can benefit from objective thinking about the leadership strategy they wish to follow. *See pp.88–89.*

❯ Even in flattened, team-based hierarchies, team leaders need to develop leadership skills to guide and support their teams. *See pp.90–91.*

❯ Despite the revolution in technology, people remain vital to organizations, as skills and knowledge are central to success. As a result, HR has an expanding role. One example is Google, which calls its HR function People Operations (POPS) and treats its staff as a valuable asset, offering a range of attractive perks to "find them, grow them, and keep them." *See pp.92–93.*

Managing projects

❯ Project management is an essential skill for managers at all levels, whether they are running regular day-to-day activities or special projects. *See pp.94–95.*

Negotiating

❯ The ability to negotiate successfully is an essential skill. Awareness of strategies and styles is key to success. *See pp.96–97.*

The human resources cycle

From the moment a company starts the process of recruiting an employee to the time that person leaves the company, the individual is in a cycle that is managed by the human resources (HR) department.

How it works

People are a significant cost to any organization—and of great value. Many CEOs talk about staff as their most important asset, and US industrialist Henry Ford famously said: "You can take my factories, burn up my buildings, but give me my people and I'll build the business right back again." The HR department is there to ensure that the right people are in the right roles so that the company can deliver the business strategy and maintain its competitive edge. The complexity of the business influences the stages in the HR cycle, but the basic elements are the same.

Recruit

A business identifies the need to fill a role, and attracts applicants. CVs are assessed and interviews held to find the best candidate.

Employ

Once terms are agreed and a contract signed, the candidate becomes the company's employee.

"Hire people smarter than you **and** get out of their way."

Howard Schultz

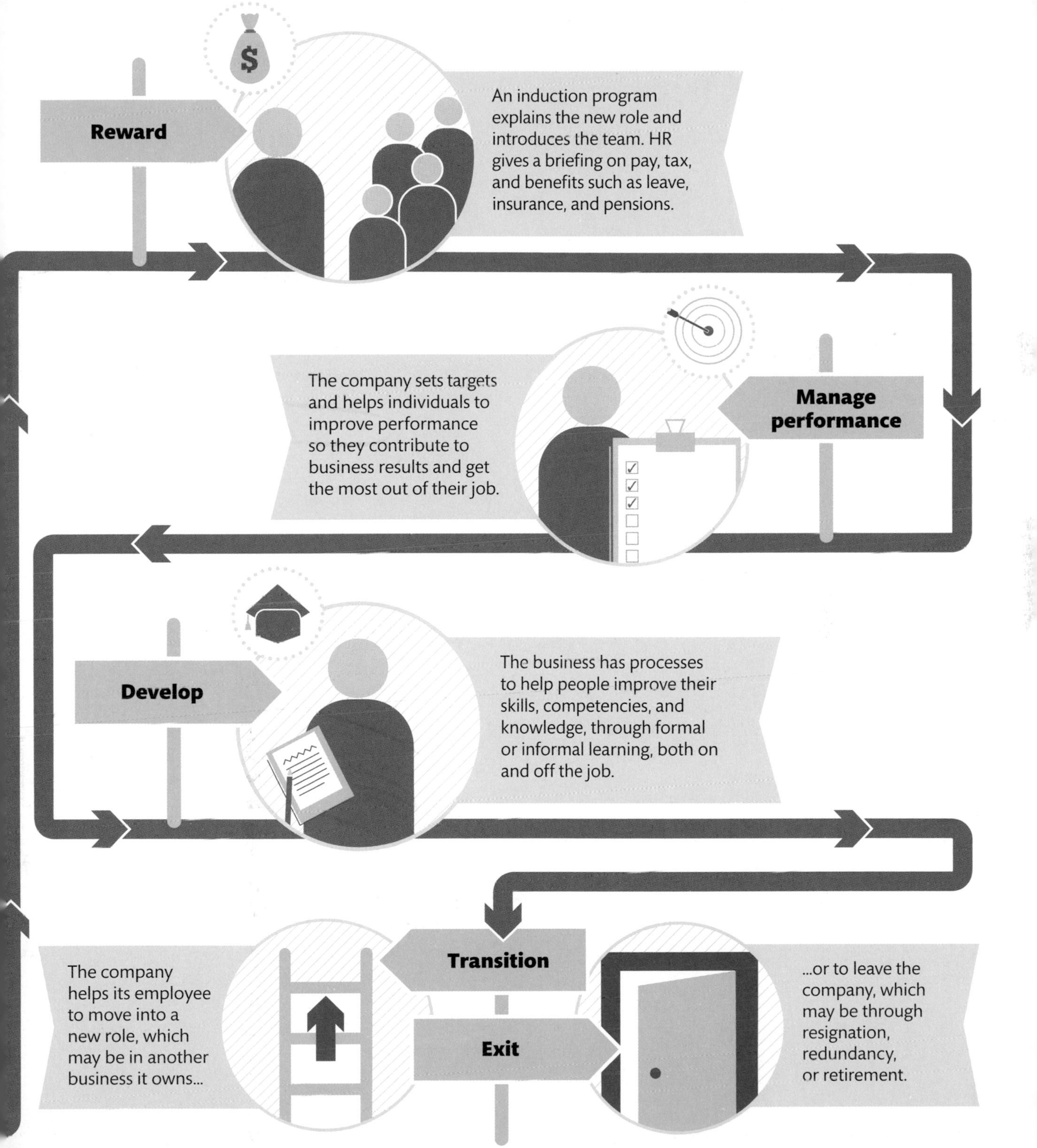

Reward

An induction program explains the new role and introduces the team. HR gives a briefing on pay, tax, and benefits such as leave, insurance, and pensions.

Manage performance

The company sets targets and helps individuals to improve performance so they contribute to business results and get the most out of their job.

Develop

The business has processes to help people improve their skills, competencies, and knowledge, through formal or informal learning, both on and off the job.

Transition

Exit

The company helps its employee to move into a new role, which may be in another business it owns...

...or to leave the company, which may be through resignation, redundancy, or retirement.

Recruitment and selection

Placing the right person in the right job is vital for the success of the organization—this is the process of recruitment and selection. Technology is changing traditional hiring pathways.

How it works

The human resources function manages the process. Increasingly, line managers are involved as well because the tools are often accessible via company intranet.

Recruitment starts with the company identifying a vacancy—the need for someone to do a job, and pulling together information about the exact nature of the role. Aspects to consider include the job's purpose, tasks required, and the outputs or deliverables of the job holder, as well as how the role fits into the organization's structure. This information forms the basis of a job description and person specification. The search can then begin. The company's own website, recruitment agencies, commercial job boards, and advertisements in the press are traditional ways of attracting the attention of people outside the organization. Internet-based routes are now common too. Today, application forms are often directly submitted online, triggering automatic responses and sorting of candidate details.

94%
of recruiters in the US **used, or planned to use,** social media for recruiting in 2013

✓ **Job description and person specification**
✓ Clear written statement
✓ of the role, including job title, purpose, duties, responsibilities, scope, and reporting structure, as well as competencies and qualities required. It is used in the recruitment process to provide a clear guide for both applicants and interviewers.

Person specification
Summarizes the necessary or desired criteria for candidate selection, including required skills and/or competencies for the role, experience, and educational qualifications.

Internal search

Looking at internal resources first creates opportunities for career development and progression, improving employee engagement and retention.

Personal recommendation

Some companies encourage existing employees to introduce friends as candidates.

External search

Increasingly, companies and candidates use professional networking sites such as LinkedIn and social media such as Facebook or Twitter. External candidates diversify the workforce but cost more to attract.

Applications

The curriculum vitae (CV) or résumé is the essential document, often with a cover letter. Companies may use an application form instead.

✓ NEED TO KNOW

❯ **Psychometric tests** Often used as an initial screening method, these aim to assess attributes such as intelligence, aptitude, and type of personality, using verbal and non-verbal reasoning tests and behavior questionnaires.

CONTRACT

Selection

After HR has drawn up a shortlist, candidates are assessed by individual face-to-face interviews, group assesssment, and psychometric testing.

Appointment

Companies may ask for references and/or request a medical examination for the chosen candidate. The employment offer is a legally binding contract that sets out the terms and conditions of the job.

Evaluating staff

For a business to achieve its goals, it needs to have a process that measures the contribution and performance of each individual against those goals.

How it works

The way in which tasks are done is becoming as important as what tasks are done, as organizations recognize the importance of creating the right culture to enable workers' performance. For any company, effective evaluation of the performance of employees should be strategic and is aimed at ensuring the maximum productivity of individuals, teams, and the organization as a whole.

Traditional performance-management cycle

Performance management is an ongoing, continuous process. Some companies are now moving away from traditional performance management to "crowdsourcing" as a way for managers to collect, evaluate, and share information on employee performance.

A WIN-WIN SITUATION

Evaluating performance is good for both the business and the individual.

Business

> Aligns individual goals with company goals.
> Offers consistent approach, with benchmarks.
> Continuously enables improvement.
> Fosters the right behaviors and relationships.

Individual

> Understands what is expected of them.
> Has the skills to deliver on these expectations.
> Is supported to fill any gaps in capability.
> Is given feedback and allowed to discuss goals.

1

Individual goals

Set personal goals to align with business strategy

> **Business goals** drive tasks and activity.
> **Culture** enables teams and individuals to deliver.
> **HR policies** give clear benchmarks.

WINNER!

5

Rewards

Promotions and pay raises in line with performance

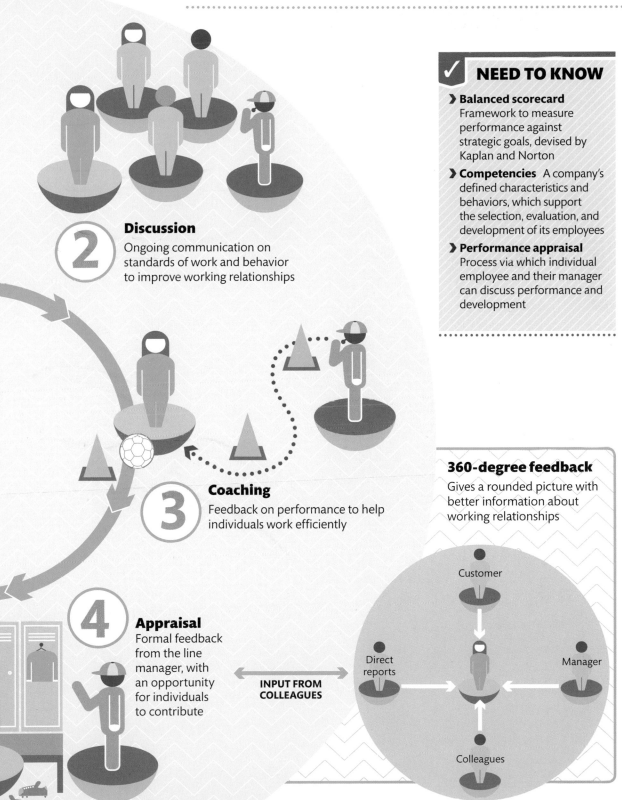

2 Discussion
Ongoing communication on standards of work and behavior to improve working relationships

3 Coaching
Feedback on performance to help individuals work efficiently

4 Appraisal
Formal feedback from the line manager, with an opportunity for individuals to contribute

INPUT FROM COLLEAGUES

✓ NEED TO KNOW

❯ **Balanced scorecard** Framework to measure performance against strategic goals, devised by Kaplan and Norton

❯ **Competencies** A company's defined characteristics and behaviors, which support the selection, evaluation, and development of its employees

❯ **Performance appraisal** Process via which individual employee and their manager can discuss performance and development

360-degree feedback
Gives a rounded picture with better information about working relationships

Customer

Direct reports

Manager

Colleagues

Motivation and rewards

People work for money, but they are also motivated by other factors such as doing a good job and being valued. Non-financial rewards drive day-to-day motivation more strongly than pay and benefits.

How it works

In the past, tangible pay and benefits were the key motivational tools for employees. These financial rewards are termed extrinsic because they are external to the actual work and others control the amount, distribution, and timing. Employers now recognize that while extrinsic incentives are clearly important, intrinsic (psychological) rewards are crucial.

Understanding motivation in the workplace

Happy staff work well, and job satisfaction comes from subtle feel-good factors as much as a paycheck. Employees who enjoy their work tend to stay—job satisfaction and turnover move in opposite directions.

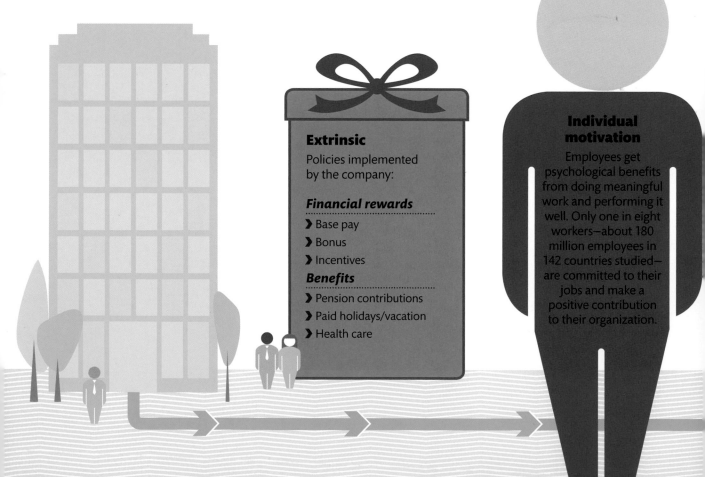

Extrinsic

Policies implemented by the company:

Financial rewards
- Base pay
- Bonus
- Incentives

Benefits
- Pension contributions
- Paid holidays/vacation
- Health care

Individual motivation

Employees get psychological benefits from doing meaningful work and performing it well. Only one in eight workers—about 180 million employees in 142 countries studied—are committed to their jobs and make a positive contribution to their organization.

13%
the percentage of employees who are fully committed to their jobs

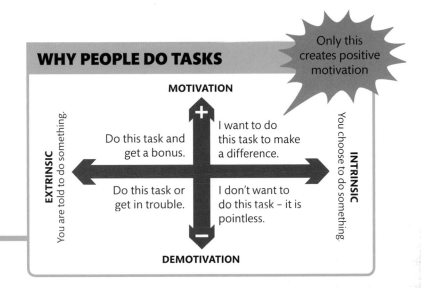

WHY PEOPLE DO TASKS

Only this creates positive motivation

MOTIVATION

EXTRINSIC You are told to do something.

INTRINSIC You choose to do something.

Do this task and get a bonus.

I want to do this task to make a difference.

Do this task or get in trouble.

I don't want to do this task – it is pointless.

DEMOTIVATION

Intrinsic

Feelings that an individual has:

- **Purpose** A sense of being able to accomplish something of value
- **Choice** Clear ownership and feeling responsible for outcome
- **Progress** As an individual, feeling and seeing evidence of moving things forward
- **Competence** Pride and satisfaction in own work

Fostering intrinsic rewards

Businesses that are successful engender trust and have employees who are passionate about what they do. All these factors contribute:

Purpose for organization and individual
- Clear vision for organization
- Understanding of where individual fits in to achieve that purpose
- Clear goals and expectations for individual

Recognition
- Continuous feedback
- Ongoing engagement
- Non-cash rewards such as praise

Career development
- Progression and promotion
- Mentoring and coaching
- Learning opportunities

Culture
- Strong teamwork and consistent behaviors
- Open communication
- Sharing of knowledge and information

INCREASING MOTIVATION

Leadership strategy and styles

Top-down leadership, in which managers give orders, is not always the best way to get results. A number of different leadership styles have been identified by business experts.

How it works

Every leader is an individual with his or her own approach. However, over the years, management gurus have identified key leadership styles that can be used to achieve different results, depending on the environment. Many frameworks are based on the ideas of psychologist Kurt Lewin, who developed his theories in the 1930s with three major styles: autocratic, democratic, and laissez-faire (non-interference).

In 2007, for example, business authors Eric Flamholtz and Yvonne Randle developed a leadership matrix based on Lewin's theories, which shows the best style to use in any given situation, ranging from autocratic (one all-powerful leader) to consensus (decisions reached by general agreement). Truly inspirational leaders encourage people to believe in themselves so that they achieve results beyond even their own expectations.

> "Outstanding leaders go out of their way to boost the self-esteem of their personnel."
>
> Sam Walton

TRANSFORMATIONAL LEADERSHIP

While different styles can suit different situations, transformational leadership, in which leaders and their followers raise one another to higher levels of integrity and motivation, was identified by guru James McGregor Burns as the most effective. This has been developed by others, including industrial psychologist Bernard Bass, who listed the qualities of a transformational leader.

- Is a model of integrity and fairness
- Sets clear goals
- Has high expectations
- Encourages others
- Provides support and recognition
- Stirs the emotions of people
- Gets people to look beyond their self-interest
- Inspires people to reach for the improbable

When to use which leadership style

A three-year study of 3,000 managers led psychologist Daniel Goleman to uncover six distinctive styles of leadership. Each style has a significant impact on how people feel about their work. The most effective leaders master a number of styles and use them appropriately according to the situation.

	Style	When to use	Drawbacks
Affiliative	**"People come before task."** Focuses on creating emotional bonds within a team and a sense of belonging within an organization.	Use in times of stress, when teammates need to recover from trauma, or when the team needs to rebuild trust.	Praise and nurturing can foster mediocre performance and lack of direction.
Coaching	**"Try this."** Helps people find their strengths and weaknesses, linking these to career aspirations and action.	Use to help teammates build lasting personal strengths that make them more successful.	Coaching is ineffective when teammates are defiant and/or unwilling to change or learn, or if a leader lacks ability.
Commanding/ coercive	**"Do what I tell you."** Demands immediate compliance, without discussion or negotiation.	Only use in times of crisis or to control a problem employee when all else fails.	Insistence should only be used when essential; it can alienate people, stifle inventiveness, and create a tense atmosphere.
Democratic	**"What do you think?"** Goal is to build consensus through participation.	Use when it is necessary for the team to buy into or have ownership of, a decision, plan, or goal.	This is not for use in crisis or when teammates are not well enough informed to be able to offer suitable guidance to the leader.
Pacesetting	**"Do as I do, now."** Expects and models excellence, creating challenging and exciting goals for the team.	Only use when the team is already motivated and competent, and when fast results are necessary.	Style can overwhelm some team members and adversely affect employee commitment; it may stifle creativity and innovation.
Visionary/ authoritative	**"Come with me."** Mobilizes the team toward a common vision and goal, leaving the means up to the individual.	Use when the team needs a new vision because circumstances have changed, or when explicit guidance is not required.	This is not effective when a leader is working with a team of experts or better-informed group.

Leadership for team building

Just as generals have to get the best from their troops, so business leaders must make the most of their teams. The key is ensuring that individuals work together to achieve a common goal.

How it works

From statesmen such as former British prime minster Winston Churchill to former General Electric CEO Jack Welch, great leaders know that to achieve a long-term goal, they must not only use their own capabilities but also maximize the combined strength of other people.

They have a passion that sweeps people along with them; they learn from mistakes and are prepared to alter their course to meet changing circumstances. Much academic work has been done to study the traits and strategies of such leaders.

How leaders inspire their teams

Academic Carl Larson and organizational effectiveness expert Frank LaFasto conducted a three-year study of more than 75 diverse teams. They identified six characteristics of leadership that steer a team toward optimum results.

Focusing on goal
> Defines goal in clear and inspirational way
> Helps each team member see how they contribute to goal
> Does not play politics

Encouraging collaboration
> Allows open discussions
> Demands and rewards collaboration
> Involves and engages people

Building confidence
> Accentuates the positive
> Shows trust by assigning responsibility
> Says "thank you"

"Leadership is the art of getting someone else to do something you want done because he wants to do it."

Dwight D. Eisenhower

BUILDING AN EFFECTIVE TEAM

In their book *The Wisdom of Teams* (1993), Jon Katzenbach and Douglas Smith make a distinction between teams and ordinary groups of people who work together. They define a team as "a small number of people with complementary skills who are committed to a common purpose, set of performance goals, and approach for which they hold themselves mutually accountable." They found that leaders who manage to build successful teams tend to:

❭ Select members for skill and potential, not personality.

❭ Focus on a few immediate tasks and goals at the beginning, to help the team to bond.

❭ Set boundaries and behavioral norms.

❭ Stimulate the team regularly with new information, encouraging open discussions and active problem-solving.

❭ Ensure that the team spends lots of time together, both in and outside of work.

> "Don't find fault – find a remedy"
>
> Henry Ford,
> *American industrialist*

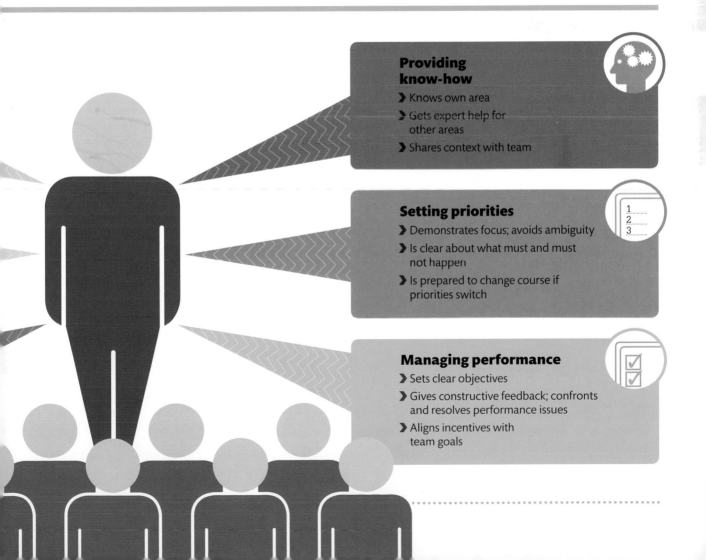

Providing know-how
❭ Knows own area
❭ Gets expert help for other areas
❭ Shares context with team

Setting priorities
❭ Demonstrates focus; avoids ambiguity
❭ Is clear about what must and must not happen
❭ Is prepared to change course if priorities switch

Managing performance
❭ Sets clear objectives
❭ Gives constructive feedback; confronts and resolves performance issues
❭ Aligns incentives with team goals

Employee relations and communications

Thriving organizations recognize the importance of harnessing people's ideas and energy to provide a competitive edge, while managers are eager to gain, retain, and build employee commitment and engagement.

How it works

Employee relations and communications are, either managed by human resources (HR) or as a function in their own right, are increasingly sophisticated. Rather than just relying on face-to-face talks and word of mouth, successful firms use added communication tools to help people understand the business goals and the individual's contribution to results. In particular, leaders no longer send only one-way messages but harness a variety of interactive media, such as video- and tele-conferencing. Individuals and teams can use customized business social media, such as Yammer, to share ideas and knowledge, but may still choose to meet in formal settings such as councils and forums.

Communication in practice

In this example, a company is establishing weekly employee forums to facilitate communication and build trust throughout the business. To strengthen employee awarenees, engagement, and commitment to the idea, various media are used, from email to webinars and discussion. Managers focus ever more on collaboration rather than just imparting information.

EMPLOYEE FORUMS

In many countries, employee communications used to focus on structured industrial relations, managed by HR. Employee relations are now based more on trust and building strong relationships. Many firms create formal works councils or employee forums.

At their best, employee forums:

> Allow representatives from across the business to share and generate ideas for improving performance.

> Encourage discussions on vision, changes, and plans for business.

> Recognize the value of employees.

Commitment

Engagement and involvement

Awareness and understanding

CONTACT
An email is sent to all employees with a short video informing them an employee forum is to be set up.

DEGREE OF COMMITMENT

TIME

CASE STUDY

John Lewis

The UK-based John Lewis chain of department stores is famous for its unique employee-owned structure, in which every worker is a partner in the business. It has a number of employee communication policies:

> **Gazette** Employees can send letters directly to management through the weekly gazette. Managers publish their responses in the gazette for all to read.

> **Partnership council** Made up of 80 elected partners from across the business, the council meets four times a year. The chairman and directors report to the council, which can remove the chairman.

> **Branch forums** Elected by employees at each branch, these forums work with management to influence the running of their store and select local charities to support.

$316 million
the amount paid in staff bonuses by John Lewis in 2013

REINFORCE AND INTERNALIZE
Regular face-to-face updates show employees how forums have made a difference.

ESTABLISH PRACTICE
A company-wide awayday illustrates to employees how the forums have changed working practices.

STIMULATE POSITIVE PERCEPTION
An inspirational seminar illustrates the benefits of the new forums.

AID UNDERSTANDING
Resources placed on the company intranet detail how employee forums will work.

ADOPT AND SHARE
Employees attend forums and then share their opinions on Twitter and Yammer so they feel involved and collaborate with managers.

CREATE AWARENESS
The purpose of employee forums is explained at a company-wide video conference.

project management

Besides day-to-day activities, a business may have projects—one-time, temporary, specific pieces of work. Projects need to be managed to deliver on time, within budget, and to specifications.

How it works

The process of project management takes a complex project from start to finish. It requires a different set of knowledge, experience, and skills from a mainstream operation because the goals set up have to be achieved within defined limitations. These constraints include scope, time, quality, and budget. A project team might include people from different organizations, diverse disciplines, and multiple locations. Successful project management involves not only overseeing the people working towards the particular objective, but also managing the risks, schedule, relationships, individual and team input, range of stakeholders with vested interests in the project, and financial resources.

Effective project management is increasingly viewed as a strategic competence (*see p.85*) for any business because it enables the introduction of new products, new methods, and new technology.

(*see p.85*)

✓ NEED TO KNOW

Project management tools

There are many different project management tools, particularly for software development. One tool is PRINCE2®, a process-based approach to project management within a clear framework. The emphasis is on dividing the project into manageable and controllable stages with a defined structure for the project management team.

Steps in project management

There are many workable project management systems, using various definitions for the key stages, all of which are encompassed in five main elements.

Initiation
> Project charter, including business case, objective, scope, budget, deliverables, and schedule
> Roles and responsibilities
> Resource allocation

Planning
> Detailed plan of work
> Critical path analysis
> Risks

Execution
> Coordinating people and resources
> Quality assurance
> Communication to team and stakeholders

HURDLES AND HOW TO OVERCOME THEM

Every project comes up against challenges. These are some of the common ones, and the ways that effective management can keep the project on track.

Obstacle	Project management	Options
Project is not on schedule, or running short of time	❯ Map out timeline of work and critical paths using tools and techniques. ❯ Review remaining work and identify risks, barriers, and mitigating strategies.	❯ Negotiate scope, budget, and resources. ❯ Inform other teams and see if any changes can be factored in.
Unclear vision or lack of clarity	❯ Review project charter and revisit vision and objective. ❯ Involve team so everyone understands direction of work and avoids stalling.	❯ Seek clarity from sponsors and/or senior management.
Scope creep (project changes once under way)	❯ Manage requests for change against business case and project objective.	❯ Communicate to identify why change is important and how to incorporate, or find alternative.

Monitoring and control
❯ Measuring effort and progress
❯ Managing and mitigating risk
❯ People management

Closure
❯ Finalizing all activities
❯ Communication
❯ Learning—project review

97%
of managers*
believe project
management
is critical
to success
*surveyed from 34 different countries

Negotiating strategy

Skillful negotiation is vital in business when two or more sides have different viewpoints and each party wants to press for their own advantage. The ideal outcome is a compromise that resolves conflict.

How it works

Like many aspects of business, negotiation is a process to find a mutually acceptable solution. Before any discussion, each party must work to understand the other's interests and decide on strategy; otherwise talks can end in stalemate, bad feeling, and loss of business. Being able to negotiate is vital to build strong working relationships, deliver a sustainable, well-considered solution (rather than a short-term fix), and avoid future conflicts.

Reaching agreement

Any strategy, from a wage negotiation between a trade union and employer to a sales negotiation between a customer and a supplier, depends on the relationship between the two parties. Good negotiation should leave each party feeling satisfied with the outcome of the discussion and ready to do business again.

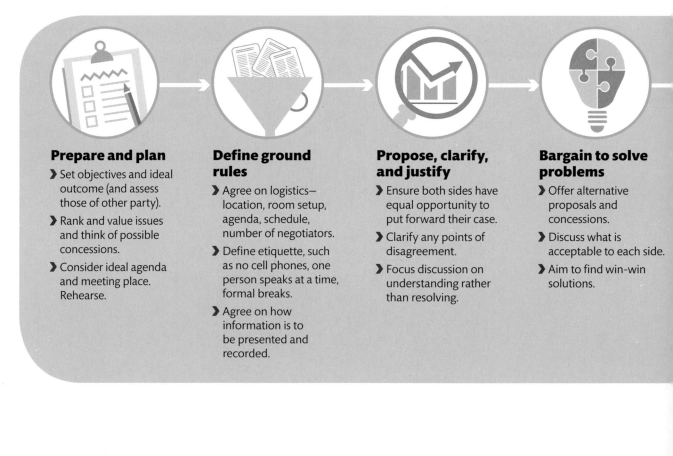

Prepare and plan

❯ Set objectives and ideal outcome (and assess those of other party).

❯ Rank and value issues and think of possible concessions.

❯ Consider ideal agenda and meeting place. Rehearse.

Define ground rules

❯ Agree on logistics—location, room setup, agenda, schedule, number of negotiators.

❯ Define etiquette, such as no cell phones, one person speaks at a time, formal breaks.

❯ Agree on how information is to be presented and recorded.

Propose, clarify, and justify

❯ Ensure both sides have equal opportunity to put forward their case.

❯ Clarify any points of disagreement.

❯ Focus discussion on understanding rather than resolving.

Bargain to solve problems

❯ Offer alternative proposals and concessions.

❯ Discuss what is acceptable to each side.

❯ Aim to find win-win solutions.

65%
of face-to-face communication is through non-verbal signals

Agree, close, and implement

> Conclude with an agreement that is mutually acceptable.

> Clearly articulate and note agreement and concessions.

> Formalize agreement in writing and follow up.

BODY LANGUAGE IN DIFFERENT CULTURES

With international negotiations, it can be hard to read body language signals, particularly since the meaning of gestures can vary.

Eye contact Chinese people avoid direct eye contact to show respect while American people see lack of eye contact as a sign of shiftiness.

Facial expressions When emotions are high in the US, it is acceptable to frown, even to swear, but not to cry. Japanese people might smile or laugh, but never frown or cry.

Head movements In much of Europe and the US, people nod to mean yes and shake their head to mean no. But in some parts of the world, such as in Bulgaria, it is the opposite way round.

Gestures Western cultures use a hand extended towards a person to indicate "Come here". Chinese people would see this gesture as offensive.

Posture In the US, being casual is valued; people might slouch when standing or sitting. In some European countries, such as Germany, a slouching posture is considered rude. Formality is also valued in Japan, particularly the ability to sit upright and still.

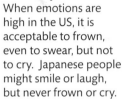

HOW
FINANCE
WORKS

Financial reporting ❯ Financial accounting
Management accounting ❯ Measuring
performance ❯ Raising financing

Financial reporting

Financial reports are everywhere: a bill at a restaurant is a financial report, as are sales receipts and bank statements. In business, however, financial reporting refers to the financial statements that make up a company's annual report and accounts. Compiled by accountants, they provide investors and lenders with information to assess a company's profitability, and enable company managers, government, tax authorities, and other stakeholders to evaluate the business.

Types of financial reports

Financial reports take many forms and can contain a vast amount of information about a company's finances, work, core business values, performance, employees, and its compliance with local, logistical, domestic, and international laws. The most important financial report, or statement, is usually the annual report—essentially a collection of many other, smaller reports—which sums up how the business has performed in the last year. There is a multitude of laws, regulations, and guidelines governing what should be put into this report.

THE ACCOUNTING CYCLE

The eight steps of the accounting cycle are used by nearly all accountants. The cycle helps by standardizing processes and makes sure that accounting jobs are performed correctly and in the same way and order for every activity.
See pp.102–103.

The annual report

Financial statements usually appear in a company's annual report and sum up its financial activities in a standardized way for different audiences to interpret quickly and clearly. These statements take diverse forms, and being able to deconstruct them is a vital skill for accountants and businesspeople, making it simple to see how well a business is performing and why.

$50 billion

the amount hidden via loans diguised as sales by Lehman Brothers in 2008

TYPES OF ACCOUNTING

There are seven widely recognized types of accounting:

❯ **Financial**   Drawn up by accountants; used by investors, creditors, and management. *See pp.110–129.*

❯ **Management**   Used by managers to control cash flow and budgets, and forecast sales. *See pp.130–143.*

❯ **Governmental**   Also called public finance accounting; used by public sector for noncommercial accounting.

❯ **Tax**   Dictates exact rules that companies and individuals must follow when preparing and submitting tax returns.

❯ **Forensic**   Engages in disputes and litigation, and in criminal investigations of fraud. *See pp.152–153.*

❯ **Project**   Deals with a particular project; a useful aid for project management.

❯ **Social and environmental**   Shows how a company makes a positive difference to the community and environment.

Financial statements

❯ **What's in an annual report?**   A full record of company performance according to various criteria, as well as accounts. *See pp.104–105.*

❯ **What are the statements?**   The main one is financial; others include sustainability, directors' pay, and charitable donations. *See pp.106–107.*

❯ **Who reads which statements?**   Sections are relevant to banks, shareholders, government, auditors, staff, and media. *See pp.108–109.*

❯ **What do the notes mean?**   Main statements are annotated in detail. *See pp.104–109.*

❯ **What are the rules?**   Accounting principles regulate financial reports. *See pp.112–113.*

❯ **Which are the most important financial statements?**   Profit-and-loss statements, balance sheets, and cash-flow statements contain key facts. *See pp.114–121.*

The accounting cycle

The accounting cycle is a step-by-step process bookkeepers use to record, organize, and classify a company's financial transactions. It helps to keep all accounting uniform and eliminate mistakes.

How it works

The cycle works as an aid to organize workflow into a cyclical chain of steps that are designed to reflect the way assets, money, and debts have moved in and out of a business. It progresses through eight different steps, in the same order each time, and restarts as soon as it has finished. The cycle can be based on any length of time—this is known as an accounting period—and usually lasts a month, a quarter, or a year. Accounts which deal with revenues and expenses return to zero at the end of each financial year, while accounts showing assets, liabilities, and capital carry over from year to year.

The eight-step cycle

The processes shown here are repeated in the same way for every accounting period. All businesses go through different phases, and the accounting cycle works by reflecting that. The financial statement, which is prepared toward the end of each cycle, is helpful in showing how strongly the business has performed during each period of time.

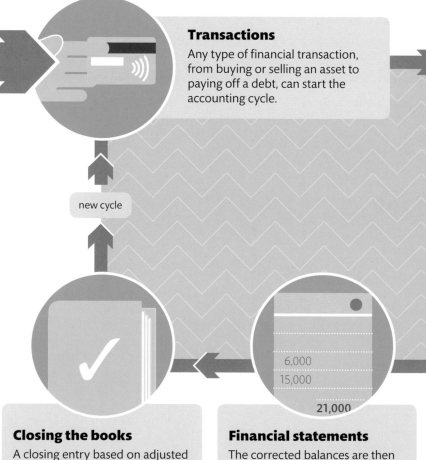

Transactions

Any type of financial transaction, from buying or selling an asset to paying off a debt, can start the accounting cycle.

new cycle

6,000
15,000
21,000

Closing the books

A closing entry based on adjusted journal entries is taken, the books are closed, and the cycle restarts.

Financial statements

The corrected balances are then used to prepare the company's financial statements.

BOOKKEEPING AND ACCOUNTING

> **Internal controls** A method of deploying, measuring, and monitoring a business's resources. This helps prevent fraud and keep track of the value of assets.

> **Double-entry bookkeeping** The process of recording all transactions twice—as a debit and as a credit. If a company buys a chair for $100, its debit account increases by $100 and its credit account decreases by $100.

> **Bad debts** Debts that cannot be or are unlikely to be recovered, so are useless to the creditor (lender), who writes them off as an expense.

NEED TO KNOW

> **Debits**   Expenses – dividends, assets, and losses. In double-entry accounting, debits appear on the left-hand side of the account

> **Credits**   Gains – income, revenue, owners' equity, and liabilities. In double-entry accounting, credits appear on the right-hand side

> **Chart of accounts**   List giving the names of all of a company's accounts, used to organize records

> **Audit trail**   Full history of a transaction, allowing auditors to trace it from its source, through the general ledger, and note any adjustments made

Journal entries

Accountants then analyze the transaction and note it in the relevant journal—a book or an electronic record.

Posting

Journal entries are then transferred to the general ledger—a large book or electronic record logging all the company's accounts.

13%
more accountants will be required in the US by 2022

Trial balance

A list of all the company's accounts is prepared at the end of the accounting period, usually a year, quarter, or month.

Worksheet

Often, trial balance calculations don't accurately balance the books (*see pp.116–117*). In such cases, changes are made on a worksheet.

Adjusting journal entries

Once the accounts are balanced, any adjustments are noted in journals at the end of the accounting period.

Financial statements

The formal records of a business's financial activities are presented as financial statements. Most jurisdictions require accurate information by law, and financial directors and auditors are liable for its contents.

How it works

Financial statements summarize a company's commercial activities clearly and succinctly, with details of the business's performance and changes to its financial position. They are aimed at several parties, so they need to be detailed but also comprehensible to the general public. The statements are usually presented together in the form of an annual report, with in-depth accounts and footnotes to give detail. Legal requirements vary, but accounts must be exact.

What's in an annual report

The contents page shows where to find the big three statements—the balance sheet, cash-flow statement, and profit-and-loss statement—and softer information such as stories about staff and opinions of other stakeholders. The annual report provides an opportunity to impress shareholders and lenders as well as fulfill legal reporting obligations. It will contain all, or most, of the following.

Chair's introduction

It is common for the chairman to write an introduction focusing on the positives and explaining any negative parts of an annual report for the benefit of shareholders.

Our environment

These pages contain much of the company's information on its environmental protocols, most of which are industry-specific. *See also pp.122–123.*

Our customers and community

This section underlines a company's social ethos, in particular its community involvement. Different types of companies may focus on different values.

Our employees

A section on employees details areas such as staff development and training, health and safety, and key statistics on staff satisfaction.

Our finances

A brief overview summarizes the key areas of finance for the company, including overall performance, turnover, operating costs, capital investment, depreciation, interest charges, taxation, and dividends. (*See also pp.114–121.*)

Our infrastructure

The infrastructure pages of an annual report are a good place to supply more detail about the company's fixed assets and explain why the company is an attractive investment for investors

CONSOLIDATED FINANCIAL STATEMENTS

In an era of globalization, large corporations are now commonly made up of multiple companies. Companies owned by a parent company are known as subsidiaries, and continue to maintain their own accounting records, but the parent company produces a consolidated financial statement, which shows the financial operations of both companies. Depending on the jurisdiction's reporting requirements, however, if a company owns a minority stake in a second company, then the latter will *not* be included in the former's consolidated financial statement.

✓ NEED TO KNOW

❯ **Subsidiary** One company that is controlled by another, usually a holding company

❯ **Holding company** A company set up to buy shares of other companies, then control them

❯ **Globalization** The process of businesses developing such large multinational presences that they transcend international borders

Our Performance indicators
Performance indicators are common across all industries. They measure areas such as customer satisfaction and the quality of goods or services provided by the company.

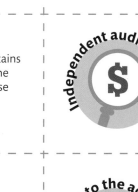
Directors' report
In the directors' report, members of the board of directors give their professional opinions on how the business has performed over the last year.

Environmental accounting
The environmental accounting section contains figures that pertain to the environment, often those stipulated by law—for example, greenhouse gas emissions.

Independent auditor's report
Auditors are independent and check the accuracy of companies' accounts. This helps to eliminate mistakes and track fraud.

Board of directors
The board of directors, governance report, and statement of directors' responsibilities sections indicate who is leading the company, showcases their credentials and roles, and reveals their pay.

Notes to the accounts
Notes to the accounts are a key part of financial statements. They provide extra detail, insight, and explanation of the bare-bones figures supplied in earlier pages of the report.

Deconstructing a financial statement

The profit and loss account shows revenues, costs, and expenses—how much money the business makes—over an accounting period. The balance sheet shows what a business is worth at the time it is published, and is relevant to investors as it reveals assets, liabilities, and shareholders' equity—all useful for gauging business health. The cash-flow statement shows the movement of cash within a business—its liquidity. However, along with the big three financial statements, an annual review contains a wealth of information about a company's performance, of interest to its stakeholder groups. It is often the notes that bring statements to life.

TAXES

The percentage of business taxes taken by governments varies from country to country but the generic types remain similar:

> **Direct taxes** are levied directly on profits or income and include income taxes, inheritance taxes, and taxes relating to sales or purchase of property and other capital assets.

> **Indirect taxes** are paid on goods or services, such as sales taxes. Indirect taxes are often targeted to reduce consumption of harmful goods, a factor relevant to companies working in the alcohol and tobacco industries.

> **Green taxes** are increasingly common and are often indirect. They are generally used as a way of prohibitively increasing the price of goods or services harmful to the environment, such as air travel, landfill sites, or fuel, to diminish their use.

> **Corporation tax** is only paid by companies, not by sole proprietors or partnerships. It is levied as a percentage of the company's total profit.

Case study: the details

Financial statements are presented as part of the annual report, which also publishes case studies, quotations, statistics, and profiles of customers, suppliers, employees, and directors. The notes, often running to 20 pages or so, contain tables and text that flesh out the financial information. The following examples are taken from the 2013 annual review of UK utility company Wessex Water.

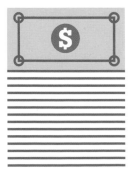

Our finance

This section contains the headline financial figures of the business, such as profits, taxes paid, assets owned, liabilities, and dividends paid out, as well as some more detailed explanation of the figures.

Sustainable investment

Wessex Water's investment in sustainability includes mandatory expenditure and extra discretionary expenditure (at the time of the review, £1 = $1.58).

	2013 £m	2012 £m
CUSTOMERS AND COMMUNITIES	55	38
ENVIRONMENT	30	25
EMPLOYEES	49	46
INFRASTRUCTURE	139	116
TOTAL	273	225

✓ NEED TO KNOW

> **Monopoly** Situation in which there is just one supplier of a particular product or service; without government control, a company with a monopoly could make prices high and quality low, as consumers would have no alternative

> **Oligopoly** Industries that have a small number of suppliers. The competition is not as intense as in the free market, so governments often impose regulations on companies to ensure quality and fair prices

> **Remuneration** Money paid for work or a service provided— the financial term for pay; may include bonuses or share options

BOARD OF DIRECTORS

Much of what might be considered personal information about directors of public companies is in the public domain. It is usually a legal obligation to disclose:

> Names of executive directors

> Names of non-executive directors, and whether they are independent or shareholders

> Shareholding

> Board attendance record

> Dates of directors' terms of office

> Remuneration, including bonus, share options, pension plans, and benefits

> Notice period

> Termination payment

> Potential conflicts of interest

Charitable donations

Companies vaunt their philanthropy in the annual report, detailing how much they have given away and how it has helped. They may support charities relevant to the nature of their business or let employees vote on recipients.

96%
Wessex Water utility's customer satisfaction score

Customer satisfaction

Overall, this section shows how the company works with customers to improve service and support. In monopoly and oligopoly industries, customer satisfaction is particularly important, as governments often set high targets. Wessex Water's annual review shows a customer satisfaction rating of 96 per cent.

Financial statements for users

The many financial statements included in the annual report are a gold mine of information for those who know how to read them. They provide headline profit figures, explanations of issues from directors, detailed financial data, and information about companies' operations and policies. For this reason, financial statements are useful to a wide range of stakeholders, from the company's employees, customers, and shareholders to potential investors, governments, tax authorities, journalists, credit-rating agencies, banks, and the general public.

Who reads what

Different stakeholders are interested in different parts of the annual review. Customers of a service provider, for instance, may look at the section on customers and community while potential lenders go to the financial statements..

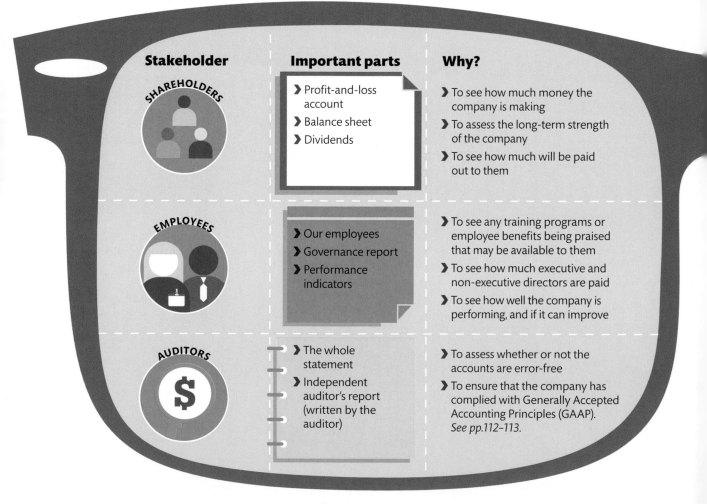

Stakeholder	Important parts	Why?
SHAREHOLDERS	❯ Profit-and-loss account ❯ Balance sheet ❯ Dividends	❯ To see how much money the company is making ❯ To assess the long-term strength of the company ❯ To see how much will be paid out to them
EMPLOYEES	❯ Our employees ❯ Governance report ❯ Performance indicators	❯ To see any training programs or employee benefits being praised that may be available to them ❯ To see how much executive and non-executive directors are paid ❯ To see how well the company is performing, and if it can improve
AUDITORS	❯ The whole statement ❯ Independent auditor's report (written by the auditor)	❯ To assess whether or not the accounts are error-free ❯ To ensure that the company has complied with Generally Accepted Accounting Principles (GAAP). See pp.112–113.

STATISTICS MADE EASY

Impressive statistics are often scattered through an annual report. These examples are from UK utility Wessex Water:

6% post-tax return on capital
> This percentage is estimated by dividing income after tax by the amount of investment. It is useful for showing shareholders the kind of returns they can expect on their investments.

64% gearing
> For most industries, gearing is a company's debt compared to its equity. In the water industry, it compares a company's net debt to its regulatory capital value (the value of the business that earns a return on investment). Gearing is expressed as a percentage. *See pp.174–175.*

A3/A-/BBB+ credit rating
> Credit ratings assess the likelihood that loans will be repaid. A3 and A- fall at the bottom of "strong capacity to meet financial commitments," while BBB+ is at the top of the adequate range. The major ratings companies in the US are Moody's, Standard and Poor's, and Fitch.

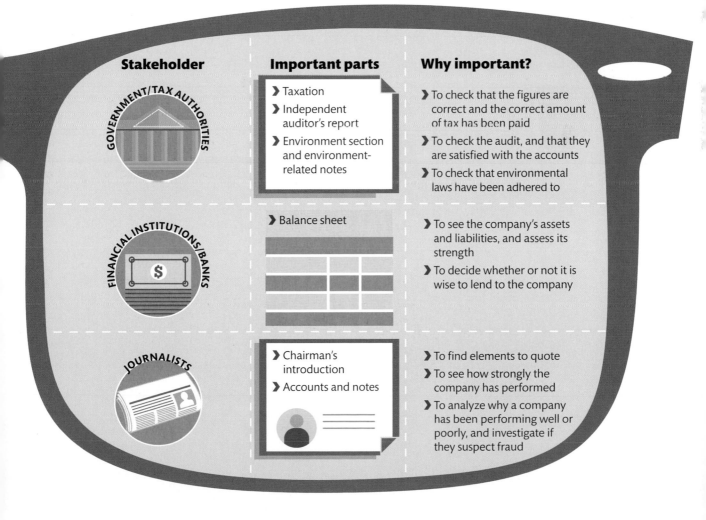

Stakeholder	Important parts	Why important?
GOVERNMENT/TAX AUTHORITIES	> Taxation > Independent auditor's report > Environment section and environment-related notes	> To check that the figures are correct and the correct amount of tax has been paid > To check the audit, and that they are satisfied with the accounts > To check that environmental laws have been adhered to
FINANCIAL INSTITUTIONS/BANKS	> Balance sheet	> To see the company's assets and liabilities, and assess its strength > To decide whether or not it is wise to lend to the company
JOURNALISTS	> Chairman's introduction > Accounts and notes	> To find elements to quote > To see how strongly the company has performed > To analyze why a company has been performing well or poorly, and investigate if they suspect fraud

Financial accounting

A company's financial accounts classify, quantify, and record its transactions. They are extremely useful for people outside the business, such as creditors and potential investors, as well as those currently involved with making investment decisions. For this reason, the accounts should be concise and clearly present the timing and certainty of future cash flows, so that people looking at the company can decide whether or not to invest in, lend money to, or do business with it.

Key elements

The profit-and-loss account, balance sheet, and cash-flow statements are the most important financial statements in an annual review, supplemented by the report's notes. To understand these statements, a knowledge of accounting principles, depreciation, amortization, and depletion is vital. Accountants also need to understand the legal requirements that the statements must satisfy and how environmental laws can affect a business and its accounts.

Accounting standards

Generally accepted principles standardize practice worldwide to ensure accuracy and prevent fraud. *See pp.112–113.*

❯ International standards simplify account reporting.

❯ Companies must meet environmental accounting rules and regulations. *See pp.122–123.*

Profit-and-loss statement

Shows how much money a company is making and is especially useful for potential investors and stakeholders. *See pp.114–115.*

❯ Outlines revenues and gains minus expenses and losses or operating costs.

❯ Informs a company if a profit warning is needed.

Balance sheet

Gives a snapshot of how much a business is worth at a certain time and is a good indication of its long-term health. *See pp.116–119.*

❯ Balances company's assets against its equity and liabilities.

❯ Lists different types of assets, including tangible fixed assets and current assets.

$74 billion

the total value lost by shareholders in the 2001 Enron accounting scandal

AUDITING

The accounts of public companies are given unbiased scrutiny by external accountants to check that they are accurate and clear. This is a legal requirement in most countries, designed to ensure market confidence in the business world and transparency in corporate finance. A company may also have an internal audit process, which means that its accounts are checked before being submitted to an external auditor.

Cash-flow statement

Reveals a company's liquidity by tracking the flow of cash—money or short-term investments—in and out of the company. *See pp.120–121.*

❯ Shows if a company can sustain itself, grow, and pay debts.

❯ Details cash flow from operating, investing, and financing activities.

Environmental accounting

Accounts for myriad environmental rules and regulations that oblige companies to mitigate the impact of business activities. *See pp.122–123.*

❯ Showcases green credentials in financial statements.

❯ Reveals compliance with environmental, social, and governance criteria.

Depreciation

Accounts for the decrease in value over time of tangible fixed assets in order to spread the cost of assets over their economic life. *See pp.124–127.*

❯ Can be calculated using a number of different methods.

❯ Tangible fixed assets include buildings, plant, and machinery.

Amortization and depletion

Account for the decrease in value over time of a range of intangible assets, loans, and natural resources. *See pp.128–129.*

❯ Intangible assets include patents, trademarks, logos and copyright.

❯ Natural resources include minerals and forests.

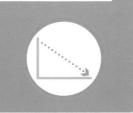

International accounting standards

With increasing globalization, international accounting standards, assumptions, and principles that help to make accounting easier across borders are essential for preparing financial statements.

	ECONOMIC ENTITY ASSUMPTION	MONETARY UNIT ASSUMPTION	GOING CONCERN ASSUMPTION	TIME PERIOD ASSUMPTION	FULL DISCLOSURE PRINCIPLE
Standard	Transactions by businesses owned by one group or individual are kept separate from transactions made by other companies owned by that group or individual.	International economic activity is expressed in monetary terms, with all units assumed to be quantifiable, constant and not affected by inflation or deflation.	The financial activities of a business will carry on indefinitely.	Different operations of a business can be divided into arbitrary time periods.	All information, past, present, or future, which could affect financial performance must be disclosed, usually in the notes of financial statements.
Example	If a group owns two companies, one manufacturing televisions and the other retailing cell phones, the financial statements for each company are separate.	Current manufacture of baseball bats is compared financially to manufacture that was carried out 30 years ago, without taking inflation into account.	Oil reserves will never run out; gold in a gold mine will last forever; a manufacturer will not go out of business.	Sales of toothbrushes can be measured daily, monthly, quarterly, and so on (when in reality they are constant, or subject to variations that are not predictable).	If a coconut importer knows that a hurricane has damaged next year's coconut crop, it must mention this in its financial statement.
Purpose	Helps the group of companies and investors compare financial statements of each company with its competitors.	Shows as much of the company as possible in financial statements, as everything a business owns can be quantified.	Offers a model for businesses to look at the long-term future of their operations.	Makes financial reporting easier.	Provides full information for shareholders and potential investors.
Pros and cons	✓ Largely beneficial ✗ Companies that operate in the same group but in different countries must prove standard market rates used for intra-company trading.	✗ It is hard to measure monetary value of, for example, the fastest worker at the baseball-bat production plant. ✗ It is hard to compare across time because of inflation/deflation.	✗ It is not applicable to companies approaching liquidation, as it assumes that any assets are worth their original value.	✓ The more often economic activity is measured, the easier it is to identify trends. ✗ Measuring activity often means more work, and such data may multiply errors.	✗ Companies may try to "bury" information likely to put off investors or lower the share price in the notes. ✗ Not all countries are equipped to root out transgressors.

How it works

International Financial Reporting Standards (IFRS) are the most widely accepted standards for accounting, and they are used in more than 110 countries. Originally introduced to harmonize accounting across Europe, they have with time spread around the world. IFRS are not to be confused with International Accounting Standards (IAS), which were in use from 1973 to 2001. Generally Accepted Accounting Principles (GAAP), which are known colloquially as accounting standards or standard accounting practice, are country-specific guidelines for recording and reporting accounts. They differ from one jurisdiction to another.

HISTORICAL COST PRINCIPLE	MATCHING PRINCIPLE	REVENUE RECOGNITION PRINCIPLE	CONSERVATISM	PRINCIPLE OF MATERIALITY
Assets and liabilities are valued at their buying price (in countries with high inflation or hyperinflation, other principles, such as fair value, are used).	The time period in which a business's expenses and revenue figures are collected always concurs.	Revenue should be recorded at the moment when: a) goods or services are exchanged; b) assets can be converted to cash; c) it is earned—not when it is received.	If there are alternatives for reporting on an item, accountants should choose to report the lower amount of income or asset gain.	Accountants may make a professional decision to go against any one of the other principles.
If a company bought a factory 50 years ago for $100,000, that will be its stated value today, even though its market value now is far higher.	A grocery store measures costs incurred and revenues gained over the same time period, because when sales are high, costs are also likely to be high, due to the need to buy more stock.	A toy-maker takes an order for 500 toys in July, delivers it in September, and is paid for it in December. The revenue is recorded in September, when the goods were exchanged.	If a company is involved in a lawsuit, it must report the potential losses rather than the potential gains, in the notes of the financial statement.	An oil refinery buys a $100 whiteboard, which could last 10 years. Under the matching principle, it should be billed for $10 each year, but the accountant enters it as a one-time cost.
Ensures uniformity and prevents the overvaluation of assets, which was a feature of the 1929 Wall Street Crash.	Avoids different time scales, which could present a distorted picture and erratic financial results—for example, with high revenues from one period and high costs in another.	Matches the time period that work was undertaken to when the payment was received, as with the matching principle.	Prevents companies from overestimating money they will make in the future, then running into debt if it does not materialize.	Saves time for small, almost insignificant transactions when there is no risk of it being applied misleadingly.
✗ Assets, especially property, acquired a long time ago are invariably represented as being worth less than their current real value.	✓ Helps to present accounts in a representative manner.	✗ Revenue may not always be received. ✓ If there are doubts about a recipient's ability to pay, the company can make an allowance for doubtful accounts.	✗ Requires a degree of objectivity from accountants: if this objectivity is absent, financial reports can be misleading.	✓ Saves time on accountancy. ✓ Makes information easier to read—for example, figures can be rounded to the nearest dollar, thousand, or even million dollars.

Profit-and-loss statement

A profit-and-loss statement is a financial statement that shows all revenues, costs, and expenses during an accounting period. It is also known as an income statement, or an income and expense statement.

How it works

The purpose of the profit-and-loss statement is to show the profitability of a business during a given period. Along with the cash-flow statement and the balance sheet, it is the most important financial statement businesses produce, as it shows investors how profitable the company is. The statement usually works by showing revenues and gains, less expenses and losses from business activities, as well as the sale and purchase of assets. Businesses that are sole proprietorships or partnerships are generally not required to submit profit-and-loss statements.

How to read a profit-and-loss statement

Profit-and-loss statements commonly illustrate the financial performance of a business over a particular month, quarter, or year. The key pieces of information are the figures for turnover (or revenue) and operating profit. If profits are going to be lower than expected, the company may put out a profit warning in advance of releasing the statement.

Case study: profit and loss statement

This statement taken from the 2013 annual review of Wessex Water, a UK utility company, shows it was making a healthy profit (at the time, the exchange rate was £1 = $1.58).

Amount of money taken by the business over a certain time; in this case, there was a 5.3 percent increase in turnover from the previous year

Profit earned from the business's core operations after expenses have been taken off, but before taxes have been deducted; it does not include money made on investments

Profit before tax after all income and expenses have been taken into account, excluding extraordinary payments

Level of profit that can be paid out in dividends to the company's shareholders.

	Year 2013 £m	Year 2012 £m
Turnover	**492.1**	**467.5**
Operating costs	(268.1)	(248.5)
Operating profit	**224.0**	**219.0**
Interest payable and similar charges	(86.9)	(81.7)
Interest receivable	2.9	1.2
Other finance costs	(1.5)	(1.0)
Profit on ordinary activities before taxation	**138.5**	**137.5**
Taxation on profit on ordinary activities	(30.6)	(44.3)
Profit attributable to shareholders	**107.9**	**93.2**

Figures in parentheses represent negative numbers.

TYPICAL EXPENSES

Payroll
Salaries and wages paid to staff, temporary contractors, and indirect labor

Utilities
Water, electricity, and gas; postage and shipping; transportation

Insurance
Insurance on fixed assets and personal liability insurance for employees

Phone/internet bills
Cost of telephone, broadband internet, and mobile devices used by employees

Advertising
Sales and marketing of the company and its products

Office supplies
Stationery such as pens, paper, and filing systems, office printers, furniture, lighting

Legal fees and professional services
Accounting and legal fees, payable to accountants, auditors, and legal advisers

Interest on loans
Interest paid on money borrowed, which counts as a business expense

Tax
Varying among jurisdictions, this may include payroll tax and corporation tax

Entertainment
Legitimate costs of business entertaining, subject to certain criteria being met

Case study: operating costs
This table breaks down the company's operating costs in more detail. It is important to read any notes regarding depreciation and ordinary and extraordinary costs and gains.

Manpower costs including basic pay and pensions, overtime payments, staff training, and maternity leave

Term given to the gradual decline in an asset's value, caused by factors such as wear and tear and market conditions.

Decrease in value over time of intangible assets or loans

Profit or loss on the sale of fixed assets

Leasing costs for buildings and equipment

Research and development carried out to improve the reliability and effectiveness of services

Directors' remuneration including base salaries and benefits, pensions, car and health benefits, share options, and bonuses

	Year 2013 £m	Year 2012 £m
Manpower costs	51.7	45.3
Materials and consumables	29.1	26.7
Other operational costs	67.6	63.8
Depreciation	120.3	114.0
Amortization of grants and contributions	(0.8)	(0.8)
Loss/(gain) on disposals of fixed assets	0.2	(0.5)
	268.1	248.5
Operating leases for plant and machinery	1.5	1.2
Research and development	0.1	0.1
Directors' remuneration	2.1	1.8
Fees paid to the auditor	0.2	0.2

Figures in parentheses represent negative numbers.

Balance sheet

A balance sheet is a financial statement that shows what a business is worth at a specific point in time. Its primary purpose is to show assets, liabilities, and equity (capital), rather than financial results.

How it works

The balance sheet essentially shows what the company owns, what it owes, and how much is invested in it. It is based on the accounting formula, sometimes called the balance-sheet equation, which is the basis of double-entry bookkeeping. This shows the relationship between assets, liabilities, and owners' capital—what the company owns (assets) is purchased either through debt (liability) or investment (capital). The equation always balances, as everything a company owns has to have been bought with its owner's funds or through borrowing.

The balance-sheet equation

As the name suggests, the balance sheet must always balance. This is because everything the business owns (its assets) must be offset against the equivalent capital (or equity) and liabilities (debt).

Company with no liabilities

For example, a young business may have assets of **$1,000**. It currently has no liabilities so its capital is equal to its assets—that is, it is the amount of equity the owners or shareholders have invested in the business. Using the accounting formula, the equation would look like this:

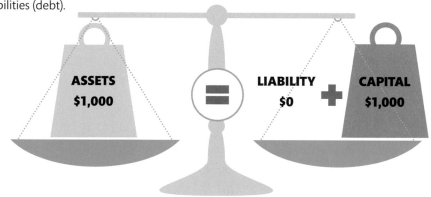

Company incurs $400 in liabilities

After spending **$400** on, for example, an illuminated sign for the storefront, the owner incurs **$400** in liabilities and so the formula changes. However, since the sign is worth **$400**, and the owner has **$600** remaining, the equation remains balanced—as it always does.

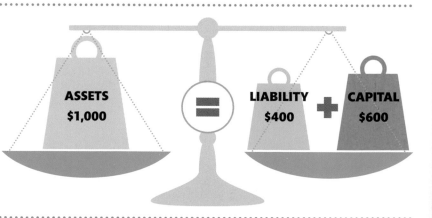

Case study: balance sheet

This example from Wessex Water, a UK public utility company, shows how a balance sheet works in practice (at the time, the exchange rate was £1 = $1.58).

Fixed assets (or non-current assets) are not easily converted into cash and usually last longer than one year. They are either tangible, such as land, or intangible, such as a logo

Current assets are assets that last one year or less, and can be easily converted into cash. Cash, cash equivalents, and inventory are the most common current assets

Creditors are the individuals or organizations to which the company owes money. Here, the money must be repaid in the current financial year

Net current assets equals current assets after money due to creditors has been deducted

Total assets less current liabilities is the sum of fixed and net current assets minus liabilities due within the current financial year

Liabilities due in more than one year are amounts due to creditors, which are deducted from total fixed and net current assets

Net assets are what is left once liabilities have been deducted from the company's fixed and net current assets to give the overall net assets

Shareholders' funds, or owner's equity, is the remaining capital; this money can be reinvested into the business or paid out as an annual dividend

ASSETS, LIABILITIES, AND CAPITAL	Year 2013 £m	Year 2012 £m
Fixed assets		
Tangible assets	**2,167.1**	**2,069.2**
Investments	–	–
Current assets		
Stock and work in progress	7.0	6.3
Debtors	162.6	153.9
Cash in the bank and in hand	181.0	211.0
	350.6	371.2
Creditors—amounts falling due within one year	(198.8)	(171.7)
Net current assets	**151.8**	**199.5**
Total assets less current liabilities	**2,318.9**	**2,268.7**
Creditors—amounts falling due after more than one year	(1,891.5)	(1,811.9)
Provisions for liabilities and charges	(114.9)	(115.3)
Retirement benefit obligations	(93.1)	(83.0)
Deferred income	(17.2)	(17.9)
Net assets	**202.2**	**240.6**
Capital and reserves		
Called-up equity share capital	81.3	81.3
Profit-and-loss account	120.9	159.3
Shareholders' funds	**202.2**	**240.6**

SYMBOLS FOR DEBITS AND CREDITS
Accountants use a number of different terms and symbols to indicate debits and credits. Some use "Dr" for debits and "Cr" for credits, others use "+" for debits and "–" for credits. On this balance sheet, parentheses are used to show credits (negative numbers).

Understanding the notes

The balance sheet is a useful indication of the health of a business, and it is important that investors know how to analyze it. It can be read in two ways—"at a glance," as on the previous page, where general information is summarized, or in depth, with more detailed information about each element. Provided after the summary, the detailed section of the balance sheet explains the specific financial workings of the business in a number of notes. It shows exactly where money has been gained or lost, in figures, and it often includes a written commentary about potential developments that may affect the company, such as court cases, staffing, or availability of resources.

Balance-sheet notes

Investors may want to know more about the figures in the summary section, so additional notes and tables give detailed breakdowns of the figures (at the time, the exchange rate was £1 = $1.58).

Case study: tangible fixed assets

This table presents details of Wessex Water's tangible fixed assets (long-term assets that cannot easily be converted into cash).

Tangible fixed assets include land and machinery

Additions are new tangible fixed assets the business has acquired this year

Disposals are any tangible fixed assets the business has disposed of or sold this year

Total value of the company's fixed assets is listed by category and in total

Depreciation is the decrease in value of assets over time

Value of depreciation of assets is listed by category and in total

Net book value of an asset is its initial cost minus all its depreciation to date

Combined value of the company's tangible fixed assets in each category, and also in total, is listed

	LAND AND BUILDINGS	INFRASTRUCTURE ASSETS	PLANT, MACHINERY, AND VEHICLES	OTHER ASSETS
	£m	£m	£m	£m
Cost				
As of April 1, 2012	676.3	1,229.7	1,204.6	105.0
Additions	9.5	67.8	49.1	2.3
Transfers on commissioning	13.7	11.2	42.2	2.8
Disposals	(0.2)	–	(13.1)	(0.5)
Grants and contributions	–	(5.0)	–	–
As of March 31, 2013	**699.3**	**1,303.7**	**1,282.8**	**109.6**
Depreciation				
As of April 1, 2012	211.3	435.5	558.8	34.0
Charge for the period	13.7	43.2	56.8	6.6
Disposals	(0.1)	–	(11.5)	(0.5)
As of March 31, 2013	**224.9**	**478.7**	**604.1**	**40.1**
Net book value				
As of March 31, 2013	**474.4**	**825.0**	**678.7**	**69.5**
As of April 1, 2012	465.0	794.2	645.8	71.0

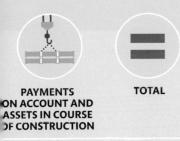

	PAYMENTS ON ACCOUNT AND ASSETS IN COURSE OF CONSTRUCTION	TOTAL
	£m	£m
	93.2	3,308.8
	96.2	224.9
	(69.9)	–
	–	(13.8)
	–	(5.0)
	119.5	**3,514.9**
	–	1,239.6
	–	120.3
	–	(12.1)
	–	**1,347.8**
	119.5	**2,167.1**
	93.2	2,069.2

Case study: debtors

Debtors are individuals or entities that owe the business money. Wessex Water has four categories of debtor.

Individuals or entities that sell assets to third parties on credit, receiving payment at a later date

Prepayments for services that will be received in the future, which the business has already been paid for, and **accrued income** that is expected in the future

	2013 £m	2012 £m
Trade debtors	48.9	48.1
Owed by group companies	31.8	35.0
Prepayments and accrued income	70.3	62.1
Other debtors	11.6	8.7
	162.6	**153.9**

Case study: creditors

Creditors are individuals or entities that the business owes money to. They are in credit of Wessex Water.

Money owed to the bank

Individuals or entities that are owed money for supplying raw materials or components

Money owed to related companies that are owned by the same group

Payment to shareholders

Tax and employee benefit payments

Any notes relating to creditors

	2013 £m	2012 £m
Bank overdraft	21.8	18.6
Inter-company loan	-	1.3
Obligations under finance leases	7.0	6.3
Trade creditors	4.3	3.1
Amounts owed to subsidiary company	18.9	14.2
Amounts owed to other group companies	0.6	0.6
Amounts owed to associate company	0.7	0.2
Dividend	23.3	21.7
Other creditors	2.4	2.0
Corporation tax	16.7	9.2
Taxation and social security	1.9	1.7
Accruals and deferred income	101.2	92.8
	198.8	**171.7**

The inter company loan was due to a fellow subsidiary company SC Technology GmbH and has been repaid.

Cash-flow statement

The cash-flow statement shows the movement of cash during the last accounting period. It is important because it reveals a company's liquidity—whether or not it has more money coming in than going out.

How to read a cash-flow statement

The statement of cash flows, to give it its official title, answers the key question of whether a business is making enough money to sustain itself and provide surplus capital to grow in the future, pay any debts, and give out dividends. Figures in parentheses are negative numbers.

Case study: cash-flow statement

By analyzing this water utility's statement, which includes a comparison to the previous year, decision-makers can base future plans on past cash flows (at the time, the exchange rate was £1 = $1.58).

Using profit before tax as a starting point, non-cash income and expenses are deducted to reach net cash inflow from operating activities

Returns on investment in this case is total interest received minus total interest paid, as well as interest paid on finance lease rentals

Taxation is the sum of all taxes paid and tax credits received

Capital expenditure and financial investment is, here, the sum of the sale of tangible assets plus connection charges, grants, and deferred income

Dividends are sums of money paid to shareholders, typically each year

This is the sum of all the figures above

Financing describes how much money the company has made or lost from loans, finance leases, and bonds

This is the change from last year's figures to this year's, and the total of the two figures above

A utility company can afford to operate with more debt than companies with a less stable base

	Year to March 31, 2013 £m	Year to March 31, 2012 £m
Net cash inflow from operating activities	334.6	303.2
Returns on investments and servicing of finance	(80.0)	(79.2)
Taxation	(21.8)	(31.5)
Capital expenditure and financial investment	(215.4)	(149.7)
Dividends paid	(129.6)	(129.4)
Cash outflow before financial investment	(112.2)	(86.6)
Financing	79.0	222.2
(Decrease)/increase in cash	(33.2)	135.6
Reconciliation of cash movement to the movement in net debt		
(Decrease)/increase in cash—above	(33.2)	135.6
Movement in loans and leases	(79.0)	(222.2)
Movement in net debt	**(112.2)**	**(86.6)**
Opening net debt	**(1,626.1)**	**(1,539.5)**
Closing net debt	**(1,738.3)**	**(1,626.1)**

How it works

The cash-flow statement is often more useful for investors assessing a business's health than other key statements, because it shows how the core activities are performing. The profit-and-loss statement, for example, obscures this by adding in non-cash factors such as depreciation. Similarly, the balance sheet is more concerned with assets than liquidity.

Three types of cash flow

Cash refers to actual money as well as cash equivalents including cash in the bank; bank lines of credit, and short-term, highly liquid investments for which there is little risk of a change in value. Cash does not include interest, depreciation, or bad debts (debts written off).

Cash flow from operating activities

The bulk of cash flow usually comes from operations, and is worked out with a formula. The change in working capital (current assets minus current liabilities) can be a negative figure.

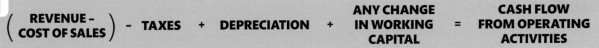

$$\left(\begin{array}{c} \text{REVENUE} - \\ \text{COST OF SALES} \end{array} \right) - \text{TAXES} + \text{DEPRECIATION} + \begin{array}{c} \text{ANY CHANGE} \\ \text{IN WORKING} \\ \text{CAPITAL} \end{array} = \begin{array}{c} \text{CASH FLOW} \\ \text{FROM OPERATING} \\ \text{ACTIVITIES} \end{array}$$

Cash flow from operating activities in practice

In this example, a juice company sells $100 worth of orange juice after spending $20 on oranges. It pays 25 percent of its $80 earnings in tax. Its juicing machine incurs a depreciation expense of $20 over the period (a positive adjustment on the orginal outlay for the machine). There is no change in working capital (short-term assets to cover short-term debt).

Cash flow from investing activities

Buying or selling assets or investments is in this category. This figure is usually a cash outflow (negative figure) due to buying more than selling, but can be positive if there are significant sales.

Cash flow from financing activities

This includes buying or selling stock or debt and paying out dividends. Money made from selling something is called cash inflow; money lost through paying out is cash outflow.

Total cash flow

Adding all three cash flows gives the total. Separating out the three types shows decision-makers the health of core activities as opposed to financing and investing, which bear little relation to day-to-day operations.

Environmental accounting

Environmental regulations force companies to consider the impact of their activities and to adopt corporate social responsibility (CSR) as they grapple with legislation, climate change, and public opinion.

How it works

Globally, there are reams of different environment acts spread across multiple jurisdictions that affect the companies operating within their borders in different ways. Areas protected by environment acts include the atmosphere, fresh water, the marine environment, nature conservation, nuclear safety, and noise pollution. International acts are usually ratified by each country individually before taking effect there. An example of a common global means of reducing greenhouse gas emissions is emissions trading ("cap and trade"), by which companies must buy a permit for each ton of CO_2 they emit over a certain level. Those emitting under the agreed level can sell their permits to other companies.

Environmental credentials

Most companies include a section on environmental accounting in their financial statement. Some details are required by law, but the statement also gives an opportunity to showcase environmental credentials to stakeholders.

Society

❯ **Programs and practices** that assess and manage the impact of operations on communities

❯ **Fines and sanctions** for noncompliance with regulations

Product responsibility

❯ **Life-cycle stages** in which the health-and-safety impact of products and services are assessed for improvement

❯ **Adherence to laws**, standards, and voluntary codes relating to marketing communications

CASE STUDY

Cleaning up rivers

Wessex Water's impressive record on pollution is mentioned several times in its statement, including in the chairman's introduction. This prominence shows that the company believes acting in an environmentally conscious manner is important to its investors. The company illustrates several areas where it has acted with others to positively affect the environment:

❯ Work with the charity Surfers Against Sewage, which campaigns for clean seawater

❯ Its river strategy: collaborating with pressure groups and organizations to reduce pollutants and the impact of habitat alteration, and so increase the numbers of aquatic plants, invertebrates, and fish in local rivers

❯ Improving water quality at swimming beaches in the region, in compliance with mandatory standards

GREENHOUSE GAS EMISSIONS

In some countries, companies are required by law to provide details of their greenhouse gas emissions. This is usually presented as a table in the environmental accounting section of the annual report. It includes direct and indirect emissions—by the company itself and by third parties—of gas, diesel, and other fuels; sulfur oxides and nitrous oxides; methane; and other ozone-depleting substances. In this table, from the Wessex Water utility company, emissions are shown as $ktCO_2$ equivalents.

Appointed business	Direct fuel use	Grid electricity	Third parties	Total 2012–13	Total 2011–12
Gas, diesel, other fuels	6	0	4	10	8
Grid electricity	0	115	0	115	107
Transportation	9	0	1	11	11
Methane	17	0	2	20	20
Nitrous oxide	10	0	7	17	19
Exported renewable	0	(3)	0	(3)	(4)
TOTAL (net emissions)	42	112	14	169	161

Economic
❯ **Financial implications**, risks, and opportunities for the organization's activities due to climate change
❯ **Financial assistance** received from the government

Human rights
❯ **Investment agreements** that include human rights clauses or that have undergone human rights screening
❯ **Suppliers and contractors** that have undergone screening on human rights; actions taken to address any issues

Labor practices
❯ **Workforce** by employment type, contract, and region
❯ **Average hours of training** per year, per employee by employee category
❯ **Ratio of basic salary** of men to women by employment category

Environmental
❯ **Direct and indirect** energy consumption
❯ **Waste by type** and disposal method
❯ **Water withdrawal** by source; discharge by destination and quality
❯ **Fines and sanctions** for noncompliance with regulations

Depreciation

When a company buys an asset, its cost can be deducted from income for accounting and tax purposes. Depreciation allows the company to spread the cost, by calculating the asset's decline in value over time.

How it works

If a business buys a long-lived asset, such as a building, factory equipment, or computer, to help it earn income, this expenditure can be offset as a cost against income earned. However, not all this income will be generated in the year of purchase and, over time, the asset will age and become less beneficial to the business, until it becomes outdated or unusable.

Accountants do two things to turn the declining value into a tax advantage. Firstly, they work out how much the asset's value decreases over a period of time—

typically a year. Secondly, they match that loss in value to the amount of income earned in that period, so depreciation becomes a deduction from taxable income.

There are several different ways to calculate depreciation. The method a company uses may depend on the kind of business, the type of asset, tax rules, or personal preference. In the United States, per IRS guidelines, companies must use MACRS (Modified Accelerated Cost Recovery System), a combination of straight-line and double declining balance methods (*see below and p.126*).

(*see below and p.126*)

✓ NEED TO KNOW

> **Fixed/tangible assets** Items that enable a business to operate but are not a part of trade; assets lasting a year or more qualify for depreciation

> **Useful/economic life** Length of time an asset is fit for its purpose and has monetary value

> **Salvage/scrap/residual value** Worth of an asset once it has outlived its useful life—often set by the tax authority

> **Book value** An asset's worth on paper at any point between its initial purchase and salvage

---

Calculating depreciation

The straight-line method is the simplest way of working out depreciation and can be applied to most assets. Depreciation is calculated along a timeline, with value loss spread evenly over the asset's economic life. Scrap value is deducted from purchase value and the remainder is split into equal portions over time.

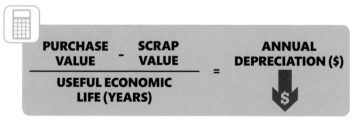

$$\frac{\text{PURCHASE VALUE} - \text{SCRAP VALUE}}{\text{USEFUL ECONOMIC LIFE (YEARS)}} = \text{ANNUAL DEPRECIATION (\$)}$$

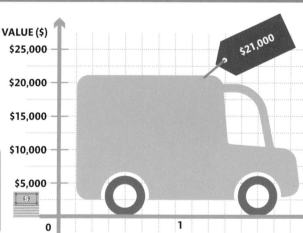

VALUE ($)
$25,000
$20,000
$15,000
$10,000
$5,000

$21,000

0   1

Example

A landscaping business buys a new van for $25,000. The IRS sets its scrap value at $5,000 after five years of use.

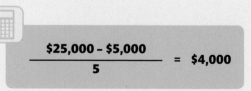

$$\frac{\$25,000 - \$5,000}{5} = \$4,000$$

Year 1 After a year, the van's value has depreciated by $4,000 (its purchase value minus its scrap value, divided by its useful economic life). Its value is now $21,000.

TYPICAL LIFE OF FIXED ASSETS

Tax authorities often specify the typical useful (economic) life of a particular asset. This helps to standardize depreciation, and to eliminate uncertainty about value and the number of years over which an asset can be depreciated.

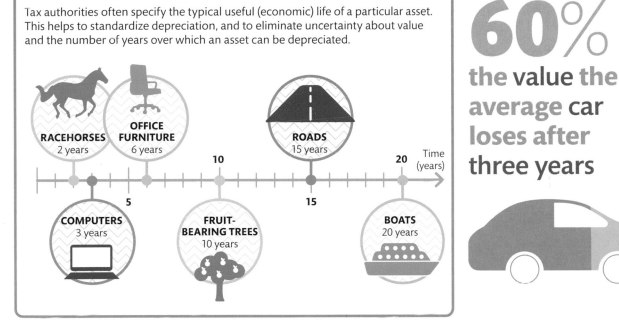

RACEHORSES
2 years

OFFICE FURNITURE
6 years

ROADS
15 years

Time (years)

COMPUTERS
3 years

FRUIT-BEARING TREES
10 years

BOATS
20 years

60%

the value the average car loses after three years

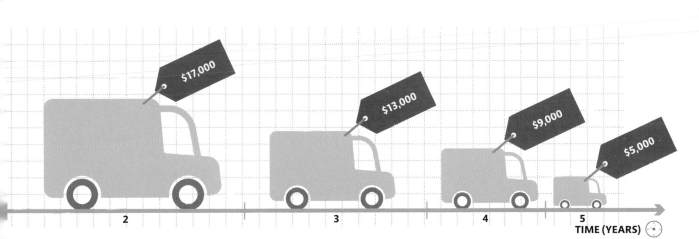

$17,000

$13,000

$9,000

$5,000

2   3   4   5

TIME (YEARS)

Year 2 After the second year, the value has depreciated by another $4,000. The van will lose an equal amount of value each year for the next three years of its useful economic life.

Year 3 At the end of the third year, the van has depreciated by another $4,000, and its book value is $13,000, although its actual value may be more or less.

Year 4 The van has depreciated by $4,000, to $9,000, at the end of four years of life.

Year 5 By the end of year five, the van is valued at only $5,000— its scrap value.

Applying depreciation

When calculating depreciation, there are a number of different factors to consider. For instance, a business needs to be able to predict the number of years an asset will last. Helpfully, tax authorities in most countries issue guidelines to accountants and businesses with estimates of the useful economic life of many common business assets.

Companies may also wonder which of the many methods of calculating depreciation to use for a given asset. Each method reflects a different pattern of depreciation, with some being more suitable for particular categories of assets. For example, the "accelerated" methods that chart rapid depreciation at the beginning of an asset's life are more suitable for technology, while the "activity" methods that link depreciation to actual hours of use or number of units produced are best suited to transport and production lines.

Again, tax authorities in most countries offer guidelines on which method to use. Although it is technically possible for a company to use two different methods for their own accounting and for tax purposes, this is best avoided.

⚠ WARNING

Misusing depreciation

> **The wrong method** A company must choose a method that is permissible for an asset type

> **Frontloading** Opting for an accelerated method can result in a taxable gain if an asset is sold early, for more than its book value

> **Claiming beyond useful life** Depreciation cannot be claimed after an asset's useful life

> **Ignoring depreciation** If a company fails to claim depreciation, it has to report a gain from the sale, despite the loss on deduction

Other depreciation methods

There are many different methods of calculating depreciation. Some are favored by particular tax codes, while others are specifically applicable to certain industries and types of assets, and their patterns of value loss.

Double declining balance method

A method used to claim more depreciation in the first years after purchase, which is useful for assets that lose most of their value early on. It reduces a company's net income in the early years of an asset's life, but generates initial tax savings.

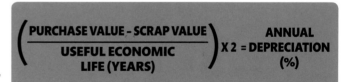

$$\left(\frac{\text{PURCHASE VALUE} - \text{SCRAP VALUE}}{\text{USEFUL ECONOMIC LIFE (YEARS)}} \right) \times 2 = \text{DEPRECIATION (\%)}$$

When to use it This accelerated method can be used for any asset that loses value early on, such as computers or a delivery truck.

Sum of the years' digits method (SYD)

Depreciation is calculated by dividing each year of the asset's life by the sum of the total years to give a percentage of the depreciable value. If the asset's useful life is 5 years, then the sum of the years as digits is 15 (5 + 4 + 3 + 2 + 1). In year 1, it loses 33 percent (5 ÷ 15), in year 2, 27 percent (4 ÷ 15), and so on.

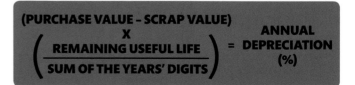

$$\left((\text{PURCHASE VALUE} - \text{SCRAP VALUE}) \times \frac{\text{REMAINING USEFUL LIFE}}{\text{SUM OF THE YEARS' DIGITS}} \right) = \text{DEPRECIATION (\%)}$$

When to use it This is another accelerated method that can also be used for vehicles that lose most of their value early on.

DEPRECIATION ON THE BALANCE SHEET

A company's accounts have to list all assets held by the company, including all fixed assets such as property and equipment. The accumulated depreciation of these fixed assets over the year is deducted from their value at the start of the year to give the year-end total. Without a depreciation figure, the accounts would give a false reflection of the finances of the business. The assets would appear as their original cost value and that might well exceed their current value.

Fixed assets are shown distinct from current assets

Depreciation of fixed assets is deducted

Total assets are calculated after depreciation has been deducted

Previous year's total assets can be compared

COMPANY NAME		BALANCE SHEET
Assets		
Current assets:	**2013**	**2014**
Cash	17,467.00	8,023.00
Investments	4,853.00	3,367.00
Inventories	1,056.00	2,138.00
Accounts receivable	2,165.00	3,600.00
Prepaid expenses	3,000.00	3,000.00
Other	860.00	976.00
Total current assets	**29,401.00**	**21,104.00**
Fixed assets:	**2013**	**2014**
Property and equipment	64,553.00	58,219.00
Building/site improvements	4,780.00	2,679.00
Equity and other investments	3,789.00	4,587.00
Less accumulated depreciation	5,625.00	4,171.00
Total fixed assets	**67,497.00**	**61,314.00**
Other assets:	**2013**	**2014**
Goodwill	1,577.00	1,650.00
Total other assets	**1,577.00**	**1,650.00**
Total assets	● **98,475.00**	● **84,068.00**

Units of production method

When a company uses an asset to produce quantifiable units, such as pages printed by a photocopier, it can claim depreciation with this method, which calculates depreciation according to the number of units an asset produces in a year.

$$\left(\frac{(\text{PURCHASE VALUE} - \text{SCRAP VALUE}) \times \text{UNITS PRODUCED PER YEAR}}{\text{LIFETIME PRODUCTION}} \right) = \text{DEPRECIATION (PER UNIT)}$$

When to use it This method is typically used by factories to calculate depreciation on machines that produce units of goods.

Hours of service method

The asset's decline in value is measured according to the number of actual hours it is in use. To calculate depreciation using this method, the company measures the hours of use per year as a percentage of the estimated total lifetime hours. It is particularly useful for transportation industries.

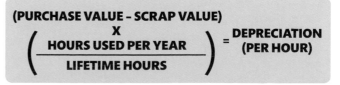

$$\left(\frac{(\text{PURCHASE VALUE} - \text{SCRAP VALUE}) \times \text{HOURS USED PER YEAR}}{\text{LIFETIME HOURS}} \right) = \text{DEPRECIATION (PER HOUR)}$$

When to use it This method may be used to match an airplane's flying hours with the revenue generated from those hours.

Amortization and depletion

Similar concepts to depreciation, amortization and depletion are used by accountants to show how intangible assets and natural resources respectively are used up.

How it works

Amortization is how the cost of purchasing an intangible asset, such as copyright of an artwork, is spread over a period of time, usually its useful lifetime. It is shown as a reduction in the value of the intangible asset on the balance sheet and an expense on the income statement. In lending, amortization can also mean the paying off of debts over time. Depletion shows the exhaustion of natural resources such as coal mines, forests, or natural gas.

Amortization in practice

There are two types of amortization, one for spreading the cost of an intangible asset, the other for loan repayment. Both are calculated in similar ways, but loan repayments are worked out as a percentage.

Intangible assets

In this example, a company buys an intangible asset— a patent for a new, revolutionary type of tennis racket—for $20,000. The patent will be useful for 10 years, so its cost is recorded as a $2,000 amortization (expense) each year rather than as a one-time cost. Unlike tangible assets, a patent does not have a salvage value (see p.124).

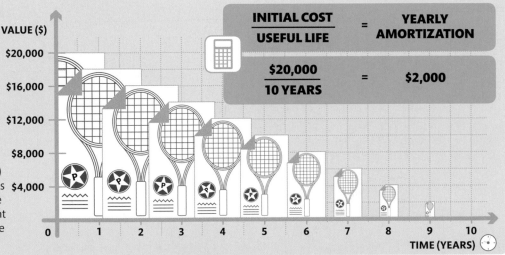

$$\frac{\text{INITIAL COST}}{\text{USEFUL LIFE}} = \text{YEARLY AMORTIZATION}$$

$$\frac{\$20,000}{10 \text{ YEARS}} = \$2,000$$

Loan percentage

If a company has an outstanding loan worth $150,000, and pays off $3,000 of this loan each year, then $3,000 of the loan has been amortized. It can also be said that 2 percent of the loan has been amortized, as it will take 50 years to repay the loan at this rate.

$$\frac{\text{COST OF LOAN}}{\text{YEARLY REPAYMENT}} = \frac{\text{YEARS TO REPAY}}{100} = \%$$

$$\frac{150,000}{3,000} = \frac{50}{100} = 2\%$$

GOODWILL

In business, goodwill describes an intangible asset based on a company's reputation, including loyal customers and suppliers, brand name, and public profile. Goodwill arises when one company buys another for more than its book value (total assets minus total liabilities). For example, if Company A buys Company B for $10 million but the total sum of its assets and liabilities is $9 million, the goodwill is worth $1 million. According to International Financial Reporting Standards since 2001, goodwill does not amortize, so it does not appear as amortization in financial statements. However, if the value of goodwill falls (through negative publicity, for example) it can be recorded as an impairment.

✓ NEED TO KNOW

> **Intangible assets** Non-physical assets, such as patents, trademarks, brand recognition, and copyright; their valuation is sometimes subjective

> **Patent** A license granted by a government or authority giving the owner exclusive rights for making or owning an invention

How to calculate depletion

Like amortization, depletion is calculated using the straight-line method (*see pp.124–125*) unless there is a particular reason to use another method.

In this example, a logging company buys a forest with an estimated 60,000 trees for $10 million. The original salvage value is $1.5 million, but the company spends $500,000 on road building in the forest, bringing it down to $1 million. The company cuts down 6,000 trees during each accounting period.

$$\frac{\text{COST – SALVAGE VALUE}}{\text{TOTAL UNITS}} \times \frac{\text{UNITS}}{\text{EXTRACTED}} = \frac{\text{DEPLETION}}{\text{EXPENSE}}$$

$$\frac{10,000,000 - 1,000,000}{60,000} \times 6,000 = \$900,000$$

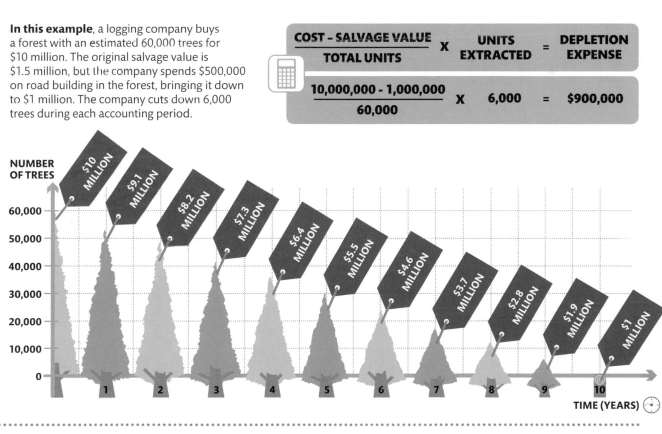

NUMBER OF TREES

$10 MILLION — $9.1 MILLION — $8.2 MILLION — $7.3 MILLION — $6.4 MILLION — $5.5 MILLION — $4.6 MILLION — $3.7 MILLION — $2.8 MILLION — $1.9 MILLION — $1 MILLION

60,000 / 50,000 / 40,000 / 30,000 / 20,000 / 10,000 / 0

1 2 3 4 5 6 7 8 9 10

TIME (YEARS)

Management accounting

For a company's management to anticipate profit and loss, plan cash flow, and set effective goals for the business, the coming year's incomings and outgoings need to be set out in detail. Unlike financial accounting, which is primarily for external users such as investors, lenders, or regulators, management or cost accounting takes place within a business to project expected sales revenue and expenses, so that the business can decide how to best use its available resources.

Management accounting process

Planning is done for the financial (fiscal) year that lies ahead—this is also called the accounting year and is made up of 12 consecutive months. Start and end dates differ from country to country.

Department budgets
Managers estimate what funds will be needed for expected outgoings. See pp.136–137.

Purchase orders (POs)
POs tell the finance department exactly how much money to reserve for payment.

Timesheets
Staff employed on an hourly or daily basis fill in timesheets; these help managers to calculate overall staff costs. See pp.140–141.

Invoices
Invoices submitted by contractors and suppliers have to be matched against purchase orders and paid out. See pp.134–135.

Goods received
Employees log receipt of merchandise, describing what the goods or services are and the quantity received.

Management
Managers create budgets and document business costs to monitor business performance, and plan for the short and medium term. The information they collate sheds light on the financial implications of ongoing projects.

Information is passed to finance department

80%
of accountants and financial professionals in the US are employed within a business or organization

COST ACCOUNTING PRINCIPLES

The Chartered Institute of Management Accounting (CIMA) in the UK and the American Institute of Certified Public Accountants (AICPA), with members in 177 countries, have established Global Management Accounting Principles.

> **Communication provides insight that is influential** Facilitate good decision-making through discussion.

> **Information is relevant** Source best material.

> **Stewardship builds trust** Protect financial and non-financial assets, reputation, and value of organization.

> **Impact on value is analyzed** Develop models to demonstrate outcomes in different scenarios.

Cost of production report (CPR)
CPR shows all of the costs that can be charged to a particular department. *See pp.140–143.*

Budget reports
Reports help management to determine the accuracy of budgets and analyze business performance. *See pp.136–137.*

Cash-flow statement
This shows how well the business will be able to meet its financial obligations and generate cash in the future. *See pp.120–121.*

Balance sheet
The balance sheet estimates the value of assets and inventory held, so that management can reduce it if necessary. *See pp.116–117.*

Profit-and-loss statement
Also called an income statement, the P&L statement tells management how much money the business made or lost over a particular time period. *See pp.114–115.*

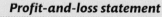

Financial analysis is passed to managers.

Finance department
Accountants in the finance department (or contracted from outside the business) receive information about the costs from managers. They then use these to generate reports and statements for the managers, who use this information to make decisions for the next financial year.

Cash flow

The money coming in and going out of a business is its cash flow; the balance of inflow and outflow is key to survival. Inflows arise from financing, operations, and investment, while outflows are expenses.

Sales revenue

Cash for goods and services sold

❯ Revenue generated by core operations

❯ Basis of profit—does not have to be repaid, unlike loans or capital

❯ Company must be able to turn revenue into cash (get paid) to maintain cash flow

❯ Also known as cash flow from operating activities

Capital

Investment and lump sums

❯ Main source of cash inflow for start-ups

❯ Additional cash injection after initial start-up or at key stages in a company's growth

❯ Revenue from flotation of private companies (going public) and shares issued by public companies

❯ Also known as cash flow from investing activities

CASH IN

CASH IN

"Cash comes in, cash goes out, but the tank should never be empty."

CASH OUT

Cash in hand

Salaries and wages

Payments to employees

❯ Money paid to employees who are directly involved in the creation of goods or provision of services

❯ Salaries paid to staff as a fixed amount monthly or weekly (based on an annual rate)

❯ Wages paid to contractors for hours, days, or weeks worked

Overheads

Payment of bills

❯ Day-to-day running costs

❯ Rental cost of commercial property; utility bills—water, electricity, gas, telephone, and internet; office supplies and stationery

❯ Salaries and wages of employees not directly involved in creating goods and services (known as indirect labor)

Loan repayments

Debt servicing and shareholder profit

❯ Interest on long-term loans for asset purchases and on short-term loans for working capital

❯ Repayments on capital loans

❯ Commission paid to factoring companies

❯ Cash distribution to shareholders via share repurchases and dividend payments

How it works

Cash flow is the movement of cash in and out of a business over a set period of time. Cash flows in from sales of goods and services, loans, capital investment, and other sources. Cash flows out to pay employees, rent and utilities, suppliers, and interest on loans. Timing is key—having enough cash coming in to pay bills on time keeps the company solvent.

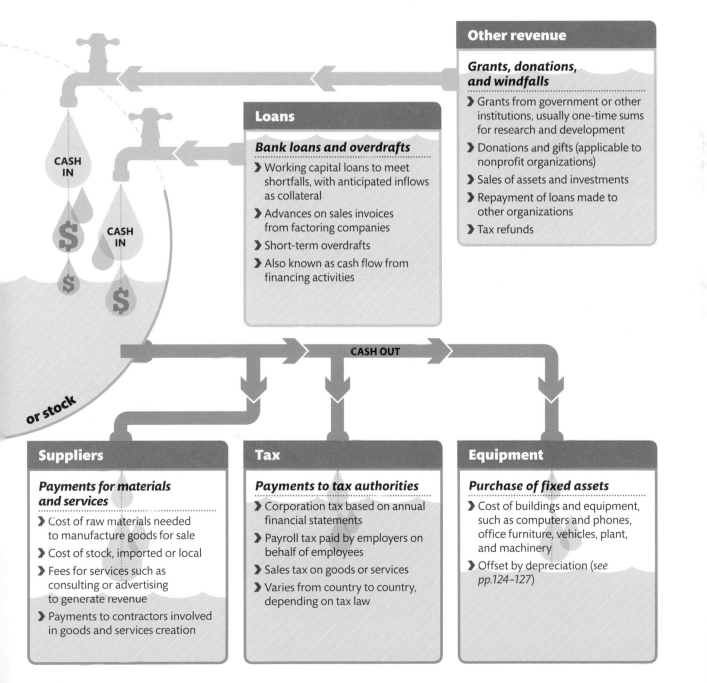

CASH IN

CASH IN

$

$

$

or stock

Other revenue

Grants, donations, and windfalls

> Grants from government or other institutions, usually one-time sums for research and development

> Donations and gifts (applicable to nonprofit organizations)

> Sales of assets and investments

> Repayment of loans made to other organizations

> Tax refunds

Loans

Bank loans and overdrafts

> Working capital loans to meet shortfalls, with anticipated inflows as collateral

> Advances on sales invoices from factoring companies

> Short-term overdrafts

> Also known as cash flow from financing activities

CASH OUT

Suppliers

Payments for materials and services

> Cost of raw materials needed to manufacture goods for sale

> Cost of stock, imported or local

> Fees for services such as consulting or advertising to generate revenue

> Payments to contractors involved in goods and services creation

Tax

Payments to tax authorities

> Corporation tax based on annual financial statements

> Payroll tax paid by employers on behalf of employees

> Sales tax on goods or services

> Varies from country to country, depending on tax law

Equipment

Purchase of fixed assets

> Cost of buildings and equipment, such as computers and phones, office furniture, vehicles, plant, and machinery

> Offset by depreciation (see pp.124–127)

Cash-flow management

The handling of cash flow determines the survival of any business. Equally important is a company's ability to convert its earnings into cash, which is known as liquidity. No matter how profitable a business is, it may become insolvent if it cannot pay its bills on time. New businesses may become victims of their own success and fail through "insolvency by overtrading" if, for example, they spend too much on expansion before payments start coming in and run out of cash to pay debts and liabilities. In order to manage cash flow, it is essential for companies to forecast cash inflows and outflows. Sales predictions and cash conversion rates are important. A schedule of when payments are due from customers, and when a business has to pay its own wages, bills, suppliers, debts, and other costs, can help to predict shortfalls. If cash flow is mismanaged, a business may have to pay out before receiving payment, leading to cash shortages. Some businesses, such as supermarkets, receive stock on credit but are paid in cash, generating a cash surplus.

! WARNING

Top five cash-flow problems

> **Slow payment** of invoices
> **Credit terms** on sales invoices set at 60 or 120 days, while credit terms on outgoings are 30 days
> **Decline in sales** due to change in economic climate or competition, or product becoming outmoded
> **Underpriced product,** especially in start-ups trying to compete
> **Excessive outlay** on payroll and overheads; buying rather than renting assets

Positive and negative cash flow

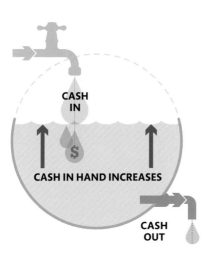

CASH IN

CASH IN HAND INCREASES

CASH OUT

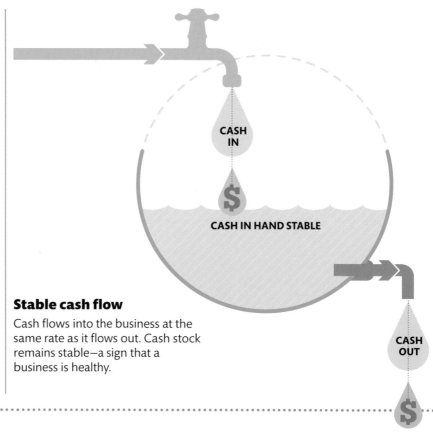

CASH IN

CASH IN HAND STABLE

CASH OUT

Positive cash flow

Cash flowing into the business is greater than cash flowing out. Cash in the tank—stock—increases. A business in this position is thriving.

Stable cash flow

Cash flows into the business at the same rate as it flows out. Cash stock remains stable—a sign that a business is healthy.

✓ NEED TO KNOW

> **Factoring** Transaction in which a business passes its invoices a third party (factor), which collects payment from the customer for a commission
> **Accounts payable** Payments a business has to make to others
> **Accounts receivable** Payments a business is due to receive
> **Aging schedule** A table charting accounts payable and accounts receivable according to their dates
> **Cash flow gap** Interval between payments made and received

Cash conversion

Successful businesses convert their product or service into cash inflows before their bills are due. To make the conversion process more efficient, a business may speed up:

> Customer purchase ordering
> Order fulfillment and shipping
> Customer invoicing
> Accounts receivable collection period
> Payment and deposit

80%
of small business start-ups across the world fail because of poor cash-flow management

HANDLING THE FLOW

Managing a surplus

> **Move excess cash** into a bank account where it will earn interest, or make profitable investments.
> **Use cash** to upgrade equipment to improve production efficiency.
> **Expand the business** by taking on new staff, developing products, or buying other companies.
> **Pay creditors** early to improve credit credentials, or pay down debt before it is due.

Managing a shortage

> **Increase sales** by lowering prices, or profit margins by raising them.
> **Issue invoices** promptly and pursue overdue payments.
> **Ask suppliers** to extend credit.
> **Offer discounts** on sales invoices in return for faster payment.
> **Use an overdraft** or short-term loan to pay off pressing expenses.
> **Continue to forecast** cash flow and plan to avert future problems.

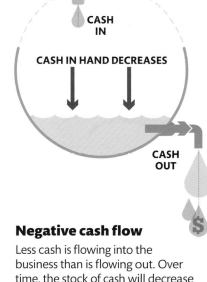

Negative cash flow

Less cash is flowing into the business than is flowing out. Over time, the stock of cash will decrease and the business will face difficulties.

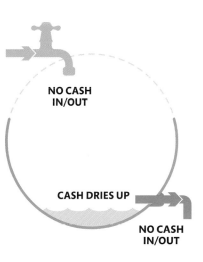

Bankruptcy

If cash flowing out continues to exceed cash flowing in, cash stock levels will drop so low that the business becomes insolvent—it has no assets left to continue trading.

Budgets

Setting the budget for a business involves planning the income and expenditure for the accounting year. This is usually broken down into months so that planned budget and actual figures can be compared.

How it works

Every business needs to budget for anticipated revenue and operating costs within the financial year. Unlike capital budgeting, in which senior management allocates what will be spent on specific projects or assets, revenue budgeting focuses on the overall projections for money coming in and money going out for each month of the coming financial, or accounting, year. Accountants compile operating budgets from each manager in the business, along with expected cash-flow projections for the business, to create a master budget. The master budget can also include figures for any financing that the company is expected to need over the coming year. As the year progresses, the projected budget and the actual money coming in and going out are monitored on a daily, weekly, or monthly basis, so that any deviations from the original budget can be identified, and, if necessary, remedied.

Setting and controlling budgets

Budget-setting is a process that takes place between the department managers, senior management, and finance department in a company to establish and control the cost of each department or project.

1%

of companies worldwide made accurate budget forecasts, from 2004 to 2007

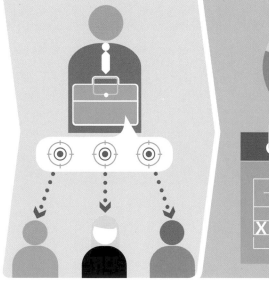

Consultation

Senior management sets out the company's objectives to the departmental managers. Each manager is then responsible for working out the budget required by their individual department, in order to meet those objectives for the coming year.

Prepare the budget

The budget is usually based on the accounting year, but broken down into shorter periods. Departmental managers submit their budgets to senior management for approval. These may cover areas such as operating costs (salaries and supplies) and administration (office expenses).

INCREMENTAL AND ZERO-BASED

There are two main approaches to setting budgets:

Incremental budget The budget for the year ahead is based on the previous year's budget. This budget takes into account any changes, such as inflation, which could have an impact on the new calculations. The downside is that previous inaccuracies may be carried forward.

Zero-base budget The coming year's budget starts afresh, with no reference to previous years. This means that each item entered into the budget is carefully scrutinized and has to be justified by the department managers. This method makes it easier to see the full cost of all planned changes.

✓ NEED TO KNOW

› **Planning, Programming, and Budgeting Systems (PPBS)** A budgeting system used in public service organizations such as city councils and hospitals

› **Virement** An amount saved under one cost heading in a budget is transferred to another cost heading to compensate for overspend

› **Budget slack** Deliberately underestimating sales or overestimating expenses in a budget

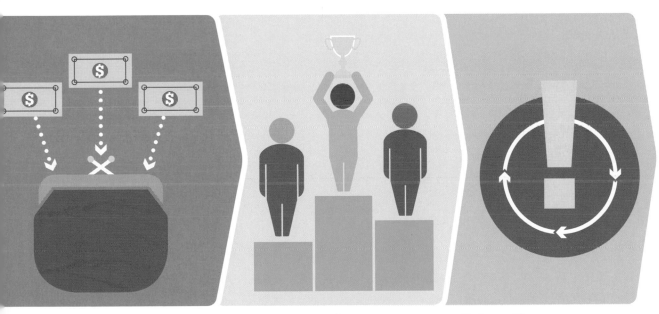

Master budget

Once approved, the budgets from each department are combined into a master budget for the year, which includes: a budgeted profit-and-loss account, a projected balance sheet, and a budgeted cash-flow statement that typically shows a month-by-month breakdown.

Measure performance

After each month (or equivalent time period set in the budget), the actual figures realized by the company are compared with the original budget projections. Variations are examined closely to work out whether they are significantly different from the figure in the original budget.

Take action

If necessary, the budget is revised to take into account any unforeseen and continued expenditure, or any savings that were not anticipated. If income is less than expected, action may be taken to alter departmental processes or campaigns in order to reach the targets set in the budget.

Assets and inventory

A company's possessions, or assets, are divided into two categories: fixed (or long-term) assets and current (or short-term) assets. Current assets consist of cash in the bank and inventory.

How it works

Fixed assets are items that enable a business to operate. They tend to be long-term holdings and cannot be easily converted into cash. Fixed assets can be categorized as either tangible or intangible: tangible assets are material objects, while intangible assets have no physical form.

Current assets are held for the short term and used mainly for trading. The most important category in terms of generating revenue is current assets. The key component of these is inventory. Inventory can be finished goods ready for sale, but it can also be the raw materials that will be used for producing the goods.

Assets and inventory in practice

The partial balance sheets below show the current assets of a branch of Super Sports Inc., a sportswear and sports accessories company. These assets include cash in the bank and inventory held by the company. The inventory in this case consists of all the items in the shop that are ready for sale.

Super Sports Inc.
May 31

Assets	$
Cash at bank	12,000
Inventories	22,000
Total assets	**34,000**

Super Sports Inc.
June 15

Assets	$
Cash at bank	54,000
Inventories	0
Total assets	**54,000**

Balance sheet as of May 31

The "Assets" section of the balance sheet shows that the company holds $22,000 worth of inventory (or goods) at this point in time, as well as $12,000 cash in the bank.

Balance sheet as of June 15

Two weeks later, the company sells all of its inventory for $42,000 and receives payment for this sale on the same day. This means that total assets have risen by $20,000—the profit made on the sale of the inventory—and increases the amount of cash in the bank by $42,000.

TYPES OF INVENTORY

Inventory can include three types of stock, depending on the kind of business being carried out: raw materials, unfinished goods, and finished goods. *See pp.316–317.*

Raw materials

Materials and components scheduled for use in making a product. For example, a chocolate factory will have:

> **Ingredients** in the form of sugar, cocoa mass, cocoa butter, additives, flavorings, and perhaps milk or nuts.

> **Foil, plastic, and paper** for the wrappers and packaging

Work in progress

Materials and components that have begun their transformation into finished goods; these may be referred to as "unfinished goods." For instance, a graphic designer will have:

> **Layouts and designs** that are being developed and are awaiting client approval

Finished goods

The stock of completed products, or goods ready for sale to customers. A bookstore, for example, will have:

> **Hardback and paperback books** of various genres and formats supplied by publishing houses

> **Gift items** such as greeting cards and notebooks

Types of fixed assets

Super Sports Inc. owns a range of tangible and intangible fixed assets. Compared to tangible fixed assets, the worth of intangible fixed assets can sometimes be harder to evaluate.

Tangible fixed assets

LAND AND PROPERTY

Retail outlets plus company headquarters

FURNITURE

Store displays and back office furniture

COMPUTER EQUIPMENT

Computers for administrative work

VEHICLES

Trucks and branded company cars

TOOLS AND MACHINERY

Warehouse and distribution equipment

Intangible fixed assets

INTELLECTUAL PROPERTY

Brands and designs, creative innovation

TRADEMARKS

Legally protected words and symbols

BRANDS

Own brands, including value and luxury ranges

COMPUTER SOFTWARE

Internet portal for online sales

COPYRIGHT AND ROYALTIES

Licensing revenue streams

Costs

Costs are the direct or indirect expenses that a business incurs in order to carry out activities that earn revenue, such as manufacturing goods or providing a service.

How it works

There are two main ways of classifying costs: direct, or variable, costs, which increase as more goods and services are sold, and indirect costs, which contribute to the overall running of the business and can either vary with the level of production or stay fixed. There are three main costs that businesses need to account for. The first is labor—wages paid to people employed to carry out a particular task. Labor can be regarded as direct or variable, or as a fixed cost or overhead. The second is the raw materials used in production and other materials used in service industries—these costs are variable. The third is expenses, which are other costs incurred in the course of the business's activities.

Fixed and variable costs

One way of looking at costs is to split them into two categories: fixed costs, which do not change with the level of business activity, and variable costs, which do change with the level of business activity. This helps accountants to determine how changes in business activity (for example, cutting or increasing production) will affect costs. In reality, some fixed costs will increase once business activity reaches a certain level–these are called stepped fixed costs.

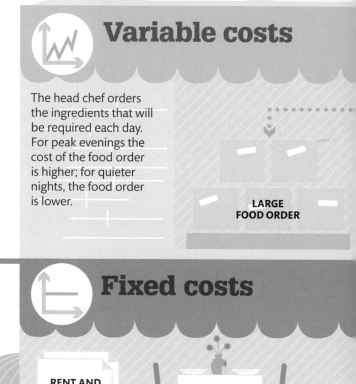

Variable costs

The head chef orders the ingredients that will be required each day. For peak evenings the cost of the food order is higher; for quieter nights, the food order is lower.

LARGE FOOD ORDER

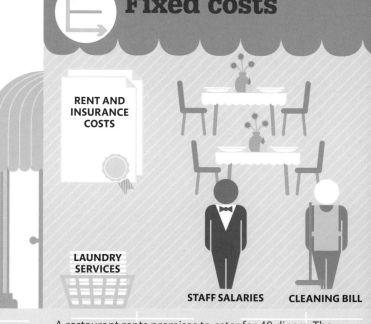

Fixed costs

RENT AND INSURANCE COSTS

LAUNDRY SERVICES

STAFF SALARIES

CLEANING BILL

A restaurant rents premises to cater for 40 diners. The fixed costs are the same whether the restaurant serves 30 or 40 diners a night.

PEAK EVENINGS

QUIETER EVENINGS

SMALL FOOD ORDER

Stepped fixed costs

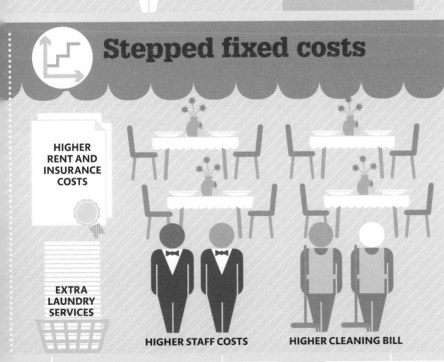

HIGHER RENT AND INSURANCE COSTS

EXTRA LAUNDRY SERVICES

HIGHER STAFF COSTS

HIGHER CLEANING BILL

40%
of business owners say that payroll is their greatest expense

The restaurant becomes popular, so the owner rents the premises next door to serve an additional 40 diners a night. The costs that were fixed at a certain level have now doubled.

Product costing and pricing

Knowing the full cost of creating each product that a business sells is vital because it helps a company price its products appropriately and assess the performance of the business.

How it works

Both direct and indirect costs contribute to the production cost of a product, whether it is a manufactured good or a service being provided. In order to calculate the cost of a product, it is treated as one unit of production. The direct and indirect costs involved in creating that single unit are then assessed and added together to create the full cost.

38%

the average total of US business costs that can be accounted for by indirect costs

✓ NEED TO KNOW

❯ **Absorption costing** Allocation of all production costs to product

❯ **Differential costing** Difference between the cost of two options

❯ **Incremental (marginal) costing** The change in total costs incurred when one additional unit is made

❯ **Throughput costing** An analysis of the impact that one extra unit of production will have on sales

❯ **Cost-plus pricing** Product price is based on direct and indirect costs, plus markup percentage

Full cost pricing

Direct costs can be measured in terms of how materials and labor are used to produce each unit. Indirect costs (overheads) are harder to assess but also need to be factored in so that the full cost of each product can be calculated. Managers and accountants must apportion indirect costs to reflect their contribution to the cost of creating a single product. Once this is ascertained, the full cost of that product can be determined. In general terms, the price is worked out by adding the direct and indirect costs of production with a profit margin that gives an appropriate selling price.

Direct costs

❯ Materials
❯ Direct labor
❯ Direct expenses
❯ All used exclusively to create a product or service for sale

Share of indirect costs

❯ Production and service overheads
❯ Administrative and management overheads
❯ Sales and distribution overheads

OTHER COSTING METHODS

There are several different approaches to costing and pricing depending on the industry, the type and size of the business, and the method of production.

JOB COSTING

Used for a customized order made to a client's specifications—for example, a printing company that prints brochures for a client

BATCH COSTING

Used when a batch of identical products is made—for example, an electrical goods company manufacturing television sets

CONTRACT COSTING

Used for a large one-time job, often the result of a tender process (when a company bids for work) and carried out at the client's site—for example, a construction company building homes in a new residential development

PROCESS COSTING

Used for an ongoing job that often involves several manufacturing processes, making it difficult to isolate individual unit costs—for example, an oil refinery which processes crude oil into diesel oil

SERVICE COSTING

Used when the product being sold is a standard service offered to customers—for example, a nail salon offering an express manicure and pedicure within a set period of time and for a fixed price

➕ Profit margin

- ❯ Must be able to generate profit for the company
- ❯ Must be in line with how the product has been marketed
- ❯ Must be pitched realistically so that customers will buy

LUXURY HOME FOR SALE

➗ Selling price

- ❯ Low: in order to gain market share, or to match competitors
- ❯ Cost-based: recover direct and indirect costs and profit margin that the market will accept
- ❯ Service-based: flexible since no manufacturing or distribution cost

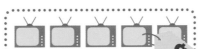

Measuring performance

There are two main ways of measuring a company's performance: financial and non-financial. To assess financial performance, a company calculates financial ratios. To assess other areas of the business, a company examines its key performance indicators (KPIs), which help management and staff evaluate performance and how it can improve. KPIs also enable interested outsiders, such as investors, lenders, or analysts, to decide whether to invest in the business.

Financial and non-financial categories

Any company that publishes a financial report will be required to set out key figures on the revenue generated and the expenses incurred during the course of its activities. These figures can be compared using mathematical calculations called financial ratios. However, financial ratios alone may not give an accurate vision of the company's future prospects. Non-financial ratios, or key performance indicators, do not measure financial performance, but they do reveal other important characteristics of a company that will ultimately affect its profitability, such as customer loyalty and research and development (R and D) productivity.

Tracking and forecasting
Financial and non-financial measures can be used to forecast company performance and track fraud. *See pp.152–153.*

Company

TREND ANALYSIS USING PERFORMANCE MEASUREMENTS

A comparison of either financial ratios or KPIs between companies in the same industry and across time is often used to track a company's performance. Current ratios are calculated by dividing current assets by current liabilities: the higher the ratio, the more liquidity a company has.

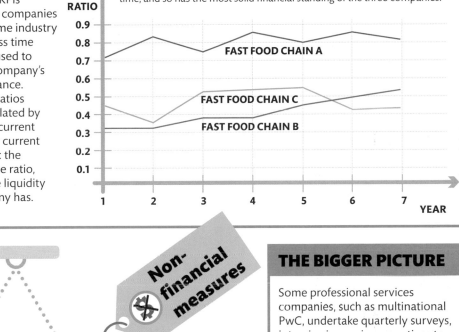

CURRENT RATIO COMPARISON OVER TIME
Fast-food chain A is shown to be a consistently better performer over time, and so has the most solid financial standing of the three companies.

CURRENT RATIO

FAST FOOD CHAIN A
FAST FOOD CHAIN C
FAST FOOD CHAIN B

YEAR

Financial measures $

Non-financial measures ✗

Financial ratios

❯ Used by investors and lenders to gauge financial health of an organization: if it's likely to survive economic slump, and what prospects it has for future growth

❯ Standard set of ratios used by the financial industry

❯ Calculated based on figures provided in financial reports

See pp.148–149.

Key Performance Indicators

❯ Used internally and by investors, as they appear in financial statement

❯ May be calculated daily or even more frequently for internal use

❯ Companies can set diverse KPIs to reflect future goals

❯ Unique to each company

See pp.146–147.

THE BIGGER PICTURE

Some professional services companies, such as multinational PwC, undertake quarterly surveys, interviewing senior executives to find out how optimistic they are about their sector and the wider economy. Such surveys help companies measure their own performance objectively.

69%
of multinationals link performance measures to future financial results

Key performance indicators (KPIs)

Key performance indicators (KPIs), or key success indicators (KSIs), are based on a company's goals and vary depending on the company and industry. KPIs are usually stated in a company's annual report.

How it works

KPIs are the non-financial measures of a company's performance—they do not have a monetary value but they do contribute to the company's profitability. Any company department can adopt KPIs to gauge its performance. A KPI for an accounts department might be the percentage of overdue invoices, as this will help determine the department's efficiency. This is an example of a lagging indicator—it is an outcome and therefore easy to measure, but not straightforward to influence. Companies also look for leading indicators, which are focused on inputs and easier to change. A leading KPI for the accounts department might be the percentage of purchase orders raised in advance.

Corporate KPIs

KPIs can be set up as dashboards on computers so that they can be checked frequently. These dashboards show examples of KPIs specific to departments in a company. Having set their KPIs, the departments are subject to managerial review, which could result in action if KPIs are sub-standard.

Accounts

Number of retrospectively raised purchase orders; finance report error rate (measures the quality of report); average cycle time of workflow; number of duplicate payments

Sales and marketing

Net promoter score (NPS – how many customers would recommend company); customer retention rate; customer lifetime value (total amount of money generated by one customer)

Customer service

Number of customer complaints; customer satisfaction (measured over time); average email response time; number of products sold compared to total sales calls made

31%
of companies use a computer dashboard to monitor KPI measurements

BALANCED SCORECARD SYSTEM

This strategic system offers a different way of monitoring a company's performance. It was proposed by Robert Kaplan and David Norton at the Harvard Business School in the 1990s, and *Harvard Business Review* has cited it as one of the most influential business ideas of the last 75 years; it is estimated that over 50 percent of large companies in the US, Europe, and Asia use the approach. The Balanced Scorecard consists of four ways to view an organization's performance:

❯ **Learning and growth**
Employee training and corporate culture

❯ **Business processes**
Includes specific measurements for monitoring daily performance

❯ **Customer perspective**
Customer satisfaction

❯ **Financial perspective**
Traditional financial data

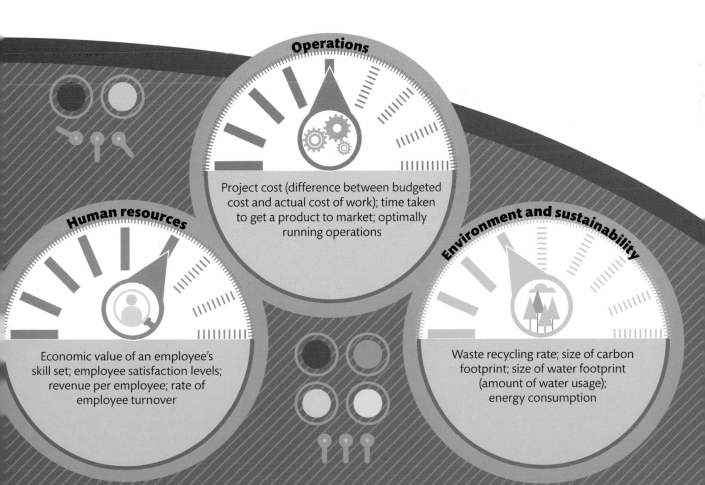

Operations
Project cost (difference between budgeted cost and actual cost of work); time taken to get a product to market; optimally running operations

Human resources
Economic value of an employee's skill set; employee satisfaction levels; revenue per employee; rate of employee turnover

Environment and sustainability
Waste recycling rate; size of carbon footprint; size of water footprint (amount of water usage); energy consumption

Financial ratios

Lenders, investors, analysts, internal management, and other interested parties calculate financial ratios to decipher what financial statements are really saying about the state of a business.

How it works

Financial ratios are used to assess the financial standing of a business and identify any problem areas that might affect its future prospects. The process involves comparing two related items in the financial statement, such as net sales to net worth or net income to net sales, and using those ratios to measure the relative performance of the company. There are many different ratios to choose from, depending on the purpose—for example, whether the purpose is to measure the company's ability to provide a good return to shareholders, its capacity to handle debt, or the efficiency with which it operates. The ratios can also be used to compare a business with its competitors or in comparison to specific benchmarks within the company to determine how consistent its financial results are.

Top financial ratios

These are some of the ratios most commonly used by people involved with assessing businesses. They are best considered comparatively and in the context of the economic climate. The ratios are for analyzing established companies, usually public ones with shares traded on the stock exchange—start-ups and small-to-medium enterprises generally do not have a full enough range of figures to provide any kind of reliable guide.

Profitability ratios

These are used to see how effective a company is at generating profit, profitability ratios may mirror investment valuation ratios. One example is the operating profit margin ratio. A high ratio is good, as it indicates that a high proportion of revenue (gross income) converted into operating income (profit minus costs).

$$\text{OPERATING PROFIT MARGIN} = \frac{\text{OPERATING INCOME}}{\text{REVENUE}}$$

Other profitability ratios

❯ **Return on equity (ROE)** is measured as net income after tax / shareholders' equity. The higher the ratio, the greater the profitability, but not if a company is relying too heavily on borrowing.

❯ **EBITDA to sales ratio** is measured as EBITDA (earnings before interest, taxes, depreciation, and amortization) / revenue. It gauges the profitability of core business operations. The higher the margin, the greater the profits.

Efficiency ratios

These show how efficiently the company uses its assets and resources to maximize profits. An example is the sales revenue to capital employed ratio, which indicates a company's ability to generate sales revenue by utilizing its assets. Similar ratios can examine how quickly the company settles its bills and invoices.

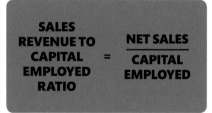

$$\text{SALES REVENUE TO CAPITAL EMPLOYED RATIO} = \frac{\text{NET SALES}}{\text{CAPITAL EMPLOYED}}$$

Other efficiency ratios

❯ **Accounts receivable turnover ratio** is measured as net credit sales / average accounts receivable. It shows how efficiently a company turns sales into cash. The higher the ratio, the more frequently money is collected.

❯ **Inventory turnover ratio** is measured as the cost of goods sold / average inventory. It shows how efficiently a company manages its inventory level. A low ratio usually equates to poor sales.

10–14%
the minimum return on investment (ROI) needed to fund a company's future

Liquidity ratios

This group of ratios reveals whether or not a company has enough cash or equivalent assets to meet its debt repayments. An example is the working capital ratio (also a measure of efficiency), which indicates whether a company has enough short-term assets to cover its short-term debt.

$$\text{WORKING CAPITAL} = \frac{\text{CURRENT ASSETS}}{\text{CURRENT LIABILITIES}}$$

Other liquidity ratios

❭ **Cash ratio** is measured as total cash (and equivalents) / current liabilities. It shows whether a company's short-term assets could repay its debts. A high ratio is seen as favorable.

❭ **Quick ratio (acid-test ratio)** is measured as current assets minus inventories / current liabilities. It shows how easily a company can repay short-term debt from cash. The higher the ratio, the more easily it can pay.

Solvency ratios

While liquidity ratios look at a company's short-term ability to meet loan repayments, solvency ratios indicate the likelihood of a company being able to continue indefinitely with enough cash or current assets to pay its debts in the long run. An example is the debt to equity ratio.

$$\text{DEBT TO EQUITY RATIO} = \frac{\text{TOTAL SHAREHOLDERS' EQUITY}}{\text{TOTAL ASSETS}}$$

Other solvency ratios

❭ **Interest coverage ratio** is measured as EBIT (earnings before interest and tax) / interest expense. It indicates how easily a company can pay the interest on its debts. The higher the ratio, the more easily they can pay.

❭ **Debt ratio** is measured as total liabilities / total assets. It indicates the percentage of the company's assets that are financed by debt. A low ratio is considered favorable.

Investment valuation ratios

Thes ratios are typically used by investors to gauge the returns they are likely to get if they buy shares in a company. An example is the dividend payout ratio. It indicates how well earnings support the dividend payments—more mature companies tend to have a higher payout ratio.

$$\text{DIVIDEND PAYOUT RATIO} = \frac{\text{YEARLY DIVIDEND PER SHARE}}{\text{EARNINGS PER SHARE}}$$

Other investment valuation ratios

❭ **Net profit margin ratio** is measured as profit after tax / revenue. Another measure of a company's profitability, it is also useful for comparing a company with competitors. The higher the ratio, the more profitable the company.

❭ **Price to earnings ratio** is measured as market value per share / earnings per share. It indicates the value of the company's share price. A high ratio demonstrates good growth potential.

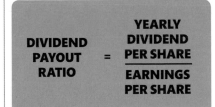

Forecasting

Predicting future business performance is necessary to estimate probable sales, income, costs, and profitability and thus gain investment and maintain confidence in the company.

How it works

Forecasting success or failure relies on historical data—financial statements, financial ratios, and Key Performance Indicators—that reflect business operation and can be tracked over time. The tracked and monitored data can provide an early warning system for potential problems. For small businesses and start-ups, accurate forecasts provide a basis for

Forecasting with Z-score models

Realizing that traditional financial ratios, such as the ratio of costs to revenue, created only a partial picture of a business's financial performance, Altman devised a set formula that combined four or five key ratios to give a Z score. The model has proven 90 percent accurate in predicting business failure over one year, and 80 percent accurate over two years.

Working capital / total assets
A measure of liquidity: the more working capital in a company, the more it is able to pay its bills.

Market value of equity / book value of total liabilities
A measure of the market confidence in the company: a ratio of less than one means the firm is worth less than it owes—it is insolvent.

Retained earnings / total assets
A measure of leverage: a high ratio indicates profits are funding growth; a low ratio indicates growth is financed by debt.

Earnings before interest and taxes / total assets
A measure of return on assets: it gauges operating income generated by assets.

Sales / total assets
A measure of efficiency: the sales generated by the assets.

Corporate success

Efficiently run companies with a healthy balance between assets and liabilities, and profit and debt inspire confidence in investors.

SS Success

Finding the Z score

Each of the above ratios is multiplied by a specific value, to give them weighting; results are added together to give Z score.

❯ A score of 0.2 or lower means the company is highly likely to fail.

❯ A score of 0.3 or higher means the company is unlikely to fail.

raising external financing, while for larger companies, this information provides an indication of financial strength for investors and markets. Predictions may range from conjectured costs and revenue to complex financial models. One of the most frequently used predictive models for forecasting business success is the Z-score model, devised by Edward Altman, a New York University finance professor, in 1968.

✓ NEED TO KNOW

> **Ohlson O score** Alternative to Z score for predicting failure

> **Overtrading** When a company's sales grow faster than its finance

> **Undertrading** When a company trades at low levels compared to its finance levels

> **Zeta analysis** Second-generation Z-score model

Signs of corporate failure

There are many signs that a company is doing badly and perhaps sliding into insolvency. These signs make investors nervous, which is likely to lower share price if they start selling their shareholding. However, most companies that fail are in profit, but run out of cash.

20%

the predicted profitability increase from 2013 to 2017 for organizations using performance measurement to make business forecasts

SS Failure

X **Selling assets** to pay off debts

X **Cuts** to employee benefits

X **Repeated dividend cuts** to shareholders

Bankruptcy occurs if the company cannot pay its debts

X **Top management** resigning and taking jobs elsewhere

X **Low cash flow**, seen in continued pattern of decline in cash holdings on balance sheet over consecutive years

X **High borrowing**, high interest payments and dwindling revenue

X **Low profitability**, seen in consistent downslide in profit on profit-and-loss statements from consecutive years

Tracking fraud

For keen observers of financial statements, warning signs that indicate fraudulent business activities may be detected in overly optimistic statements and evasive attitudes of senior management.

How it works

Public companies are required to have their annual financial statements audited (checked) by an independent auditor. It is typically during this process that any financial shenanigans—creative accounting tricks used to manipulate the figures and improve the performance of a company in its financial statements—and outright fraudulent activity is uncovered. It is the auditor's job to ensure that business records and statements are accurate and have been honestly reported. Auditors carry out a systematic examination of the company's records and may identify any irregularities that may indicate fraud. If evidence of fraud is found, the next step is to involve forensic accountants and criminal investigators, who may prosecute the perpetrators.

✓ NEED TO KNOW

❱ **Asset stripping** Selling off the assets of a company for a profit to raise funds, often resulting in the closure of the business

❱ **Tunneling** A particular type of fraud in which assets and funds are illicitly transferred to management or shareholders

Red flags indicating fraud

Auditors may be alerted to fraud by a number of recognized warning signs or "red flags"; these may be either directly to do with the behavior of the CEO or other top executives, or in the form of irregularities within the financial statements.

Suspicious figures on financial statements

❱ Cash flows that are negative for three quarters, then suddenly and dramatically become positive

❱ Sudden increase in gross margin, at odds with industry average and company's previous performance pattern

❱ Large sales to companies with dubious track records

❱ Sales recorded before they have been made

❱ Made-up, nonexistent sources of revenue

❱ Expenses moved from one company to another, or classified as assets

❱ Ongoing, long-term growth of earnings per share

❱ High payments to executives compared to base salary

89%
of US corporate fraud cases in 2010 typically involved the company's CEO or CFO

How to detect fraud

Procedures should be in place to hold accountable anyone who handles expenses. When these fall short, internal and external auditors need to take more drastic measures.

Applying ratio analysis to reveal key long-term trends (*see pp.148–149*)

LINE-UP: TOP FIVE NOTORIOUS FRAUDS

Some of the worst frauds stem from the most prestigious companies.
Enron was one of the top seven US companies, while JPMorgan Chase
& Co. was the largest American bank when measured by assets.

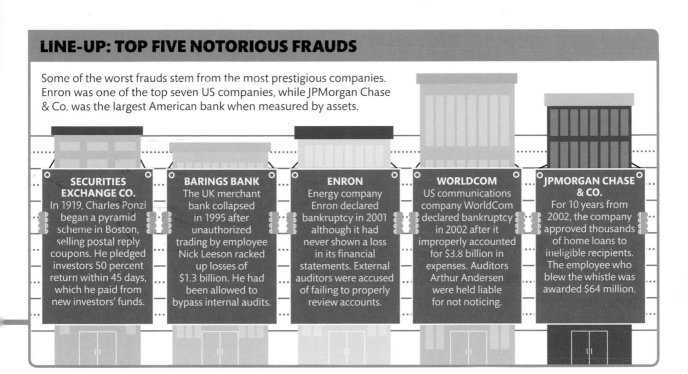

SECURITIES EXCHANGE CO.
In 1919, Charles Ponzi began a pyramid scheme in Boston, selling postal reply coupons. He pledged investors 50 percent return within 45 days, which he paid from new investors' funds.

BARINGS BANK
The UK merchant bank collapsed in 1995 after unauthorized trading by employee Nick Leeson racked up losses of $1.3 billion. He had been allowed to bypass internal audits.

ENRON
Energy company Enron declared bankruptcy in 2001 although it had never shown a loss in its financial statements. External auditors were accused of failing to properly review accounts.

WORLDCOM
US communications company WorldCom declared bankruptcy in 2002 after it improperly accounted for $3.8 billion in expenses. Auditors Arthur Andersen were held liable for not noticing.

JPMORGAN CHASE & CO.
For 10 years from 2002, the company approved thousands of home loans to ineligible recipients. The employee who blew the whistle was awarded $64 million.

CEO behavior
> Evasive behavior by executives over important financial details
> Attempts by CEO to steer auditors away from certain documents

Technicalities
> Late entry of sales or earnings adjustments
> Missing approvals or signatures
> Photocopied documents presented in place of originals

Setting up confidential hotline for current and past employees or others with knowledge of the company

Using element of surprise, such as undertaking an aggressive internal audit without prior warning

Conducting a surprise cash count to determine whether current cash flow matches statements

Data mining with auditing software to detect any mismatch between past patterns and current statements

Raising financing

When a company needs additional funds, it can use either internal or external sources, or both, depending on whether it seeks large amounts of funding for long-term growth, such as an expansion, or smaller amounts for short-term expenses, such as to cover operating costs. In addition, the number of external sources available depends on whether the business is well established or whether it is relatively new and without much of a track record.

Sources of financing and capital

When considering the prospect of raising financing, the financial directors will first evaluate the financial health of the company. They will then decide what proportion of the company will be funded by equity (the company's own reserves of cash and money raised from issuing shares) and what proportion will be funded by borrowing money from an outside source, such as a bank, so that the company takes on debt.

59% of US financial managers say financial flexibility is the most important factor in deciding how much debt the company takes on

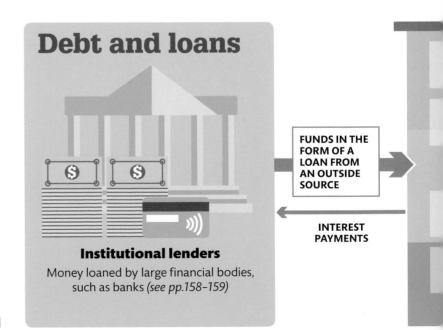

Debt and loans

Institutional lenders
Money loaned by large financial bodies, such as banks (*see pp.158–159*)

FUNDS IN THE FORM OF A LOAN FROM AN OUTSIDE SOURCE

INTEREST PAYMENTS

EVALUATING CAPITAL STRUCTURE

When investors consider buying shares in a company, they look at its capital structure to assess the future prospects of the business. The capital structure refers to the percentage of a company's finances made up of funds from shares and earnings, called equity, and the percentage made up from borrowed funds, or debt. When evaluating capital structure, investors consider the following:

❯ As a general rule, companies with more equity than debt are considered less risky to invest in because their assets outweigh their liabilities. So a company with significantly more equity than debt has a low debt-to-equity ratio and is generally seen to be a low-risk investment.

❯ A company with significantly more debt than equity has a high debt-to-equity ratio and is more risky as an investment.

❯ Debt is not always bad. If interest rates are low a company could take on more debt to fund expansion, as long as the revenue it makes from the borrowed funds is greater than the interest payable. So although this company may be more risky, it may also have greater potential for growth—this is known as "gearing" (see pp.174–175).

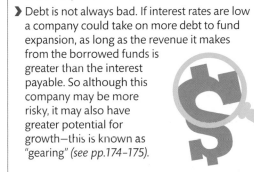

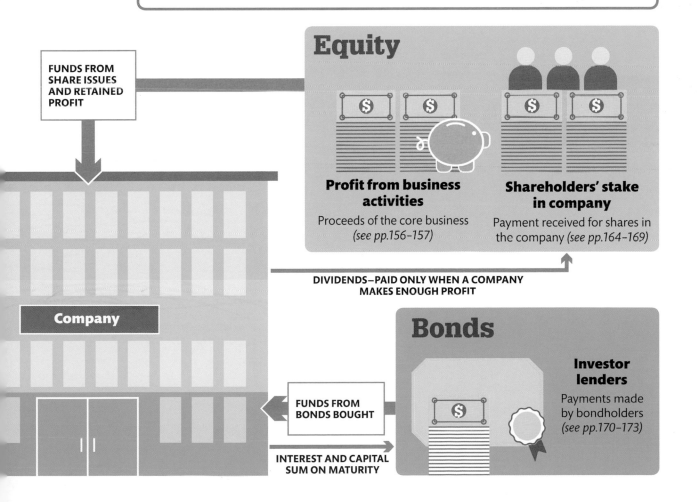

FUNDS FROM SHARE ISSUES AND RETAINED PROFIT

Equity

Profit from business activities

Proceeds of the core business *(see pp.156–157)*

Shareholders' stake in company

Payment received for shares in the company *(see pp.164–169)*

DIVIDENDS—PAID ONLY WHEN A COMPANY MAKES ENOUGH PROFIT

Company

Bonds

Investor lenders

Payments made by bondholders *(see pp.170–173)*

FUNDS FROM BONDS BOUGHT

INTEREST AND CAPITAL SUM ON MATURITY

Internal financing

Most companies prefer to secure funding from their own internal resources, rather than either take on debt through borrowing or give up a stake in the company by issuing shares, both of which cost more.

How it works

When a business needs funds, or capital, to pay for expansion or investment in order to maintain its current operations, it is faced with two choices: either find the money from outside sources, or find the money from within the organization itself. Since there are costs attached to bringing in funds from external sources, such as interest that has to be paid on a bank loan, the business managers must weigh up the opportunity cost of using its own funds—the profit it could earn by investing those funds—against the cost of financing.

Raising internal financing

Whether a company's need for additional funds is long- or short-term, steps can be taken to increase the level of funds within the company.

Short-term financing

For businesses wishing to raise funds without recourse to external sources, there are three main strategies they can implement to maximize the amount of cash available for day-to-day operations and capital expenditure.

Tighten credit control

Actions include chasing debtors so that invoices are paid on time; ensuring new customers are creditworthy by conducting strict credit checks; and setting a 30-day payment term.

Delay payment

Large suppliers may offer a discount for early payment, but they may also allow a company longer terms for payment, boosting cash levels in the short term.

THE RECENCY BIAS

When a company receives timely payments for its invoices, this helps maintain its levels of funds. Interestingly, invoices issued right after completion of work tend to get paid sooner than those invoices that are sent later. A theory called recency bias explains this phenomenon: the brain prioritizes recent events over those that occurred longer ago.

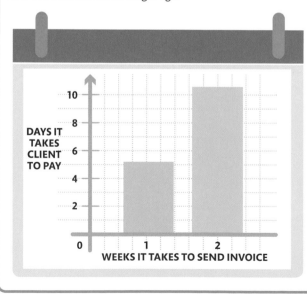

DAYS IT TAKES CLIENT TO PAY (y-axis: 2, 4, 6, 8, 10)

WEEKS IT TAKES TO SEND INVOICE (x-axis: 0, 1, 2)

Company

Long-term financing

For a business needing long-term financial help, its own resources should act as the primary support.

Reduce inventory

It is expensive for a business to retain a large inventory of unsold goods. Cutting the inventory back reduces storage costs, the cost of production, and replacement of goods that go out of date or become obsolete.

Retained profits

A portion of profits may be pumped back into the business. A company may also decide to sell assets to raise cash.

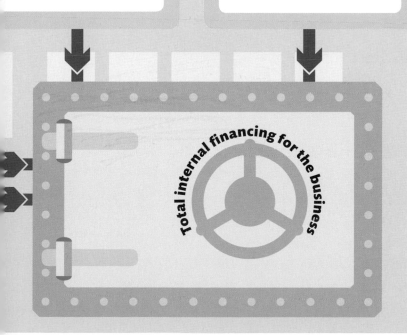

Total internal financing for the business

USING PROFITS TO FUND EXPANSION

A company seeking to grow may choose to fund the expansion with its profits. This option offers both advantages and disadvantages.

Pros

❯ The use of profits means that no interest payment has to be made, unlike on money that is borrowed

❯ Existing owners and directors are able to retain full control over the business, rather than sharing it with new investors

❯ The company is able to keep a low debt profile, which will appeal to future investors and lenders

Cons

❯ Profits can take time to build up sufficiently to fund expansion

❯ Withholding dividends may upset some shareholders who prefer to receive the profit as dividends

❯ Lost opportunity to earn funds from investing profit rather than spending it

44

the average number of days it takes a limited company in the UK to pay a 30-day invoice

External financing

When business growth or unforeseen expenses cannot be met using internal sources of financing, such as retained profit, organizations must rely on finding funds from lenders or investors.

How it works

External financial support comes in various forms, including bank loans and issuing shares. The available sources of outside financing depend on the amount a company requires, and whether the money is needed to resolve a short-term issue, such as cash flow, or for the long-term growth of the business. While short-term financing is easier to secure, finding larger sums for an expansion is more challenging. A company that is either already listed on a stock exchange or is preparing to enlist will be able to raise the capital through the sale of shares. However, an unlisted company may struggle to raise a comparable amount. A company with a large amount of debt will also find it hard to raise funds, since lenders or investors will see the business as risky.

✓ NEED TO KNOW

- ❭ **Term loan** A bank debt repaid over a set period of time
- ❭ **Loan note** A form promising payment to the holder at an agreed future date
- ❭ **Eurobond** A bond issued in a currency other than the currency of the country in which it is issued

Raising external financing

Generating funds from external sources can be a challenge, especially when securing investors. However, revenue does not necessarily need to take the form of a loan. There are a number of strategies that can be implemented through working with external parties in order to provide a company with good working capital.

80%
of external corporate financing is provided by domestic banks

Short-term financing

A range of financial agreements that help provide a company with immediate funds can be made with outside parties as a way of raising cash short-term.

Bank line of credit
Borrow from business checking account up to an agreed limit, with interest typically at a high rate.

Debt factoring
Sell unpaid invoices to an external source for an agreed amount in order to receive immediate payment minus a commission fee.

Invoice discounting
Borrow money against sales invoices customers are yet to pay (again, often at a disadvantageous rate).

DEBT FACTORING PROCESS

To get money immediately, a company sells unpaid invoices (accounts receivable) to a third party, known as a "factor." The factor advances the company a major portion of the amount, retains the rest until the account is paid, then charges a fee.

 →  →  →  →

Company negotiates an agreement in which its unpaid receivables (invoices) are sold at a discount to a "factor."

Company sends invoices out to customers, and copies these to the factor. Customer now owes payment to factor.

Factor pays company an agreed percentage of the invoices (typically 80–90 percent) within a few days of receipt.

Customer pays factor the invoice amount after 30 days (or more if terms of payment are longer).

Factor pays remaining invoice amount to company, minus a fee (usually 2–5 percent of the invoice amount).

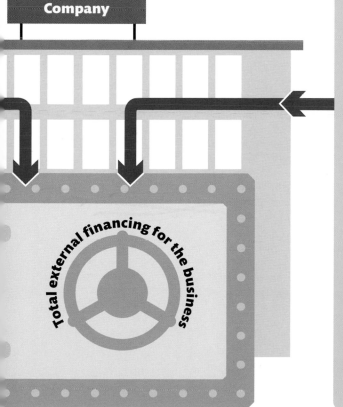

Company

Total external financing for the business

Long-term financing

Putting effective measures in place to provide ongoing revenue is essential for a company's long-term growth.

Shares

Raise capital by issuing shares to finance growth. The company then retains less profit, as it pays dividends to shareholders, who also benefit from any capital gains in the company's value (see pp.164–165).

Borrowing

Secure long-term loans from banks and other financial institutions, usually on better terms than a bank line of credit.

Finance leases

Sell expensive assets such as computers to finance companies to release capital, and then lease them back.

Rent-to-own agreements

Pay for expensive assets, such as vehicles, in installments. Overall cost may be higher, but capital is not tied up.

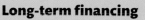

Going public

When a company changes from private to public, it offers shares for sale to members of the public. This process is known as going public and enables the company to raise money for growth.

How it works

The process by which an organization goes public (also known as flotation) marks the end of its life as a private company, after which it is no longer owned by a small number of shareholders or company members. A company may choose to go public when it needs capital to finance growth. Going public usually happens over several months; the company makes legal and financial preparations before the final stage, when it releases company shares for sale, either to selected investors or to the general public, or to a combination of both. Each share represents a "stake" in the company, and the money that the company receives from the sale of shares becomes capital, or wealth, which it now owns.

! WARNING

> **Underestimation** If the initial valuation of shares by the underwriters is too cautious, then the company will fail to realize the true value of its stock

> **Overestimation** If underwriters overestimate the value of shares newly on the market (new issue), it may flop due to lack of demand

> **Volatility** Share prices in the first few days of an IPO may fluctuate dramatically due to political or economic events

Ways to list on a stock exchange

There are three primary ways to take a company public, each of which has different associated costs. The type of public offering that a company chooses will be determined by its size and how much capital it needs to raise.

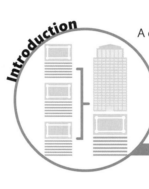

Introduction

A company joins a new stock exchange without raising capital, but by trading its existing shares. To do this, over 25 percent of the shares must already be in public hands (on other stock exchanges) and no one shareholder can own a majority of shares.

Placing

Select groups of institutional investors are invited to buy shares. This involves fewer costs than undertaking a full public share offering (see below) but the amount of capital that can potentially be raised is limited since there are fewer shareholders.

Initial public offering (IPO)

Institutional and private investors are invited to subscribe to or buy from the first round of shares that the company issues. This is the most expensive way to go public, but allows for a company to raise large amounts of capital.

20% the typical minimum annual growth potential of public companies in the US

TEN LARGEST IPOS IN HISTORY

When a well-known private company undertakes an IPO, there is fierce competition between investors to buy its shares, and record-breaking activity can ensue. This graph shows the largest IPOs until 2014, based on proceeds from shares sold on the first day they went public.

Stock exchange

A financial market in which company securities (stocks and shares) are bought and sold according to current market rates. *See pp.170–171.*

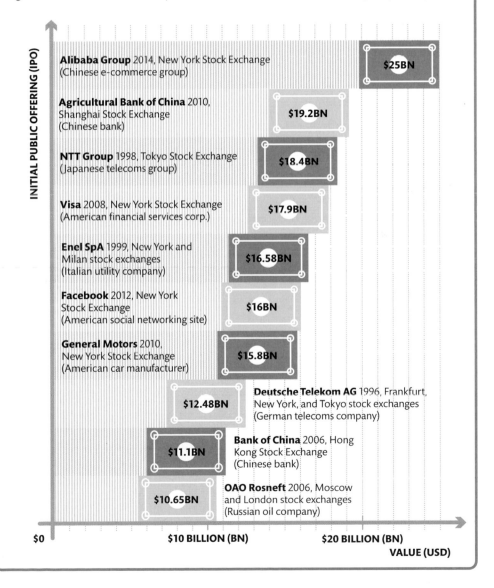

INITIAL PUBLIC OFFERING (IPO)

Alibaba Group 2014, New York Stock Exchange (Chinese e-commerce group) — **$25BN**

Agricultural Bank of China 2010, Shanghai Stock Exchange (Chinese bank) — **$19.2BN**

NTT Group 1998, Tokyo Stock Exchange (Japanese telecoms group) — **$18.4BN**

Visa 2008, New York Stock Exchange (American financial services corp.) — **$17.9BN**

Enel SpA 1999, New York and Milan stock exchanges (Italian utility company) — **$16.58BN**

Facebook 2012, New York Stock Exchange (American social networking site) — **$16BN**

General Motors 2010, New York Stock Exchange (American car manufacturer) — **$15.8BN**

Deutsche Telekom AG 1996, Frankfurt, New York, and Tokyo stock exchanges (German telecoms company) — **$12.48BN**

Bank of China 2006, Hong Kong Stock Exchange (Chinese bank) — **$11.1BN**

OAO Rosneft 2006, Moscow and London stock exchanges (Russian oil company) — **$10.65BN**

$0 $10 BILLION (BN) $20 BILLION (BN)

VALUE (USD)

A closer look at IPOs

An Initial Public Offering (IPO) is the first time that shares in the company are offered for public sale. It is the most common way for a private company to go public if it needs a large injection of capital to fund major expansion. There are other reasons for going public—for example if a government wants to privatize a state-owned company, such as a national railroad, or if the members of a large family-owned enterprise want to sell their stake.

WORLD'S TOP 10 STOCK EXCHANGES

The largest exchanges manage shares belonging to some of the world's most lucrative businesses and, as a result, substantial sums of money flow through them. The following exchanges are listed in order of the size of market capitalization—in other words, by the total monetary value of shares issued by the companies listed on each exchange.

1. New York Stock Exchange
2. NASDAQ OMX, New York
3. Tokyo Stock Exchange
4. Euronext (Pan-European)
5. London Stock Exchange
6. Shanghai Stock Exchange
7. Hong Kong Stock Exchange
8. Toronto Stock Exchange
9. Deutsche Borse
10. SIX Swiss Exchange

The IPO process

Before a company can issue shares, it has to be listed on a stock exchange where trading (the buying and selling of shares) can take place. The company must then fulfill the criteria necessary to secure investors. This process is lengthy, subject to strict financial regulations, and is extremely expensive to undertake. Only once all stages of the process are complete can the share offering be officially declared on a stock exchange.

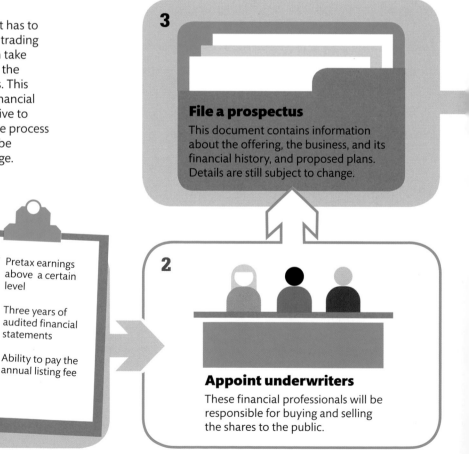

3

File a prospectus

This document contains information about the offering, the business, and its financial history, and proposed plans. Details are still subject to change.

1

Meet the qualifications

The specific requirements are set by the stock exchange where the company plans to list. Listing conditions vary between exchanges, but typically demand:

✓ Pretax earnings above a certain level

✓ Three years of audited financial statements

✓ Ability to pay the annual listing fee

2

Appoint underwriters

These financial professionals will be responsible for buying and selling the shares to the public.

$16.6 trillion

the total market capitalization of companies listed on the New York Stock Exchange*

* as of October 2014

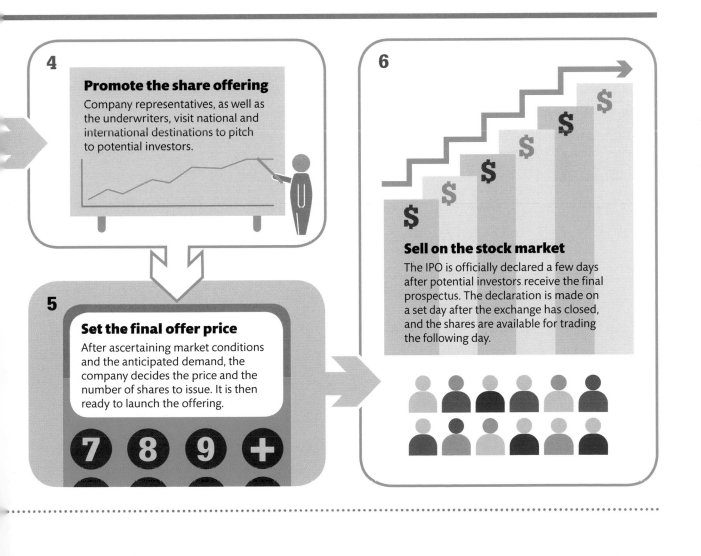

4

Promote the share offering

Company representatives, as well as the underwriters, visit national and international destinations to pitch to potential investors.

5

Set the final offer price

After ascertaining market conditions and the anticipated demand, the company decides the price and the number of shares to issue. It is then ready to launch the offering.

6

Sell on the stock market

The IPO is officially declared a few days after potential investors receive the final prospectus. The declaration is made on a set day after the exchange has closed, and the shares are available for trading the following day.

Shares and dividends

When a company goes public, it sells shares to investors, who become part-owners in return for capital investment. The number and type of shares bought by each investor determines the size of their ownership.

How it works

Before floating on a stock exchange, a company undergoes a valuation process to set the initial price of its shares. This process involves the directors, prospective investors, and an investment bank, which is appointed to assess the company's value. Together, they reach a decision on the most financially viable price for the shares that will be offered on the exchange. Upon going public, a company issues ordinary shares to investors as the basic unit of ownership, commonly referred to as a stake in the business. A company may also issue shares privately, rather than publicly to investors via the stock exchange, to retain greater management control.

A share of the pie

Ordinary shares, issued by all companies when they go public, are the most common type of shares. There are also other share types, which give the company more flexibility to control rights available to different shareholder groups. Most shares are sold on the stock exchange, but non-voting and management shares are issued directly to holders. Different types of shares entitle the holder to different rights.

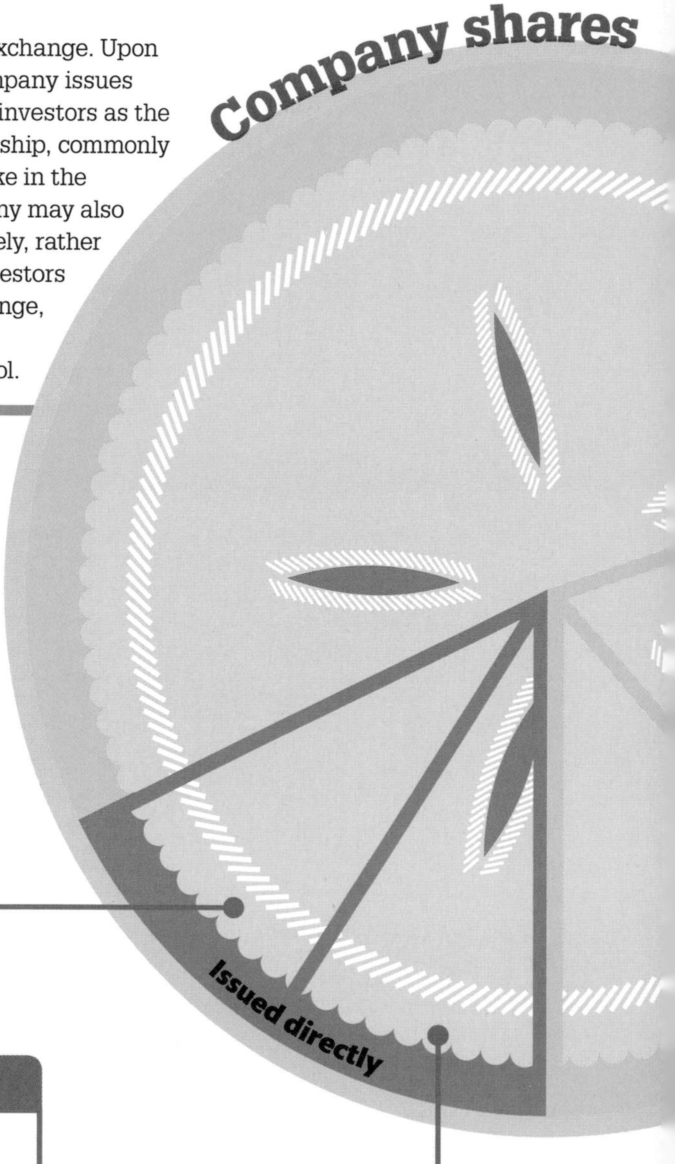

Management shares

Issued (usually given not sold) to owners and members of company management, who have:

✓ Extra voting rights, so control of company stays in the same hands

Non-voting shares

Issued to employees, who:

✓ Receive a part of remuneration in the form of dividends

✗ Have no voting rights

✗ Receive no invitation to attend annual meeting

Common stock

Shareholders:
- ✓ Share in the company dividends
- ✓ Share in the company's assets
- ✓ Have right to attend AGM
- ✓ Have right to vote on important company matters such as appointment of directors
- ✓ Receive the company's annual report and financial statements

Sold via stock exchange

Preferred stock

Shareholders:
- ✓ Receive fixed dividend, paid ahead of any dividends paid out to ordinary shareholders
- ✓ Take priority in receiving a share of any assets left after debts are paid if company is insolvent
- ✗ Have fewer, if any, voting rights

Deferred stock

- ✓ Shareholders receive company dividends and share of assets, but only after all other shareholders

✓ NEED TO KNOW

- 》 **Flipping** Buying and quickly reselling IPOs for a large profit
- 》 **Redeemable shares** Shares that may be later bought back by the issuing company for a cash sum

698%
the increase in share price of IPO VA Linux Systems in one day on the New York Stock Exchange, in 1999

RAISING MORE SHARE CAPITAL

After the initial sale of shares, when a company goes from private to public, the business can raise additional funds by issuing more shares. There are three main ways to do this:

- 》 **Rights issue** entitles existing shareholders to buy additional shares from the company within a set time frame, before they are offered to other buyers.
- 》 **Public issue** is a process by which the company issues a new allotment of shares to sell to the public on the stock market.
- 》 **Private placement** is a practice by which the company sells its shares (or other securities) directly to private investors, usually large institutions, bypassing the stock exchange all together.

Establishing share value

The forces of supply and demand set the price of shares. Companies issue only a limited number of shares to the public, which can then be bought and sold on the stock exchange. Demand for those shares is determined by whether investors think the company has good future economic prospects. If investors believe that the company is primed for substantial growth, they will want to buy shares in it, which consequently drives up the share price.

25%

the drop in share value over four days during the Wall Street Crash of 1929

SPLITTING SHARES

A company occasionally carries out a "share split" to its existing shares. This increases the total number of shares, although the combined value of shares stays the same. A share split allows a company to lower the price of its shares to bring them in line with the price of competitor shares. The share split is usually a two-for-one or three-for-one increase, whereby the shareholder sees the number of their shares double or triple.

Rising value of shares

Financial market observers believe that the emphasis on optimizing the value of shares for shareholders began in 1976, when the idea of maximizing profit for shareholders became a priority. Since then, the market has experienced a general upward trend with occasional deep dips. The graph tracks the average value of all shares on London's FTSE from 1964 to 2013.

✓ NEED TO KNOW

❯ **Bear market** Market that has seen decline of 20 percent over a period of 2 months or more

❯ **Bull market** Market where share prices are rising and investor confidence is high

❯ **Market correction** Short-term decline in share prices to adjust for an overvaluation

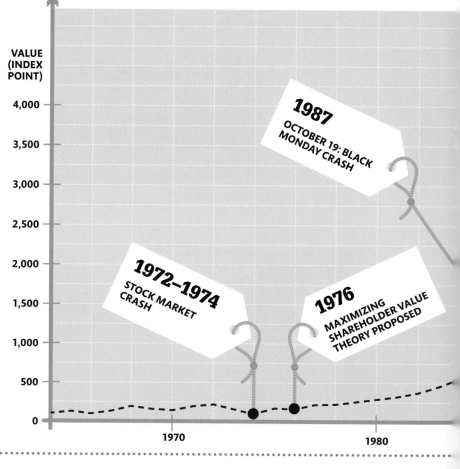

VALUE (INDEX POINT)

4,000
3,500
3,000
2,500
2,000
1,500
1,000
500
0

1987
OCTOBER 19: BLACK MONDAY CRASH

1972–1974
STOCK MARKET CRASH

1976
MAXIMIZING SHAREHOLDER VALUE THEORY PROPOSED

1970   1980

SHARE PRICE TOO HIGH
A company listed on the stock exchange has seen its share price increase so that its shares now cost more than its competitors'. The high price puts off investors.

SHARES SPLIT
The company decides on a share split. It halves the price of each existing $3 share, so each share is now worth $1.50.

SHARE CERTIFICATES ISSUED
It issues new share certificates to holders, doubling shares held: a shareholder with 1,000 shares at $3 each now has 2,000 at $1.50 each. Total worth is still $3,000.

SHARE VALUE ALIGNED
The value of shares is now similar to that of competitors. The price encourages new investors to make a purchase.

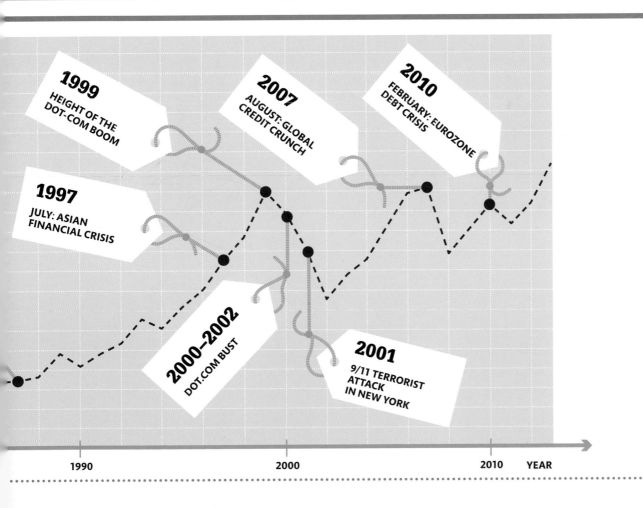

1999
HEIGHT OF THE DOT-COM BOOM

2007
AUGUST: GLOBAL CREDIT CRUNCH

2010
FEBRUARY: EUROZONE DEBT CRISIS

1997
JULY: ASIAN FINANCIAL CRISIS

2000–2002
DOT.COM BUST

2001
9/11 TERRORIST ATTACK IN NEW YORK

1990   2000   2010   YEAR

What is a dividend?

Shareholders in a company are usually entitled to a payment of cash from its profits. The company pays a dividend sum on every share it has issued, but it is up to the company's board to decide how much profit to reinvest and pay out. Investors may look at a company's rate of dividend payout, along with its capital growth, to gauge its financial health and decide whether to invest in it. Investors who rely on shares for income are likely to invest in companies that reliably pay out dividends. In a good economic climate, they win twice—the dividend provides income and the capital value of the shareholding increases. However, there is always a risk that the value of shares will go down, and companies only pay dividends if they have made a profit.

Paying dividends is a good way for a company to attract investors. It is essentially a reward for putting money into a company so that it can fund its existing output and develop and expand the business.

> **NEED TO KNOW**
>
> ❯ **Dividend yield ratio** Measure of how much a company pays out in dividends relative to the price of each share
> ❯ **Dividend per share** Sum paid on each share after retained profits have been calculated
> ❯ **Dividend payout ratio** Percentage of a company's net income that is paid out in the form of dividends

How it works

Shareholders usually receive a dividend if the company in which they hold shares has retained enough profit in that financial year to make the payment. The decision to make a payment is made by the board of directors. The dividend might be paid every quarter (four times a year), or in two parts—an interim dividend may be made partway through the year, with the final dividend paid just after the end of the financial year.

Announcing retained profits

At the end of the financial year, the company announces its retained profits: the sum it intends to keep for reinvesting or paying off debts rather than pay out as dividends.

Making the decision for dividends

The board of directors makes a decision on whether there is enough to warrant a dividend payment, and if so, how much. It records details of each payment in dividend vouchers.

INTEREST RATES AND DIVIDENDS

When interest rates are low, shares with high dividend payouts become extremely attractive to investors because they provide a better return than investments that yield an interest payment. This economic climate encourages companies to pay out top-rate dividends and so attract as many investors as possible, which in turn increases the share value.

Conversely, when interest rates are rising, investors may prefer to put their money into fixed-income assets, which will pay high rates as a result of the hike without the risk attached to buying shares.

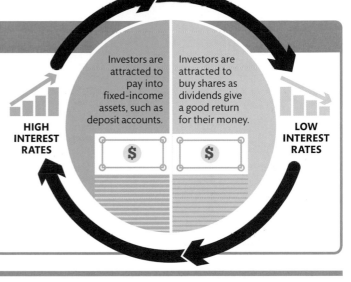

HIGH INTEREST RATES

Investors are attracted to pay into fixed-income assets, such as deposit accounts.

Investors are attracted to buy shares as dividends give a good return for their money.

LOW INTEREST RATES

Keeping funds for growth

The company keeps some of its profit to put back into the business. It needs to strike a balance between pleasing investors and expanding its operation.

1602

the year the Dutch East India Company became the first company to issue stocks and bonds

Making the payment

Most dividends are cash dividends. Sometimes companies distribute stock dividends, issuing more shares instead of cash to shareholders.

Paying taxes

Shareholders must declare dividends on their tax return and pay taxes on them.

The capital market

The capital market is a global financial marketplace for trading long-term securities—bonds with a maturity of at least a year, and shares. It is where governments and businesses can raise funds and investors make money.

How it works

There are two types of product sold on the capital market: shares (equity) and bonds (debt investments). Shares and bonds are sold first on the primary market, where they are originally issued, and later traded on the secondary market. The capital market is crucial to a functioning economy, because it channels funds to users of capital, such as businesses and government, and capital is what enables goods and services to be produced. The original issuers of the shares and bonds do not gain from trading activity in the secondary market, which is purely for investors. However, share value and bond trading levels reflect confidence in a company or institution, reinforcing its financial position.

The structure

The capital market encompasses the debt capital market, where bonds are sold, and the stock exchange, where shares are sold. Both have a primary and a secondary market.

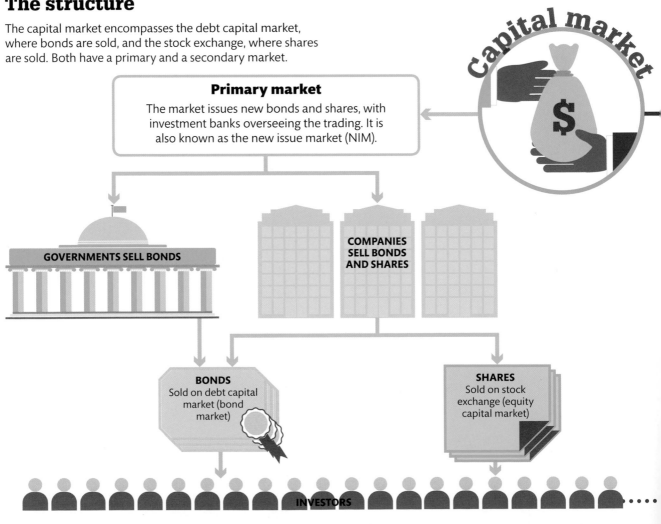

Capital market

Primary market
The market issues new bonds and shares, with investment banks overseeing the trading. It is also known as the new issue market (NIM).

GOVERNMENTS SELL BONDS

COMPANIES SELL BONDS AND SHARES

BONDS
Sold on debt capital market (bond market)

SHARES
Sold on stock exchange (equity capital market)

INVESTORS

WHAT IS A BOND?

A bond is a debt security that a company issues to investors. By buying bonds, an investor is effectively loaning money to the issuers, who in return agree to pay interest to the investor. A bond has a set term of maturity (a limited number of years of validity) and until that time the interest is paid to the investor annually. When the bond matures, the issuer repays the original sum of the loan to the investor. Companies or governments issue bonds to raise money that can then be put back into the business or used to fund government.

$100 trillion

the estimated value of global debt markets

Secondary market

Investors buy bonds and shares from other investors, not from issuing companies. The cash proceeds go to an investor, not to the underlying company or entity.

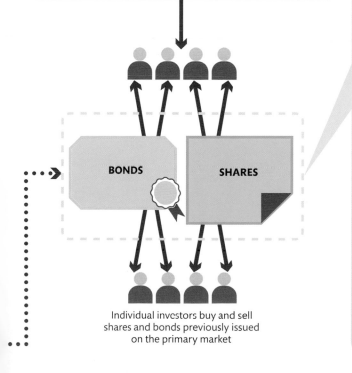

BONDS

SHARES

Individual investors buy and sell shares and bonds previously issued on the primary market

Bonds or shares: pros and cons

Bonds (debt investments)

✓ Sellers are contractually obliged to pay interest

✓ Bonds are less risky: debt capital markets are less volatile than stock exchanges; if the issuing company has trouble, bondholders are paid before other expenses and before compensation to shareholders

✗ Buyers of bonds have no stake in the company

✗ Buyers cannot access principal sum until bonds mature

Shares (equity)

✓ Buyers of shares gain a stake in the company

✓ Sellers of shares have to pay dividends, although these can be reduced or suspended if the company feels it is necessary

✗ Shares are more risky: changes in company profits and in the economy as a whole can cause share prices to rise and fall; if the company fails, the shares become worthless

How do bonds work?

Bondholders effectively buy a slice of a larger loan with each bond, for which they receive interest, along with the original sum on maturity. Issuing, buying, and selling bonds takes place in the debt capital market. The marketplace has several functions: it offers bonds and other types of loans to investors; it operates as a fixed-income market, because the issuer is required to pay regular interest; and it enables companies and governments to raise long-term funds. Overall, the debt capital market is much larger than the stock exchange (equity capital market), where shares are bought and sold. It attracts investors because bonds provide more protection from risk than shares. There are various types of bonds, some safer than others—the risk lies in whether the issuer will be able to pay the interest and repay the principal sum on maturity. A secured bond is backed by an asset, such as property; an unsecured bond is not and so carries more risk.

Both bonds and shares may be referred to as securities. The term describes the share or bond itself, and the certificate of ownership or creditorship that gives the holder the right to receive a dividend, in the case of shares, or interest payments, in the case of bonds.

✓ NEED TO KNOW

❭ **Debt instrument** Official term for bond or other long-term debt

❭ **Convertible bond** Bond that can be converted into shares of the issuing company, or cash

❭ **Warrant** Security that allows the holder to buy stock in a company at a fixed price for a certain period of time

❭ **Callable bond** Bond that gives the issuer the right to redeem it before maturity

❭ **Non-callable bond** Bond that cannot be redeemed or sold back to the issuer before maturity but continues to provide interest

Investing in the debt capital market

A company wants to raise $100 million to finance growth but does not wish to issue further shares. Instead, it raises the money by issuing bonds on the debt capital market.

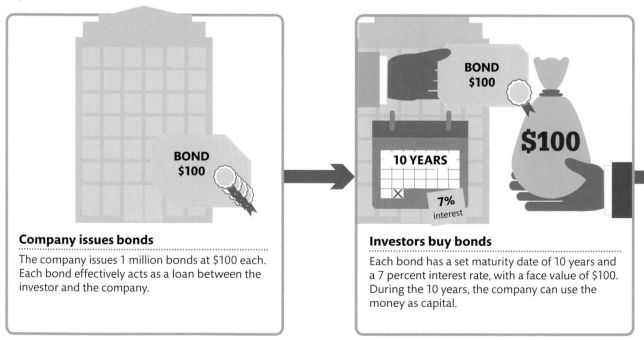

Company issues bonds

The company issues 1 million bonds at $100 each. Each bond effectively acts as a loan between the investor and the company.

Investors buy bonds

Each bond has a set maturity date of 10 years and a 7 percent interest rate, with a face value of $100. During the 10 years, the company can use the money as capital.

TYPES OF BONDS

Government bonds

GOVERNMENT BONDS

Secured

Government bonds are the safest type of bond since governments in developed capitalist economies are unlikely to default on interest payments on the loan or on the principal sum.

Corporate bonds

SECURED BONDS

Secured

Secured bonds are secured by the assets of a company, making them a less risky investment than shares. Examples include equipment, trust certificates, and mortgage bonds.

UNSECURED BONDS

Unsecured

Unsecured bonds are not backed by pledged collateral and are a riskier investment—if the company fails, investors are paid only after secured bonds have been paid out. Because they are more risky, investors expect a higher return (interest) on their investment.

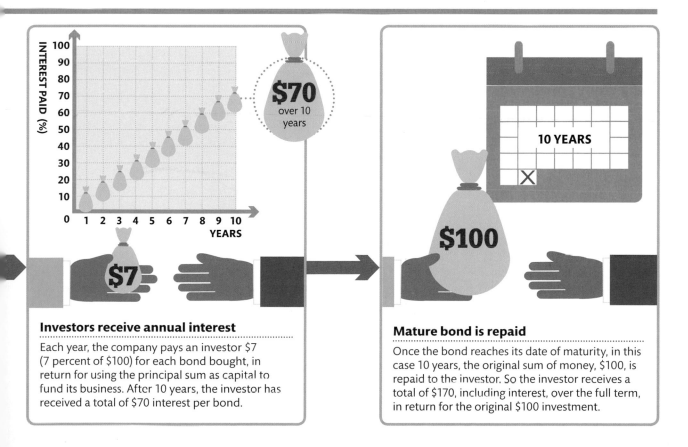

Investors receive annual interest

Each year, the company pays an investor $7 (7 percent of $100) for each bond bought, in return for using the principal sum as capital to fund its business. After 10 years, the investor has received a total of $70 interest per bond.

Mature bond is repaid

Once the bond reaches its date of maturity, in this case 10 years, the original sum of money, $100, is repaid to the investor. So the investor receives a total of $170, including interest, over the full term, in return for the original $100 investment.

Gearing ratio and financial risk

Capital gearing is the balance between the capital a company owns and its funding by short- or long-term loans. Investors and lenders use it to assess risk.

How it works

Most businesses operate on some form of gearing (also called financial leverage). They partly fund their operations by borrowing money, via loans and bonds, on the condition that they make regular repayments of a fixed amount to the lender. If the level of gearing is high (in other words, the business has taken on large debt), some investors will be concerned about its ability to repay and see this as an insolvency risk. However, if the amount of operating profit is more than enough to repay interest, high gearing can provide better returns to shareholders. The optimum level of gearing for a company also depends on how risky its business sector is, how heavily geared its competitors are, and what stage of its life cycle it is at.

Equity finance (shares)

Pros
> Does not have to be repaid
> Shareholders absorb loss
> Good for start-ups, which may take a while to become profitable
> Angel investors share expertise
> Low gearing seen as a measure of financial strength
> Low risk attracts more investors and boosts credit rating

Cons
> Shared ownership, so company has limited control of decisions
> Shared profit in return for investors risking their funds
> Legal obligation to act in the interests of shareholders
> Heavy administrative load
> Complex to set up

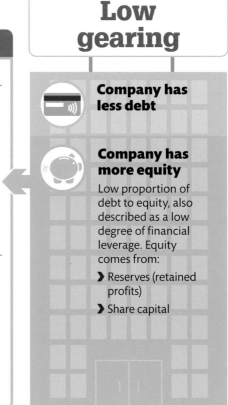

Low gearing

Company has less debt

Company has more equity
Low proportion of debt to equity, also described as a low degree of financial leverage. Equity comes from:
> Reserves (retained profits)
> Share capital

Gearing ratio calculation

Analysts and potential investors assess the financial risk of a company with this calculation, presented as a percentage.

$$\left(\frac{\text{LONG-TERM DEBT}}{\text{SHARE CAPITAL} + \text{RESERVES} + \text{LONG-TERM DEBT}} \right) \times 100$$

Low gearing

A software company is going public. Its ratio of 21.2 percent tells investors that it has relatively low gearing and is well positioned to weather economic downturns.

$$\left(\frac{\$1.2 \text{ MILLION}}{\$2 \text{ MILLION} + \$2.455 \text{ MILLION} + \$1.2 \text{ MILLION}} \right) \times 100 = 21.2\%$$

High gearing

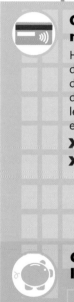

Company has more debt

High proportion of debt to equity, also described as a high degree of financial leverage. Typical examples of debt are:

> Loans
> Bonds

Company has less equity

Debt finance (loans)

Pros

> If the company makes a profit, it can reap a larger proportion
> Paying interest is tax deductible
> Does not dilute ownership
> Company retains control of decisions
> Repayment is a known amount that can be planned for
> Quicker and simpler to set up
> Small business loans at favorable rates may be available to start-ups

Cons

> Loan must be repaid
> Interest must be paid, even if operating profit shrinks
> Debt may be secured on fixed assets of company
> Unpaid lender can seize assets and force bankruptcy
> Lenders first to be paid in the event of insolvency
> High gearing considered a measure of financial weakness
> High risk may put off investors and adversely affect credit rating

✓ NEED TO KNOW

> **Interest cover ratio** An alternative method of calculating gearing—operating profit divided by interest payable
> **Overleveraged** A situation in which a business has too much debt to meet interest payments on loans
> **Deleverage** Immediate payment of any existing debt in order to reduce gearing

25%
the ratio at or below which a company is traditionally said to have low gearing

High gearing

A water utility is the only water provider in the area, with several million customers. The ratio of 64 percent is acceptable for a utility company with a regional monopoly and a good reputation.

$$\left(\frac{\$360\ \text{MILLION}}{\$82\ \text{MILLION} + \$120\ \text{MILLION} + \$360\ \text{MILLION}} \right) \times 100 = 64\%$$

HOW
SALES AND MARKETING
WORKS

Marketing mix **>** Marketing approaches
Outbound marketing **>** Inbound marketing
Business development **>** Information management

Marketing mix

The successful marketing of a product depends on the consideration of four key elements—the product itself, its price, how it is promoted, and where it is sold. This combination is called the marketing mix, and it is used as a tool for planning product launches and campaigns. Before focusing on the marketing mix, marketers need to define the target market for their product by determining which groups of customers are most likely to purchase it.

The 4Ps and 4Cs of the marketing mix

First proposed in 1960, the classic marketing mix tool contains the 4Ps: product, price, promotion, and place. In the 1990s, these were recast as the 4Cs, which emphasized the customer-oriented dimension of the tool.

The 7Ps of the marketing mix

Some marketers use a more detailed model of the marketing mix, which has three additional elements.

> **Product** See pp.180–183.
> **Price** See pp.186–187.
> **Place** See pp.188–189.
> **Promotion** See pp.190–191.
> **People** Does the business employ the right people to deliver optimum service to customers?
> **Process** Are effective systems in place for handling orders and dealing with customer questions and complaints?
> **Physical environment** Does the design and layout of the business premises appeal to customers?

Commodity
> **Has the product been specifically engineered** and designed to meet and exceed customer expectations?

Product
> **Is the product the right design, size, and color** to appeal to customers?
> **What are its unique features?** How does it compare with competitors?

Communication
> **What is the most meaningful way** to get marketing messages to customers and provide them with useful information?

Promotion
> **What combination** of marketing and media channels will be most effective?
> **When is the best time** to run promotions?

"Product, promotion, and place create value. But price harvests value."

DEFINING THE MARKET

In order to establish a marketing strategy for the product they are introducing to the marketplace, businesses have to define the customers they aim to sell to by researching and segmenting the market.

Market research
See pp.192–193.

❯ Identifies gaps in the market for the launch of new products

❯ Measures customer reactions to new offers and campaign messages

Market segmentation
See pp.194–195.

❯ Breaks down the market into smaller customer groups with similar needs

❯ Allows more focused campaigns with a greater chance of success

Price

❯ **What is the value of the product** to prospective customers?

❯ **What is the usual price point** for this type of product?

Cost

❯ **How much will the product cost the customer**, and will it be seen to represent a good buy?

Place

❯ **Where should the product be sold**—stores, online, or catalogs?

❯ **Where do competitors sell**, and is there a way to stand out in the same place?

Convenience

❯ **How easy is it for busy customers to find** and buy the product?

The 7Cs of the marketing mix

This model offers a customer-focused variation of the 7Ps, adding three more elements to the 4Cs.

❯ **Commodity**

❯ **Cost**

❯ **Convenience (or Channel)**

❯ **Communication**

❯ **Corporation** How do company structure, stakeholders, and other competitors affect marketing?

❯ **Consumer** What are the customer's needs and wants? Is the product safe? What product information is available?

❯ **Circumstances** Can the business deal with external factors, such as laws, weather, economy, culture?

Product

The goods and services a company sells are its product. A product can be defined in terms of features, design, size, packaging, service type, return policies, and warranties, together intended to meet the customer's needs.

How it works

Consumers can be said to buy benefits rather than products. For the marketer, the product itself is that benefit to the consumer, as packaged and presented.

Marketers identify the goods and services they sell in three or five product levels, with the benefit at the core. The marketer's job is to translate and communicate each product level as an offer to the consumer.

Total product concept: three product levels

From a marketer's perspective, a product is more than the end commodity bought by a customer. It is a total product concept with several layers of benefit, and these must be conveyed to the consumer.

Core product
Product's basic function and its core benefit to consumer

Actual product
Packaging, brand name, quality level, design, and additional features that set it apart from rival products

Augmented product
Additional benefits, such as delivery and credit, warranty, after-sales service

Takes rider from A to B

eco-friendly • traditional design • 3 gears • high-tech tires

free delivery • pay in installments • 2-year warranty • 6 months' free service

42%
of new product launches can be expected to fail

Variation: five product levels

This variation on the total product concept is more detailed. It introduces two more levels by breaking down the actual product level into a generic and an expected product, and also includes an extra level of benefit—the potential product.

Core product Product's core benefit to consumer

Generic product Basic functional benefits

Expected product Additional desirable benefits

Augmented product Extra features and benefits

Potential product Future, improved version

Takes rider from A to B

2 wheels · 3 gears · brakes

sturdy · reliable · smooth ride

design · color choice · well-known brand

lighter frame · auto lock to prevent theft · built-in collision protection

Product positioning

A vital step in the process of deciding how to market a product is defining how it is distinct from the competition—what is unique about it and what are the qualities that make it better than rival products.

How it works

Before a company launches a product, the marketing department has to decide how to position it in the marketplace compared to competitors' products. To determine the positioning of a product, marketers must define the most important features and values of the product or brand, and clarify how it is different from similar types of products offered by competitors. They also need to identify the criteria that customers are most likely to use when choosing a particular product or brand. With this information the marketers can then create a product positioning matrix or map.

Product positioning maps

Marketers commonly create a perceptual "map," using a product's two most important attributes, presented as variables on an x and y axis, to work out where to position it. Attributes may include price, quality, status, features, safety, and reliability. Once the map is labeled, existing products are placed on it to reveal the best position or gap for the proposed launch.

FOUR POSITIONING STRATEGIES

> **Value positioning** A product plotted on the map so that it has an attractive price while delivering good functional qualities.

> **Quality positioning** A product that is located on the map on the basis of its perceived quality or superiority.

> **Demographic positioning** A product mapped according to its appeal to a specific population segment, such as consumers with a particular occupation.

> **Competitive positioning** A product that is very similar to those of competitors, relying on correct pricing to find a viable position in the marketplace.

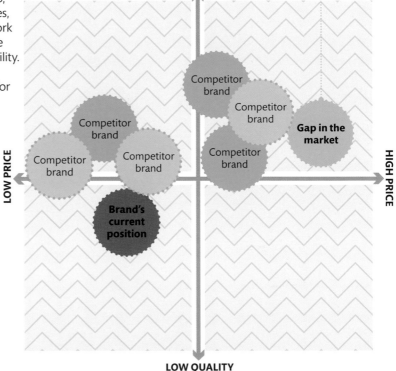

Product positioning template

The map shows how marketers position competing products in the marketplace according to the price/quality variables (the most commonly used) to identify a gap for the new product.

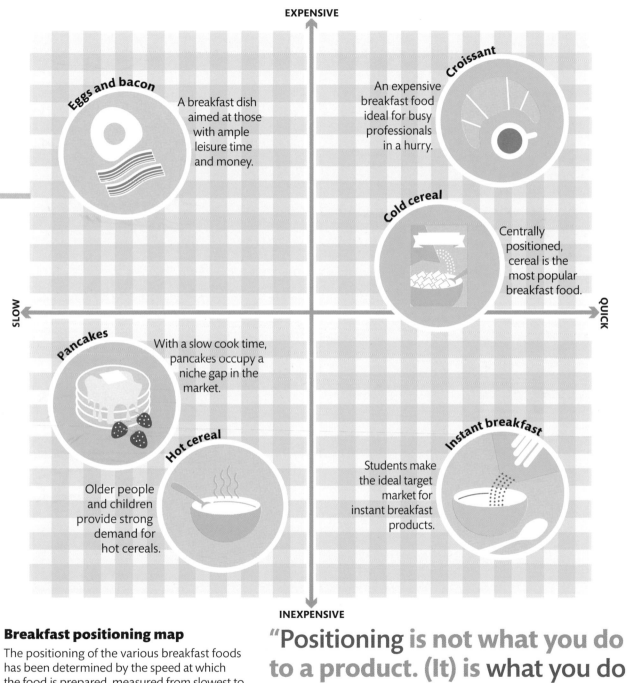

EXPENSIVE

Eggs and bacon
A breakfast dish aimed at those with ample leisure time and money.

Croissant
An expensive breakfast food ideal for busy professionals in a hurry.

Cold cereal
Centrally positioned, cereal is the most popular breakfast food.

SLOW

QUICK

Pancakes
With a slow cook time, pancakes occupy a niche gap in the market.

Hot cereal
Older people and children provide strong demand for hot cereals.

Instant breakfast
Students make the ideal target market for instant breakfast products.

INEXPENSIVE

Breakfast positioning map

The positioning of the various breakfast foods has been determined by the speed at which the food is prepared, measured from slowest to fastest, and the price of each food type, from the least expensive to the most expensive.

"Positioning is not what you do to a product. (It) is what you do to the mind of the prospect."

Al Ries and Jack Trout

Product life cycle

Every successful product launched on the market experiences growth followed by decline. To maximize profitability, business managers must recognize and manage each stage of the product's life span.

How it works

There are typically six identifiable stages in a product life cycle, with the product's rate of growth measured by time and revenue. Most businesses have more than one product on the market at any time, and strategic manipulation of the portfolio of products at their different stages in the cycle is crucial to maintaining business growth. The life of older products may be prolonged by extension strategies, but if they are no longer grabbing new market share, the business must consider launching new products in order to continue generating revenue.

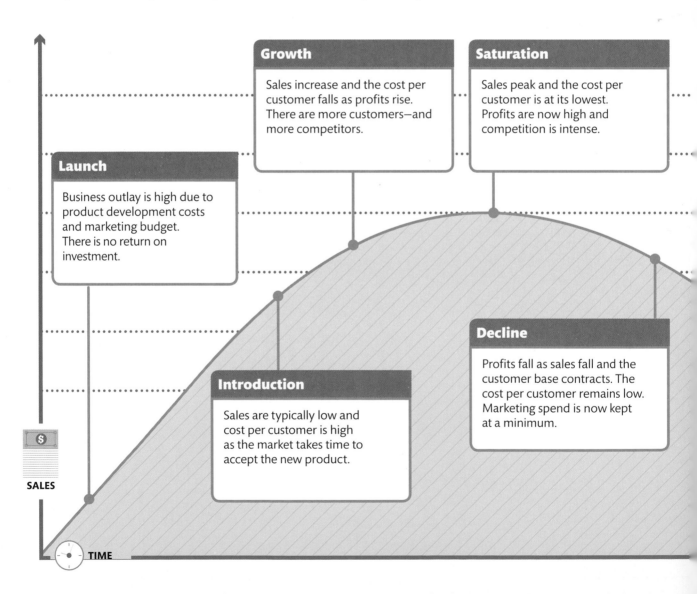

Growth

Sales increase and the cost per customer falls as profits rise. There are more customers—and more competitors.

Saturation

Sales peak and the cost per customer is at its lowest. Profits are now high and competition is intense.

Launch

Business outlay is high due to product development costs and marketing budget. There is no return on investment.

Decline

Profits fall as sales fall and the customer base contracts. The cost per customer remains low. Marketing spend is now kept at a minimum.

Introduction

Sales are typically low and cost per customer is high as the market takes time to accept the new product.

SALES

TIME

6 months

the length of time a product can be labelled as "new"

Withdrawal

The product is phased out as sales stall or continue to fall. The business introduces a replacement product before the old one is withdrawn.

Diffusion of innovation (consumer uptake) %

Marketers identify five distinct customer types according to how quickly they pick up on a new product.

INNOVATORS — 2.5%
EARLY ADOPTERS — 13.5%
EARLY MAJORITY — 34%
LATE MAJORITY — 34%
LAGGARDS — 16%

✓ NEED TO KNOW

❯ **Extension strategy** Revival of a product by rebranding, or repackaging, repricing it, or finding new markets

❯ **Portfolio analysis** Each of a company's products measured by growth rate and market share to determine marketing spend

❯ **Product life cycle management (PLM)** Tracking of product data from inception to withdrawal

PORTFOLIO ANALYSIS

Rising stars
Products with a high market share in a high-growth market; they require a big marketing spend to keep them growing.

Cash cows
Products with a high market share in a low-growth market; they generate money to support rising stars.

Problem children
Products with a low market share in a high-growth market; they need a big marketing spend.

Dogs
Products with low market share and low growth; they may stay in portfolio to keep customers happy.

Price

Price is a crucial variable of the marketing mix: it generates revenue, while product, promotion, and place yield costs. Pricing may also be the marketer's most potent tool because even minor tweaks affect returns.

How it works

To set the price of a product, marketers adopt a pricing strategy based not only on the actual cost of production but also on the perceived attractiveness of the product to consumers. If consumers think a product has a high value, they will be prepared to pay more for it, but if they believe the value of the product is low they will look for the cheapest price among competing products.

A business must also take into account the price charged by rival organizations, particularly in competitive markets. Setting a price above that charged by competitors can only work if the product is superior to others.

Pricing strategies

A number of different strategies can be used to determine the price of a product. Cost-plus pricing is a retail markup used by many companies to ensure a profit is made. For example, adding a markup of 50 percent to a product that costs $2 to make means that every unit will sell for $3, generating a $1 profit.

Pricing matrix: price vs. quality

A product's quality affects its price tag—the higher the quality, the more money consumers will pay for it—but marketers use strategies that play on the interaction between price and perceived quality.

5%
increase in price is worth more than a 5% increase in market share

Low price

High price

Low quality

Economy

❯ **High prevalence** Manufacture a product that is very similar to others in the same category.

❯ **Low price** Undercut competitors' pricing and gain a larger share of the market.

❯ **Minimal marketing** Keep the marketing and branding spend as low as possible.

Skimming

❯ **High launch price** Charge more than usual in the short term while a product is seen as unique.

❯ **Correct timing** Set a higher price when the business has a temporary advantage in the marketplace, before competing products appear.

❯ **Price adjustment** Reduce the price once competitors enter the market, or to draw more customers.

PRICING MARKUP COMPARISON

Different industries adopt different approaches to markups. A markup of two to five times the cost is typically applied to drinks served in bars and restaurants. The highest markup is usually applied to the second-cheapest bottle of wine on the wine list, as people tend to avoid the cheapest item.

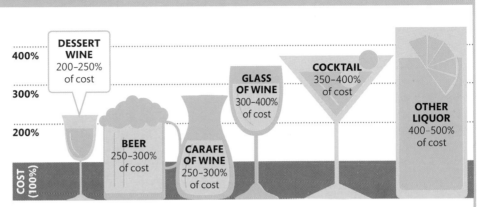

400%

DESSERT WINE
200–250% of cost

300%

BEER
250–300% of cost

200%

CARAFE OF WINE
250–300% of cost

GLASS OF WINE
300–400% of cost

COCKTAIL
350–400% of cost

OTHER LIQUOR
400–500% of cost

COST (100%)

$

High quality

Market penetration

> **Low price** Charge the lowest price possible in order to lure customers away from competitors.
> **Price adjustment** Increase the price to a normal level once the product has a loyal following.
> **Pricing flexibility** Reassess pricing; initial high-volume sales lower cost of production, allowing price tweaks.

$$$$

Premium

> **High price** Charge as much as the market will pay for an item.
> **Unique value** Apply premium prices to products that have no comparable substitute, such as famous brand-name goods.
> **High production cost** Charge a premium price because a product is customized and offers no savings through volume manufacturing.

Other pricing strategies

Psychological pricing
Manipulate a customer's emotions, appealing to their thrifty side or desire for prestige.

Bundle pricing
Offer several products for an overall price, providing better value than buying separately.

Geographic pricing
Charge different prices for the same product in different locations.

Non-pricing strategies
Avoid adjusting the price to attract sales, promoting superiority of product instead.

Place

Knowing where customers shop, where a product is sold, and how efficiently goods can be delivered to the consumer—called "place" in marketing terms—is essential to sales success.

How it works

Whether a company sells goods or services, customers must be able to find and buy those products as easily as possible. Businesses have to decide on the best sales outlet and sales channel to get their products to customers in a way that benefits both parties.

A sales outlet is the place where a product is sold, suchas stores, catalogs, or e-commerce sites. Sales channels are the merchants, agents, and distributors who take a product from the seller and bring it to the consumer.

70.5%
of device sales by 2017 are forecast to be smartphones

Main distribution channels

A product reaches the marketplace through one of four main types of distribution channels. The most suitable distribution channel is usually dictated by where customers prefer to buy the product.

Producer
A producer chooses the distribution channel, or a combination of channels, that will maximize the number of customers it can reach while keeping costs as low as possible.

Selling direct to consumers
Product is sold directly by the producer, online, or through a mail-order catalog, and delivered to customer without intermediary.

Selling through retailers
Goods are delivered by producer directly to retail outlets; retailer adds a markup onto the price they pay to producer.

Selling through wholesalers and retailers
Products are distributed in two stages: by producer to wholesaler and then wholesaler to retailer.

Selling through an agent
Products are distributed in three stages: from producer to agent, from agent to wholesaler, and then on to retailer.

PROS AND CONS OF USING INTERMEDIARIES

Pros

> Allows wider market coverage so producer can reach more customers, especially those in distant areas.

> Minimizes distribution cost for producer as intermediaries are responsible for this service.

> Provides producer with specialized knowledge of customer buying habits, as well as delivery logistics.

Cons

> Raises difficulty of making direct communication with customers to learn about their preferences.

> Increases the risk of slow, inefficient delivery, especially if several intermediaries are involved.

> Takes away control over how products are handled and displayed at point of sale.

✓ NEED TO KNOW

> **Channel margin** The cost intermediary adds to producer's selling price, which is added to price paid by customer

> **Push strategy** Method in which producer promotes products to wholesalers, wholesalers to retailers, and retailers to customer

> **Pull strategy** Use of advertising and promotion to sell to customer

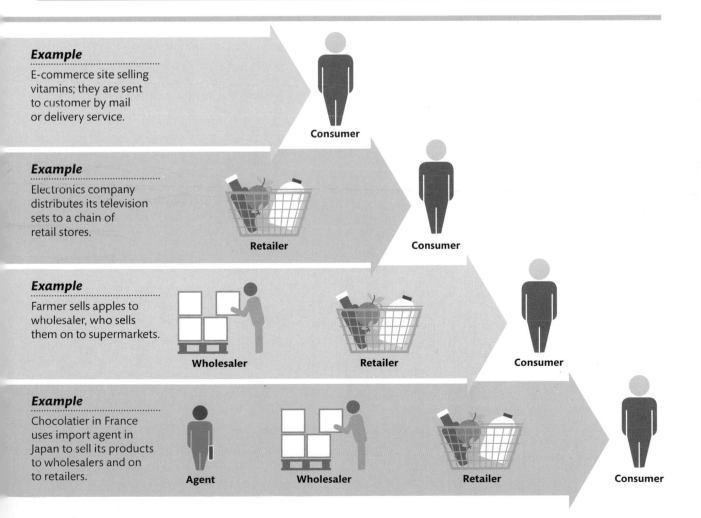

Example
E-commerce site selling vitamins; they are sent to customer by mail or delivery service.

Consumer

Example
Electronics company distributes its television sets to a chain of retail stores.

Retailer   **Consumer**

Example
Farmer sells apples to wholesaler, who sells them on to supermarkets.

Wholesaler   **Retailer**   **Consumer**

Example
Chocolatier in France uses import agent in Japan to sell its products to wholesalers and on to retailers.

Agent   **Wholesaler**   **Retailer**   **Consumer**

Promotion

Promotion is necessary for generating interest in and sales of a product or service. A complex and expensive part of the marketing mix, it involves communicating to customers and influencers such as peer groups.

How it works

The primary purpose of promotion is to boost sales by attracting new customers, while enticing existing ones to try out something new. Most companies use a number of communication activities to inform and remind their target audience of a product's benefits (*see pp.196–231*).

One of the long-term benefits of communicating with customers is that it helps to build brand loyalty.

✓ NEED TO KNOW

> **Integrated Marketing Communication (IMC)**
> Promotion of the same brand message across all media channels

> **MarCom (Marketing Communication)** Full range of promotional activities used to reach out to the market

25%
the percentage of digital promotion budgets spent on mobile advertising in 2013

Consumer bee

Personal selling
Interact with customers face to face and tailor sales messages to their needs.

Customer service
Provides customers with information about the product; offers updates and special deals.

Below the line (BTL)
Describes promotional activities a business carries out in-house, such as direct mail or telemarketing, to reach customers directly.

Advertising
Run ad campaigns through media channels most likely to reach target market, and stick to budget appropriate for the product.

Direct marketing
Send product offers and information directly to the potential consumer, via mail or email.

Interactive marketing
Build long-term relationships with customers using two-way communication, especially online.

Sales promotion
Entice customer with offers, free samples, gifts, competitions, packaging, and point-of-sale displays.

Public relations
Generate positive interest in the company by sponsoring events and charities, or pitching news content to media.

Above the line (ATL)
Refers to online and offline advertising a business pays for to target customers.

Market research

Asking customers what they think about a product is a vital part of the decision-making process for marketers. Research offers insights into how a product might perform and lowers the risk of marketing campaigns.

How it works

Market research is used during product development and then to monitor customer satisfaction and competitor activity. Researchers draw on existing data, observations, and their own research. New research is broken down into quantitative (number-based) research—closed (multiple choice) questions asked of a large group of people—and qualitative (in-depth) research—into how a consumer uses and feels about a potential new product. The marketing department's research budget is usually split between the two types of surveys. Quantitative research is often used when developing a new product, followed by qualitative research to help refine the product.

Primary data collection

New research to answer specific question

"Research + Intuition = Decision"

Observations
- Researchers may watch from a distance as customer interacts with product, or identify themselves and talk to customer.
- They observe customer using equipment such as eye tracking analysis and checkout scanners.
- They study credit card records or computer history to observe past consumer behavior.

Quantitative surveys
- Researchers question many people for a broad view (numerical data).
- They carry out online surveys to obtain a quick result from a large sample.

Qualitative surveys
- Researchers probe small groups or individuals for in-depth view.
- They conduct focus group discussions.

?

Marketer has a question

✓

Marketer reaches a decision

DATA REQUESTED

DATA RETURNED

CASE STUDY

Coca-Cola launch

In 1985, Coca-Cola launched a new kind of cola. The launch followed two years of taste tests, costing $4 million, to refine the product. However, the drink failed and had to be withdrawn in the face of overwhelming disapproval from the public. In the marketing postmortem, analysts concluded that the company's researchers had failed to ask customers a very important question: "Do you want a new Coke?"

Secondary data collection
Published material on a subject

Agency
Carries out original research and organizes research data into meaningful results

32%
the projected increase **in the** hiring of **market research analysts in the US by 2022**

Internal sources
❯ Web usage data (for example browser logs and online sales records)
❯ Customer profiles with buying history and demographic data
❯ Accounting records, such as statements and balance sheets
❯ Original data from past market research reports

External sources
❯ Industry reports by trade bodies, institutions, and private research companies
❯ Reports by broadcast, print, and internet media
❯ Academic papers, university think tank reports, and research library holdings
❯ Government surveys, reports, and statistics

Market segmentation

In order to make decisions about who to sell their product to, marketers try to identify distinct groups of consumers with similar wants and habits who together form a "segment" of the market.

How it works

Marketing departments use a strategy of market segmentation to find the potential customers who are most likely to buy a particular product, thereby increasing the chances of a successful product launch. They divide a broad group of consumers into subgroups based on many factors, including age, lifestyle preferences, location, family structure, household income, and occupation. This process narrows down a potentially huge market into segments, allowing marketers to identify the ones more inclined to buy a given product. For example, after applying this strategy, a company trying to launch premium-price organic baby food realizes that instead of marketing to all women who have young children, it should aim its product at working mothers with children under six months, above-average incomes, and an interest in healthy eating.

Defining market groups

To establish different consumer groups, marketers create five segments and focus on each individually. Besides identifying groups by geography and demographics, marketers also explore psychology to ascertain how consumers behave, so that they gain a better idea of which products might appeal to which consumer groups. (See also pp.258–261.)

Behavioral

Focuses on behavioral patterns when it comes to shopping. Understanding this helps marketers adapt campaigns to target specific groups. Potential focus areas include:

❯ Brand loyalty
❯ Regularity of purchases
❯ Credit card usage
❯ Typical expenditure
❯ On- or offline shopping
❯ Heavy product user

"Market segmentation is a natural result of the vast differences amongst people."
Donald Norman

Sociographic

Identifies individuals' connections on social media, or membership of political and other groups, helping marketers learn about consumers' passions and interests. Potential focus areas include:

> Group memberships
> Number of friends on social media

Psychographic

Focuses on consumer's interests, values, and opinions to help marketers develop relevant messages and find the right media channels to target a segment. Potential focus areas include:

> Risk taker
> Charitable
> High achiever
> A tendency towards expensive tastes
> A preference for email contact

Geographic

Concentrates on a customer's place of residence, so that any product launched is made relevant to their environment. Potential focus areas include:

> Post code
> Continent
> City
> Neighbourhood
> Population density
> Climate

Demographic

Uses basic consumer data, such as gender or age, to accurately categorize needs and target products appropriately. Potential focus areas include:

> Income
> Nationality
> Family size and age
> Ethnic background
> Occupation
> Religion

Marketing approaches

Every product launch requires strategic planning to make sure messages about a new product reach the right types of consumers, are communicated through the most effective combination of channels, and have the most relevant content and style. Once marketers have researched the market and defined their target audience, they face several key decisions on how to make their approach.

Types of approaches

Whom to target and how to go about it are crucial to success. Marketers may use several complementary approaches to different groups of potential consumers.

Rather than sending the same message via different media, they usually adjust the tone and style of the marketing pitch to suit the channel as well as the target consumer.

Niche marketing
"I only have eyes for you."

Mass marketing
"I love you all."

The big choice
The first decision is whether to go for a narrow, specialized market or to appeal to as large an audience as possible. *See pp.198–199.*

85%
of all purchasing decisons in the US are made or influenced by women

Engagement marketing
"Come dance with me." It entices the customer to collude in product sales. *See pp.204–205.*

Sensory marketing
"Wake up and smell the roses." It seduces the customer with sights, sounds, and smells. *See pp.206–207.*

Traditional channel allied with a dominating style. "Let me tell you," it blares. *See pp.200–201.*

Digital channel allied with a soft approach. "Let me woo you," it whispers. *See pp.202–203.*

Relationship marketing
"Let's be friends." It builds a rapport with its audience of consumers. *See pp.208–209.*

How to tell the customer
Marketers often get the best of both worlds by using traditional and online channels in varying styles.

Making a move
Turning the buying transaction into an experience the consumer enjoys can help sell a product.

Niche vs. mass marketing

Two fundamental choices traditionally face marketers: whether to try to sell a product with broad appeal to as many people as possible, or to focus on selling a tailored product to a defined group.

How it works

Both niche and mass marketing strategies offer businesses the potential to make a high return on investment. A niche approach generally works on the basis of low-volume sales at a premium price to a specific group of consumers, while a mass approach tends to use heavy promotion to a wider audience and aims to achieve high-volume sales.

In reality, businesses tend to mix up both approaches, launching a niche product and then expanding it to a mass market. Marketers also use internet channels to promote the same product to different groups of customers within a mass audience.

20%
of sales can make up to 80% of profit

✓ NEED TO KNOW

Long-tail marketing

Coined by *Wired* magazine editor Chris Anderson, the term "long-tail marketing" takes its name from a demand curve (see below) depicting products with low demand or sales volume—niche products—that continue to sell and make profit over time.

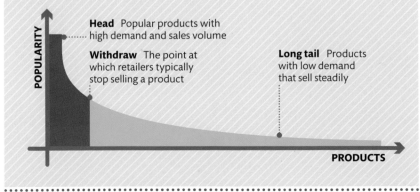

POPULARITY

Head Popular products with high demand and sales volume

Withdraw The point at which retailers typically stop selling a product

Long tail Products with low demand that sell steadily

PRODUCTS

Niche market

Who and how

> Business targets a select group of consumers with specific need and wants.

> Customers often prepared to pay a premium price for an uncommon product.

> Sales volume of niche product low, so does not benefit from production economies of scale (manufacturing large quantities to decrease the unit cost of production).

HYBRID APPROACHES

Using social media to identify and reach more than one target market, marketers have developed hybrid approaches that are more flexible than conventional niche or mass-market positioning of products.

Mass market
An unfocused strategy that aims at the broadest customer base.

Large segment
Channels marketing resources to one large segment of the mass market.

Adjacent segment
Once large segment is fully penetrated, product expands into related segment.

Multi segment
Markets to several segments at once, with a customized strategy for each.

Small segment
Markets to a small segment with few competitors, if resources are limited.

Niche segment
Focuses marketing resources on a specific group of customers.

Mass customization
Customizes a strategy for each sub-segment within the mass market.

Mass market

Who and how

> Business targeting a large group of consumers with generalized wants and needs.

> Requires high marketing spend to promote products, which must be widely distributed.

> Marketplace often crowded with other competitors selling a similar product.

Traditional marketing

Before the digital age, marketers relied exclusively on non-digital channels, such as TV, radio, and print media, as well as direct mail, events, and cold-calling, to convey their message to the consumer.

How it works

Traditional marketing encompasses a number of tried-and-tested ways of building a brand and pushing a product to sell more. It remains a key facet of marketing. Nowadays, however, most businesses use a mix of traditional and digital marketing methods. One of the advantages of traditional marketing is that companies have face-to-face contact with customers through person-to-person selling, special events, and event sponsorship.

Events
Staging sports activities, themed displays, parades, or exhibits to promote a product, cause, or brand.

TV
Promoting sales through TV ads, program sponsorship, or product placement.

Traditional marketing process

Small and large businesses use a range of conventional marketing channels, and often integrate them with digital marketing strategies.

Direct mail
Mailing catalogs or circulars to a targeted list of consumers, often promoting special offers on products.

Face-to-face
Approaching customers directly to create brand awareness or persuade them to buy a product.

Telemarketing
Calling potential customers who have an identifiable need for a product with a sales pitch.

Product samples

Offering free samples of a product to customers, giving them the opportunity to try it before making a purchase—an effective way to launch new products and build a customer base.

Billboards

Renting large outdoor advertising spaces to market products. Cost depends on the size of space, its visibility, and the amount of traffic that passes the location.

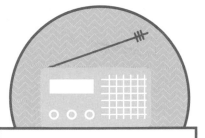

Radio

Using commercial slots on radio to promote products either locally or nationally, depending on the station's reach.

Newspapers and magazines

Buying space in print media to run advertisements, or creating advertorials to market products or services.

25%

Traditional
marketing
Digital
marketing

75%

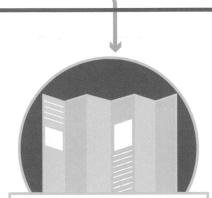

Brochures and flyers

Promoting through mailing or locally hand-distributing printed materials to promote businesses.

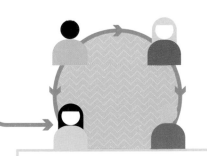

Networking

Interacting with other people at special events to develop professional contacts.

25%

of US companies surveyed in 2012 valued traditional marketing while 75% valued digital marketing

Digital marketing

Using the internet, marketers can connect directly and instantly with current and potential customers to build brand recognition, collect data, and encourage word-of-mouth recommendations.

How it works

Unlike traditional offline marketing, digital marketing gives a business direct, two-way communication with customers. Digital marketing employs some conventional approaches, such as "pop-up" or "banner" ads on web pages, but it also relies heavily on the power of social media for raising awareness of a product or brand. This makes it harder to measure return on investment. Digital marketing is often used in conjunction with traditional marketing techniques, a hybrid known as "tradigital" marketing.

Tradigital in practice

A new health club is launched using a tradigital approach to marketing. TV ads are aired with a call to action to visit the gym's website and schedule a free workout with a fitness trainer. Print ads feature a coupon or a QR (quick response) code to scan and present at the health club for a free trial. At the club, members get free Wi-Fi access. The Wi-Fi landing page has a link to the gym's free app. The club may also use pop-up ads, podcasts, email, and text messaging to attract or retain members.

Consumer experience

CUSTOMERS VISIT THE GYM

Customer blogs about the gym

Blog links to website

Directs customer to

QR code is taken to gym on cell phone

Customer takes coupon to gym

Customer schedules a free workout on website

Traditional marketing

POSTER WITH QR CODE FOR TRIAL

PRINTED AD WITH TRIAL COUPON

QR code is scanned with cell phone

Directs customer to

POSTER IN GYM ADVERTISING FREE WI-FI

TV ADS AIRED DURING TENNIS TOURNAMENT

Directs viewer to

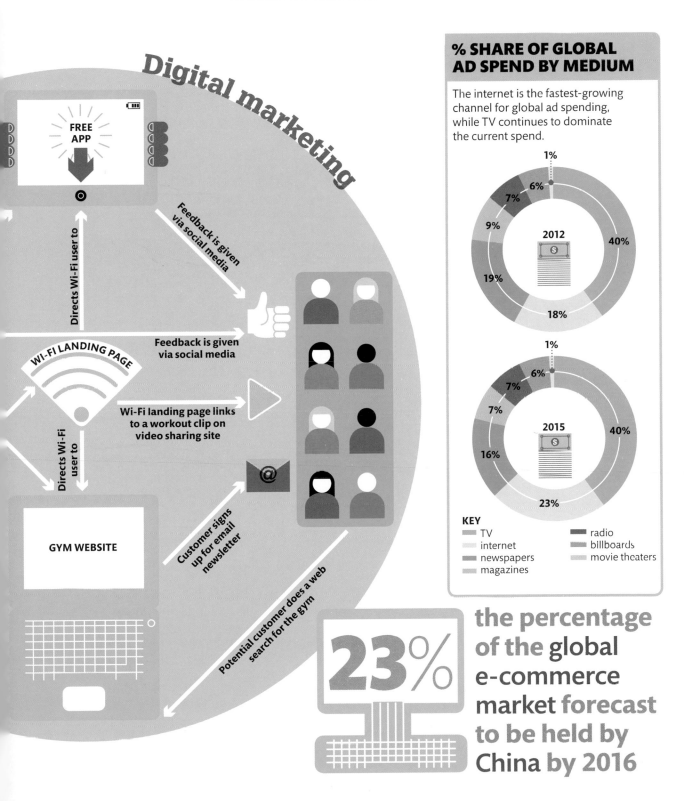

Digital marketing

FREE APP

Directs Wi-Fi user to

Feedback is given via social media

WI-FI LANDING PAGE

Feedback is given via social media

Wi-Fi landing page links to a workout clip on video sharing site

Directs Wi-Fi user to

Customer signs up for email newsletter

GYM WEBSITE

Potential customer does a web search for the gym

% SHARE OF GLOBAL AD SPEND BY MEDIUM

The internet is the fastest-growing channel for global ad spending, while TV continues to dominate the current spend.

2012
- 1%
- 6%
- 7%
- 9%
- 19%
- 18%
- 40%

2015
- 1%
- 6%
- 7%
- 7%
- 16%
- 23%
- 40%

KEY
- TV
- internet
- newspapers
- magazines
- radio
- billboards
- movie theaters

23% the percentage of the global e-commerce market forecast to be held by China by 2016

Engagement marketing

By involving customers directly in the development of a brand, marketers hope to build a strong two-way relationship with customers and win long-term loyalty.

How it works

Engagement marketing harnesses several online and offline strategies to draw a customer's interest and get them talking about products and services. This contrasts with the more traditional style of marketing in which a brand concept and product proposal are presented to the customer as fixed, to be either accepted or rejected. Engagement marketing, on the other hand, encourages customer input so that they feel closer to the brand. The goal is to lure potential customers to the website with an initial experience, and then work hard to keep them there.

Start with a "wow" experience

Provide interesting, informative, or entertaining content to draw potential customers to a web page.

Sale

Once customer makes purchase, follow up with after-sale call, full of feel-good reinforcement.

PURCHASE

✓ NEED TO KNOW

> **"Sticky" customers** Consumers who are loyal to a company and return to make more purchases

> **Decision simplicity** The ease with which consumers can find trustworthy information about a product

> **Churn rate** The percentage of customers that cut ties with the company in any given time period

> **WOM** Word-of-mouth marketing, which relies on satisfied customers recommending products to others

New prospects

Offer incentives to existing customers for recommending product or sharing content.

COMMENTS AND SHARES

Social visibility

Post interesting and relevant content on social media, and encourage dialogue.

71% of UK business leaders believe that customer experience is the next corporate battleground

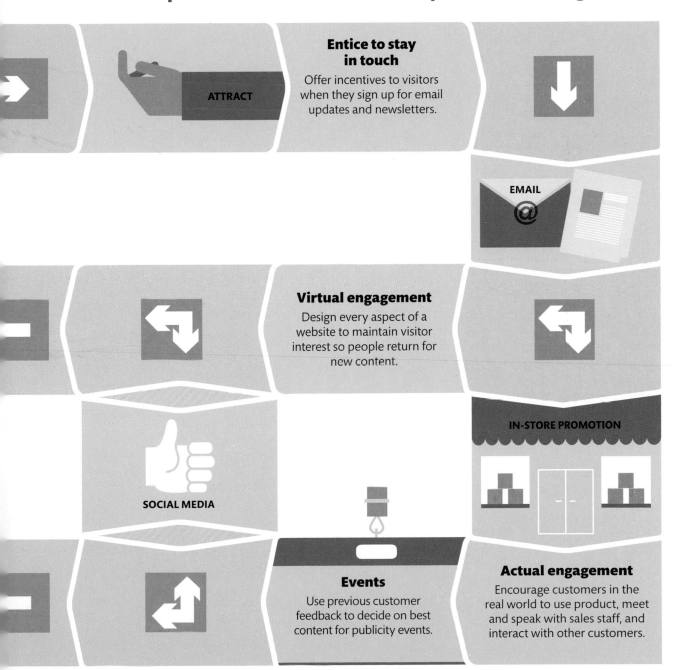

ATTRACT

Entice to stay in touch
Offer incentives to visitors when they sign up for email updates and newsletters.

EMAIL

Virtual engagement
Design every aspect of a website to maintain visitor interest so people return for new content.

IN-STORE PROMOTION

SOCIAL MEDIA

Events
Use previous customer feedback to decide on best content for publicity events.

Actual engagement
Encourage customers in the real world to use product, meet and speak with sales staff, and interact with other customers.

Sensory marketing

Sensory marketing targets multiple senses to sway purchasing decisions. Based on research showing how the brain responds to sensory input, this type of marketing acts covertly on the customer.

How it works

Sensory marketing is most obviously used by the food and drinks industries, but its use extends to diverse products and services: computers designed with tactile materials, hotels scented to relax customers, and even fireworks displays featuring edible confetti.

Typical channels for sensory marketing include field marketing (in-store events, samples, and person-to-person sales), direct mail, and product delivery. For online businesses, however, finding a way to use it remains a challenge.

Sight
Technology is making advances with this, the most stimulated sense in marketing, by using optical illusions, digital effects, 3-D, and 360-degree photography.

Touch
Marketers use 2-D and 3-D textural print techniques for promotional materials and packaging, as well as to sell products with tactile appeal.

Smell
Customers are willing to pay more for a product sold in an environment that is scented appealingly.

81%
of consumers born from 1980 to 2000 value experience over material items

Taste
Taste sensations can be enhanced or subtly altered by combining them with touch, sight, and especially the closely linked sense of smell.

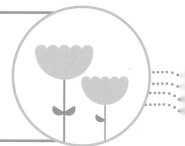

Attitude, memory, behavior, and mood

The sensory input results in a short- or long-term effect on attitude, memory, behavior, and mood. This can be influenced by the intensity of sensory data and by using it to stimulate more than one sense at the same time.

Perception

The brain receives stimuli from one or more senses.

Emotion

Sensory stimuli tap into the store of emotional memories, as both are processed by the same area of the brain.

Cognition

After processing sensory stimuli, the brain embeds memory, regulates emotion, and makes decisions.

Hearing

Sound is more effective than sight in triggering the brain areas that process emotions.

Relationship marketing

The strategy of relationship marketing is to develop and manage a trusting, long-term association with customers and other markets that have links with the company.

How it works

Relationship marketing aims to replicate the type of interaction that village stores once had with their customers, offering a high level of personalized service to win them over for a lifetime. While small, local businesses naturally work this way, large corporations have now changed their focus from making the sale to relationships, and from short-term reward to long-term gain. The marketer can extend the network beyond the engaged customer to include employees, suppliers, and others.

Supplier markets
Building a relationship of collaboration with suppliers makes good commercial sense.

Six markets model

Relationship marketing has established a strategy for communicating with the customer. This strategy defines six markets—not just traditional customer markets—where companies should direct their marketing efforts.

CASE STUDY

Starbucks

The strategy of coffee-shop chain Starbucks exemplifies effective relationship marketing. Centered on core customer and internal markets, it also involves suppliers, referrals, and recruitment (employee) markets.

Marketing to customers
> Social media
> Business crowdsourcing
> Familiarity with customers
> Loyalty program
> Reward card app
> Mobile payments

Marketing internally
> Barista training
> Tech development opportunities

Marketing via referrals
> Word of mouth
> Social media shares

Marketing to employees
> Stock options
> Medical insurance
> Partnership

Marketing to suppliers
> Fairtrade programs
> Quality control

Influence markets
To maintain good public relations, the company works with regulators and consumer or environmental groups.

Referral markets

Customers can be word-of-mouth advocates for a company. Related businesses may also refer trade.

"Ignore the human element of marketing at your own peril."

Bob Garfield

Internal markets

A company's employees are its internal customers, working together to represent its goals, mission, and strategy.

Customer markets

The main marketing focus is on customers, but activities are based more on building long-term customer relationships than on acquiring new customers.

Recruitment markets

To attract the best employees, a company may market itself by offering incentives to staff.

✓ NEED TO KNOW

❯ **Key account management (KAM)** System that coordinates departments in a business-to-business (B2B) company to serve big clients

❯ **Frequency marketing** Promotion aimed at increasing repeat sales by rewarding customers for repeat purchases

❯ **Direct response (DR)** Marketing that invites consumers to respond directly to the advertiser, by mail, telephone, or email

❯ **Transaction marketing** Strategy that aims to persuade customers to make additional one-time purchases at the point of sale

Outbound marketing

Also called interruption marketing, outbound marketing involves a marketer pushing a message to consumers. With this type of marketing, businesses typically reach out to a wide audience by paying for advertisements on various media channels. Although the audience may have no interest in the advertisement, outbound strategy relies on delivering a high-impact message and generating a response by creating familiarity through repetition.

Outbound marketing process

Outbound marketing takes a traditional approach to grabbing consumers' attention, but may use both non-digital and digital media platforms. There are two stages to the outbound process. First, the company broadcasts a message to an audience and tries to convert them into customers; second, it analyzes the results to identify the channels and campaigns that have generated the most sales.

Broadcast

Marketers select a media channel with proven reach to the target audience, then communicate the message about brand or product to that audience.

Broadcast channels

> **Ads on prime time TV** to find widest possible audience—ideal for raising brand awareness.

> **Direct mail** sent to a general audience using mailing lists, or to existing customers who have previously bought by mail order. *See pp.212–213.*

> **Print advertisements** in special interest, hobby, or trade magazines with proven circulation to find a defined target market.

> **Presence at trade events** for increasing corporate visibility and to reach a business audience.

Convert

Marketers link offline outbound campaigns with digital channels as part of an overall strategy to persuade potential customers to respond.

Means of conversion

> **Radio advertisement** that repeats easy-to-recall phone number to elicit immediate action.

> **Direct mail** that makes high-impact call for customer response; includes postage-paid reply form and customer service contacts.

> **Online advertisement** that has prominent position on web page and clear click-through point that invites customers to click, find out more about product, and buy.

> **Flyer** distributed door to door that includes an appealing introductory offer on the product for a limited period of time.

32%
of UK brands cut outbound marketing spend in favour of spending more on content marketing, in 2013

Analyze

Marketers monitor the progress of outbound campaign and adjust the mix of media or other paid-for channels, then measure campaign results.

Actions

❱ **Run control and test streams** to compare the success of different media or campaign strategies.

❱ **Examine click-through-rate** analytics, which look at how many customers have clicked through to find out about or buy product, to determine online ad success.

❱ **Measure direct mail response rates**, including breakdown of different mailing lists or target demographics.

❱ **Analyze sales by outbound spend** to establish which channels offer the best return on marketing investment (ROMI).

TYPES OF OUTBOUND MARKETING

Offline

❱ **Cold calling**   Campaign can be more effective if conducted at the right time of day to suit target audience; message should be scripted carefully and delivered in a genuine tone. *See pp.218–219.*

❱ **TV commercials**   Although many consumers now switch off TV advertisements, they are familiar with and open to this type of media, and repetition gets the message across. *See pp.212–213.*

❱ **Radio**   This medium is the world's most popular mass communication channel with a global reach, and is ideal for outbound messages aimed at an international market. *See pp.212–213.*

❱ **Guerrilla marketing**   The use of a creative and unconventional approach in high-traffic public places can be a cost-effective way to raise brand awareness. This is a form of engagement marketing. *See pp.204–205.*

Online

❱ **Social media**   The types of advertising on social media sites are increasing and include sponsored posts, promoted pins, and direct forms, such as banner ads. *See pp.228–229.*

❱ **Mobile technology**   Advertising that is tailored for mobile devices takes the form of text and images, or both, to offer special deals to users; promotions are also made via apps. *See pp.214–215.*

❱ **Social lead targeting**   This strategy taps into individual profiles from social media and tailors messages, which are sent via online networks, such as Twitter and LinkedIn.

❱ **Search engine optimization (SEO) keywords**   Paying for popular SEO keywords relevant to a brand can improve exposure by raising them in internet search engine listings pages. *See pp.230–231.*

Traditional offline advertising

Offline advertising uses traditional media channels, such as magazines, TV, radio, and billboards, to market a product or service. Although online advertising is growing fast, globally most advertising is still offline.

How it works

The common criteria for both online and offline advertising is that businesses pay for ads that are intended to catch a consumer's attention with a brand or product message.

Businesses calculate the success of their advertisement by looking at the return on investment (ROI) for every ad dollar spent. And to maximize the ROI, they must make sure they choose the right channel for their target audience.

Marketers choose different channels according to the target market defined for the product or service being advertised. The choice may also be based on the ROI that a company has previously experienced for that channel. However, tracking the response rate of offline advertising is more difficult and less accurate than tracking online advertising (*see pp.214–215*).

83% of all advertising in India **in 2013 was via** television or print; **digital comprised just 6.5% of the total**

OFFLINE ADVERTISING AND RETURN ON INVESTMENT (ROI)

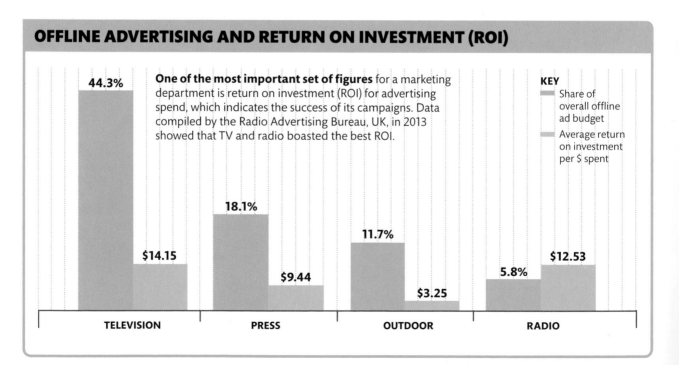

One of the most important set of figures for a marketing department is return on investment (ROI) for advertising spend, which indicates the success of its campaigns. Data compiled by the Radio Advertising Bureau, UK, in 2013 showed that TV and radio boasted the best ROI.

KEY
- Share of overall offline ad budget
- Average return on investment per $ spent

	Share of overall offline ad budget	Average return on investment per $ spent
TELEVISION	44.3%	$14.15
PRESS	18.1%	$9.44
OUTDOOR	11.7%	$3.25
RADIO	5.8%	$12.53

Offline advertising channels

	Pros	Cons
Television	Offers local, national, and global reach; mix of sound and vision creates high-impact message	Expensive; ad repetition may cause viewer fatigue; viewers likely to skip ads on recorded shows
Radio	Inexpensive; quick and easy production process; most stations play to specific demographic	Competition for prime "commute" slots; radio on as background noise renders ad ineffective
Newspapers	Fast publication process; themed newspaper sections allow for more targeted advertising	Ads compete for attention with other material on page; usually black and white, and text only
Magazines	May remain in circulation for months; niche trade and special-interest titles allow focused advertising	Real circulation figures hard to source; securing ad slot requires planning months in advance
Direct mail	Cost-effective; delivered straight to people's homes and offices; targets specific markets	May be perceived as junk mail and instantly thrown away; response rate usually low
Billboards	High reach makes channel cost-effective; advertiser's message visible 24 hours a day	Heavy competition for prime sites; format limits message length and complexity
Movies	Potential to impress with sophisticated, creative production; it has captive audience members	Audience numbers limited; members may choose to enter theater after ads are shown

✓ NEED TO KNOW

> **Television rating point (TVR)** Indicates percentage of target viewers in program audience

> **Cost per thousand (CPT)** Figure used to measure outlay to reach a thousand people via any channel

> **Advertising to sales ratio (A/S)** Method of measuring money spent on advertising and sales generated

> **Share of voice** Percentage of total activity claimed by one advertiser for a product sector

58%
of marketers' ad budget globally was spent on TV advertising in 2010, although 86% of people skip television ads

Online advertising

Marketers are increasingly advertising online to push marketing messages to consumers. Online channels include display and mobile technologies, email, search engines, and social media marketing.

How it works

When marketers advertise on the internet, they have to choose both the form of the ad and a location that has an audience matching their target market. There are several advertising channels, but the two most often used are display advertising and search advertising.

Display advertising includes banners with text and images, which appear on websites known to be used frequently by target consumers, such as news, social media, or video content sites.

Search advertising is a method of placing ads in the web pages that appear in the results of search engine queries. While display advertising is likely to get more views overall, search advertising has a better chance of reaching the target audience.

Other forms of digital advertising include mobile advertising, which embeds advertisements in mobile content viewed on smartphones and tablets, or sends text messages; email, which delivers ad copy directly to an email address; and social media advertising, which a company uses to promote products via its social media profile.

A major advantage of online over offline advertising is that response rates can be tracked effectively.

210%
the growth rate of mobile advertising in China, between 2013 and 2014

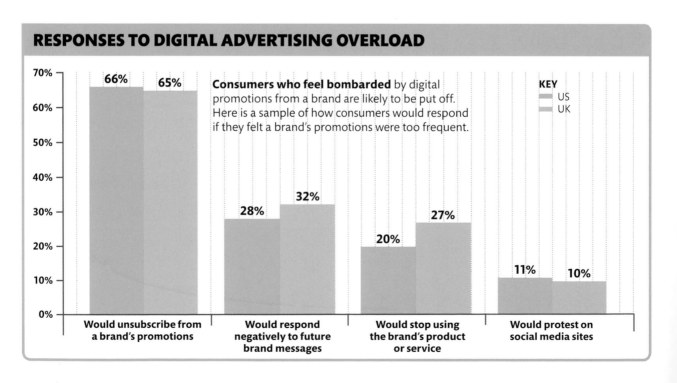

RESPONSES TO DIGITAL ADVERTISING OVERLOAD

Consumers who feel bombarded by digital promotions from a brand are likely to be put off. Here is a sample of how consumers would respond if they felt a brand's promotions were too frequent.

KEY
US
UK

	Would unsubscribe from a brand's promotions	Would respond negatively to future brand messages	Would stop using the brand's product or service	Would protest on social media sites
US	66%	28%	20%	11%
UK	65%	32%	27%	10%

Online advertising channels

	Pros	Cons
Display advertising	Attention-grabbing; if ad is clicked on, success can be tracked with pay-per-click system	Hard to target consumer precisely; internet users suffer ad fatigue and ignore advertisements
Search advertising	Good for targeting consumers, as search user keywords are matched to advertiser keywords (*see pp.230–231*)	Potentially expensive if using premium keywords; can take time to see results
Mobile	Cheaper to develop content for mobiles than for computers; easy to track ad effectiveness	Different screen sizes and systems can distort ad layout; user may feel annoyed by interruption
Email	Offers opportunity to reach millions of potential customers, especially with bulk emailing (*see pp.216–217*)	Recipient may delete email without reading it, and is more likely to do so if feeling bombarded
Social media	Easy to target specific audience; offers chance of ad going viral and achieving many views (*see pp.228–229*)	Continual posts and updates can easily distract user's attention away from placed ad

✓ NEED TO KNOW

> **Clickstream** User activity profile that summarizes what an individual has clicked on

> **Behavioral targeting** Process whereby websites capture data from landing page visitors and use it to improve ad effectiveness

> **Interstitials** Ads that precede the content page a user expects to land on, or appear right after it

🔍 CASE STUDY

Click fraud and botnets

With pay-per-click (PPC) advertising, a business pays a website for every click made on one of its ads, but click fraud has become a serious issue. Fraudsters set up a website and sell PPC advertising, then infiltrate the computers of unsuspecting users with a computer virus known as a "botnet" to generate fake traffic to the website. Advertisers on the site end up paying the fraudsters for the large number of clicks received. In 2013, one London company uncovered a botnet that was generating nine billion fake clicks per month.

46%
of e-commerce sales in 2014 came from the Asia–Pacific region

Direct mail

By targeting a large number of potential customers via mail or email, marketers hope to convert some into actual customers. This is achieved through the timing, design, and wording of the message.

How it works

Direct mail is one of the oldest forms of marketing. It works on the basis of sending a product offer to a large group of consumers in the knowledge that at least some will take up the offer and become customers. Direct mail relies on lists of names and addresses, which could be a company's existing clients or a list bought from a specialist agency. Almost any business, from a small company to a corporation, may use direct mail to sell. Typical companies that sell through direct mail include mail-order companies, financial institutions, and nonprofit organizations seeking donations. The percentage of people who respond to direct mail, take up the offer, make a purchase, and become customers—a category known as the conversion rate—is extremely low, but nevertheless proves to be profitable.

✓ NEED TO KNOW

> **Cleaning** Correcting name and address details on mailing lists

> **Lettershop** Company that specializes in printing and mailing out letters and catalogs

> **Merge/purge** Software system that pulls together different mailing lists, searches for duplicates, and makes corrections

Direct mail and email—A/B testing

A/B testing compares the effectiveness of two versions of a marketing email or direct mail copy. The two versions are sent to different groups of potential customers, and the response to each is measured.

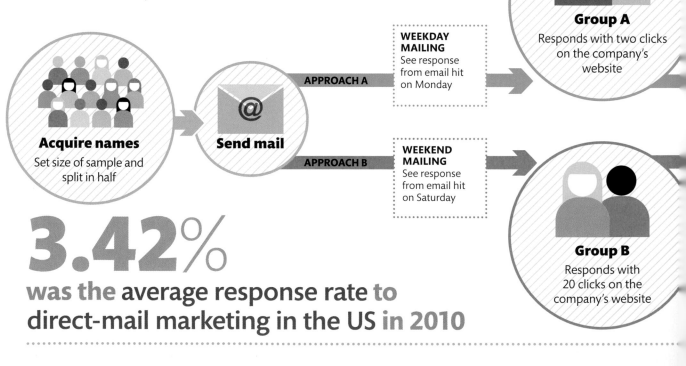

Acquire names
Set size of sample and split in half

Send mail

APPROACH A

WEEKDAY MAILING
See response from email hit on Monday

Group A
Responds with two clicks on the company's website

APPROACH B

WEEKEND MAILING
See response from email hit on Saturday

Group B
Responds with 20 clicks on the company's website

3.42%
was the average response rate to direct-mail marketing in the US in 2010

HOW TO SEND DIRECT MAIL

1

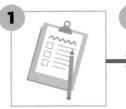

Acquire names

Buy in mailing lists or trade with other companies.

2

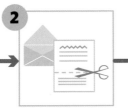

Prepare direct-mail copy

Write offer/response instructions; include prepaid envelope.

3

Send letters or emails

Send mail (staggered dispatch controls flow of response).

4

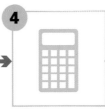

Work out response rate

Calculate responses as percentage of mail sent out.

5

Evaluate effectiveness

Assess performance of campaign compared to others.

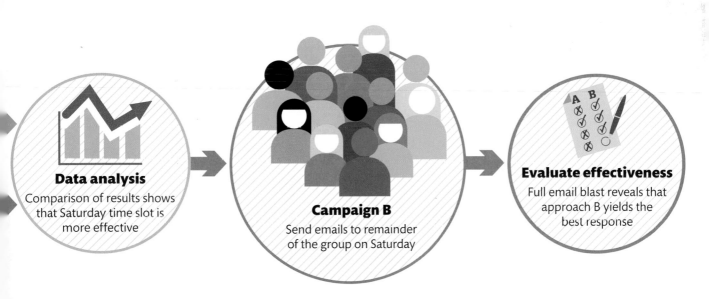

Data analysis
Comparison of results shows that Saturday time slot is more effective

Campaign B
Send emails to remainder of the group on Saturday

Evaluate effectiveness
Full email blast reveals that approach B yields the best response

Telemarketing

Businesses use telemarketing to initiate direct contact with existing and potential customers. Customers can also contact the company directly. Telemarketing offers businesses a way to retain and acquire customers.

How it works

Telemarketing works in two directions: inbound and outbound. A customer making a call to a business (with a question or complaint, for example) is referred to as an inbound call. It gives the business a chance to retain a customer who may be dissatisfied with a product or service, or to win over a new customer contacting the company for the first time. When a business makes an outbound call, it is to sell additional products or services to an existing customer, or to entice a new customer to make a purchase. Telemarketing sales can be monitored in orders per hour; for example, agent A may make 140 calls per hour and generate $400. A more effective measure is revenue per call—if agent B makes 60 calls per hour but $450 worth of sales, the conversion rate per call is higher for agent B than agent A.

60%
of all call centre staff in France and India have college degrees

Outbound and inbound telemarketing process

Telemarketers usually refer to a list of telephone numbers retrieved from a database to contact new or existing customers. Call center agents have access to product information to help them deal with questions and complaints.

Customer inquiry
The customer may have a question about service or billing.

INBOUND
Customer telephones call center

Call center
Agents in the call center receive inbound calls and make outbound calls.

WARM OUTBOUND
Call made to promote new products/offers to existing customer

COLD OUTBOUND
Call made to establish first-time contact with prospective customer

TOP FIVE CALL CENTER LOCATIONS

The Philippines is the top call center location for US firms, followed by India. This is because of the high number of Filipinos who have a US education and knowledge of American culture.

Ireland
Poland
China
India
Philippines

✓ NEED TO KNOW

❯ **After-call work (ACW)** Tasks the agent has to complete after making a call, such as processing sales forms

❯ **Average handling time (AHT)** Typical length of calls made to customers

❯ **Automatic call distributor (ACD)** Computerized telephone system that connects each call to the correct agent

❯ **Average speed of answer (ASA)** Measure of the time it takes to answer inbound calls

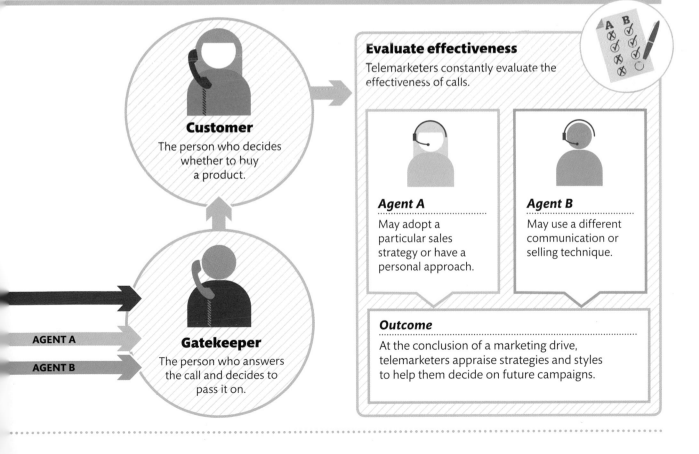

Customer
The person who decides whether to buy a product.

AGENT A
AGENT B

Gatekeeper
The person who answers the call and decides to pass it on.

Evaluate effectiveness
Telemarketers constantly evaluate the effectiveness of calls.

Agent A
May adopt a particular sales strategy or have a personal approach.

Agent B
May use a different communication or selling technique.

Outcome
At the conclusion of a marketing drive, telemarketers appraise strategies and styles to help them decide on future campaigns.

Inbound marketing

Inbound marketing lures customers by offering them appealing content, and engaging with them. The approach pulls customers into a relationship with a brand rather than "pushing" them into making a purchase, which is how advertising works. Inbound marketing is also known as permission marketing as potential customers are giving a business permission to communicate with them. In other words, they are actively interacting with the company or brand.

Inbound marketing process

Content forms the core of inbound marketing. It includes text, images, and video that consumers seek out online, especially on social media sites, or in person at events, such as trade fairs, and share with their network of friends, family, and colleagues. Potential customers respond to inbound marketing because the business or brand is offering interesting and relevant information, entertainment, or content with emotional value. Businesses expect this interaction to culminate in a sale, or create brand recognition that leads to a sale.

✓ NEED TO KNOW

❯ **Top of funnel marketing (TOFU)**
Offers content to grab the initial attention of potential customer

❯ **Middle of funnel marketing MOFU** Offers more detail and encourages participation

❯ **Bottom of funnel marketing (BOFU)** Attempts to win a sale with low pricing, offers, or via customer recommendations

Top types of content marketing

1. Blogs
2. How-to guides
3. Images
4. Infographics
5. Videos
6. Testimonials/reviews
7. Case studies
8. Internet memes
9. Email newsletters
10. E-books
11. Podcasts
12. Twitter chat
13. Newsjacking (giving content to news media)

Exploration
Publish and actively promote content; use search engine optimization (SEO) to attract consumers online

Decision-making
Ensure that content captivates potential customers or solves problems for them; encourage two-way communication

Purchase
Entice interested site visitors to become customers; make shopping online an easy and positive experience

Advocacy
Provide excellent customer service; spur customers to make recommendations and share on social media

41%

of marketers **surveyed in 2013 believed** inbound marketing **produced** measurable return on investment (ROI)

Search engines, social media networks, web publishers, and third-party blogs

Company website, blog, podcast, community, and interactive tools

E-commerce process, product, price, discount, and promotion

Customer championing of product or service

INBOUND MARKETING STRATEGIES

Offline

❯ **Optimize retail space**
Provide a well-designed physical environment that will both draw customers in and encourage them to come back.

❯ **Engage media**   Generate press releases to gain media coverage. Focus on topics of real interest, especially ones that can be backed up by statistics and research.

❯ **Interact face to face**
Conduct events in stores that provide a new experience/benefit to customers; rent a stand at a trade event and offer key information.

Online

❯ **Post blogs**   Update company blog with appealing content to attract visitors. *See pp.224–225.*

❯ **Create podcasts**   Produce content relevant to customers searching for information; engage experts to add value. *See pp.226–227.*

❯ **Produce other content**   Post articles, photos, and videos on social media sites; target influential users to encourage viral sharing. *See pp.228–229.*

❯ **Apply search engine optimization (SEO)**   Fill search engine listings with key phrases that answer specific questions; add inbound links from popular sites. *See pp.230–231.*

Outbound vs. inbound marketing

Outbound marketing interrupts consumers to promote a product or brand, but inbound marketing needs consumers' permission—they have to seek out information that leads to the marketing message.

How it works

Before the rise of the internet and the phenomenon of social media, most marketing strategies were outbound. In other words, marketers pushed messages at consumers by interrupting them with advertisements or direct mail. The same principle applies to outbound marketing that appears on the internet, with pop-up ads interrupting the content the consumer wishes to access. However, because consumers from all over the world now use the internet to search for information and entertainment, marketers have adopted inbound strategies instead, providing content that draws the consumer to the brand or product, rather than pushing marketing messages at them.

Pros and cons

Marketers interrupt consumers with hundreds of outbound marketing messages every day, but they also use subtle inbound marketing tactics to attract consumers. Each strategy has its advantages and drawbacks.

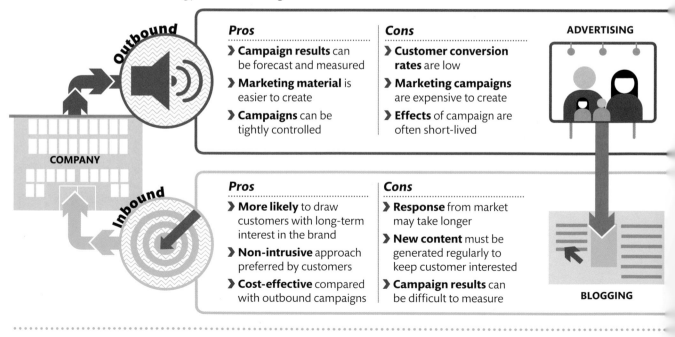

Outbound

Pros
❯ **Campaign results** can be forecast and measured
❯ **Marketing material** is easier to create
❯ **Campaigns** can be tightly controlled

Cons
❯ **Customer conversion rates** are low
❯ **Marketing campaigns** are expensive to create
❯ **Effects** of campaign are often short-lived

ADVERTISING

COMPANY

Inbound

Pros
❯ **More likely** to draw customers with long-term interest in the brand
❯ **Non-intrusive** approach preferred by customers
❯ **Cost-effective** compared with outbound campaigns

Cons
❯ **Response** from market may take longer
❯ **New content** must be generated regularly to keep customer interested
❯ **Campaign results** can be difficult to measure

BLOGGING

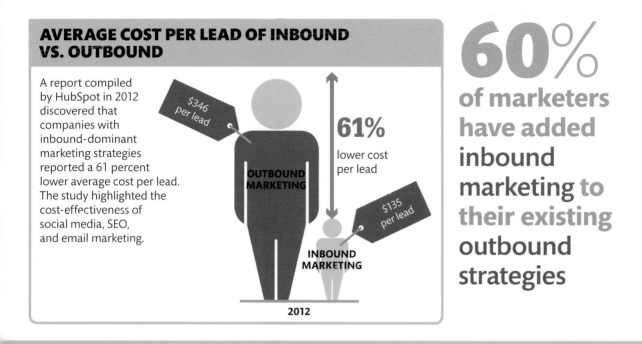

AVERAGE COST PER LEAD OF INBOUND VS. OUTBOUND

A report compiled by HubSpot in 2012 discovered that companies with inbound-dominant marketing strategies reported a 61 percent lower average cost per lead. The study highlighted the cost-effectiveness of social media, SEO, and email marketing.

$346 per lead

OUTBOUND MARKETING

61%
lower cost per lead

$135 per lead

INBOUND MARKETING

2012

60% of marketers have added inbound marketing to their existing outbound strategies

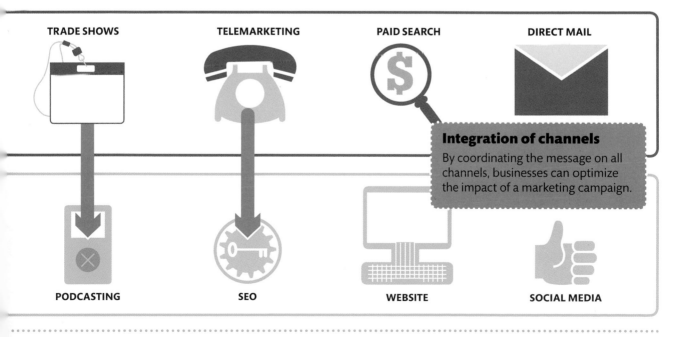

TRADE SHOWS

TELEMARKETING

PAID SEARCH

DIRECT MAIL

Integration of channels
By coordinating the message on all channels, businesses can optimize the impact of a marketing campaign.

PODCASTING

SEO

WEBSITE

SOCIAL MEDIA

Blogging

Businesses post information articles on web logs, or blogs, as a way to attract consumers to their websites. They may blog on their own website or rely on independent bloggers to achieve this goal.

How it works

Unlike a conventional website, a blog is a site that consists purely of informational posts or entries that appear in chronological order, starting with the most recent. Blogs first started appearing in the mid-1990s, when new web tools made it possible for non-experts to publish material online. This type of web content has since become one of the most common sources of information and opinion on the internet. Although it was once only individuals who published blogs, many are now commissioned or professionally edited and produced by the company's marketing department.

Blogging process

Marketers may use SEO tools (*see pp.230–231*) to gain insight into what's being talked about online, which helps them to determine the most suitable topics for blogs. Many companies have the in-house talent to create blog content.

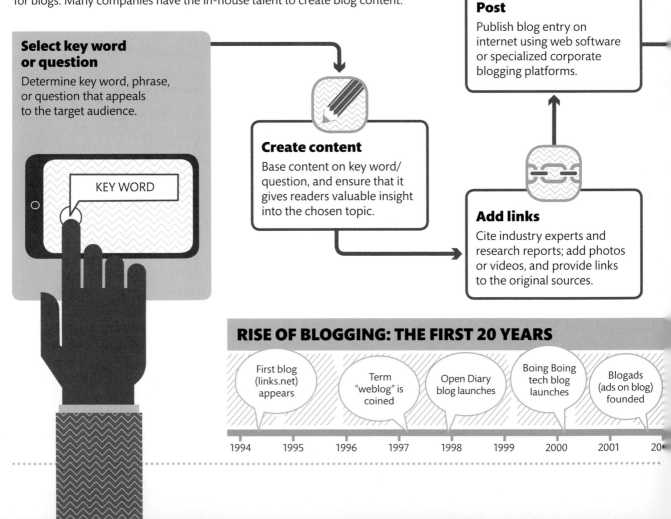

Select key word or question
Determine key word, phrase, or question that appeals to the target audience.

KEY WORD

Create content
Base content on key word/question, and ensure that it gives readers valuable insight into the chosen topic.

Add links
Cite industry experts and research reports; add photos or videos, and provide links to the original sources.

Post
Publish blog entry on internet using web software or specialized corporate blogging platforms.

RISE OF BLOGGING: THE FIRST 20 YEARS

First blog (links.net) appears

Term "weblog" is coined

Open Diary blog launches

Boing Boing tech blog launches

Blogads (ads on blog) founded

1994   1995   1996   1997   1998   1999   2000   2001   20

85.2%
of internet users in Brazil visited blog sites in 2011

✓ **NEED TO KNOW**

> **Disclosure** Statement of whether blog is sponsored, or if reviewed products are given to blogger or were independently bought

> **Splog** Spam blog containing fake articles designed to increase the search engine rankings of specific websites

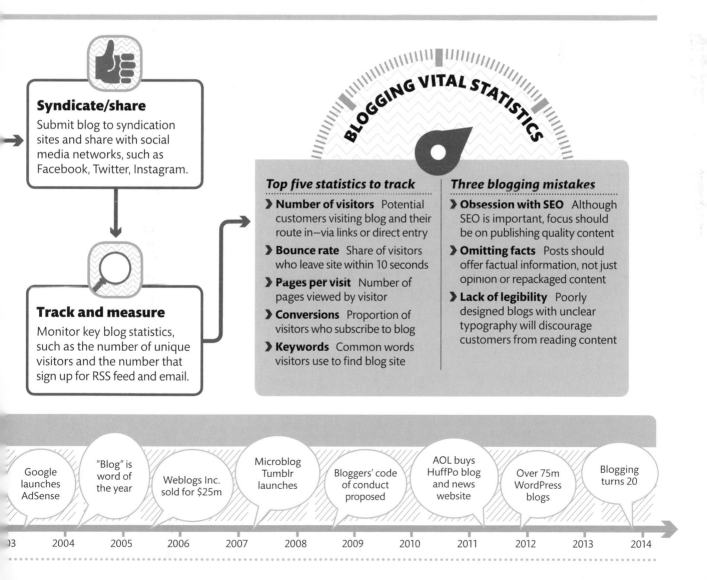

Syndicate/share
Submit blog to syndication sites and share with social media networks, such as Facebook, Twitter, Instagram.

Track and measure
Monitor key blog statistics, such as the number of unique visitors and the number that sign up for RSS feed and email.

BLOGGING VITAL STATISTICS

Top five statistics to track

> **Number of visitors** Potential customers visiting blog and their route in—via links or direct entry

> **Bounce rate** Share of visitors who leave site within 10 seconds

> **Pages per visit** Number of pages viewed by visitor

> **Conversions** Proportion of visitors who subscribe to blog

> **Keywords** Common words visitors use to find blog site

Three blogging mistakes

> **Obsession with SEO** Although SEO is important, focus should be on publishing quality content

> **Omitting facts** Posts should offer factual information, not just opinion or repackaged content

> **Lack of legibility** Poorly designed blogs with unclear typography will discourage customers from reading content

Google launches AdSense	"Blog" is word of the year	Weblogs Inc. sold for $25m	Microblog Tumblr launches	Bloggers' code of conduct proposed		AOL buys HuffPo blog and news website	Over 75m WordPress blogs	Blogging turns 20		
2004	2005	2006	2007	2008	2009	2010	2011	2012	2013	2014

03

Podcasting/vidcasting

Businesses may post audio or video files on the internet to attract and engage website users; the goal is to convert first-time users into subscribers. Once consumers engage with podcasts or vidcasts, companies try to sell products either through advertising on the podcast or the podcast download page, or by sponsoring the podcast or vidcast to create brand reinforcement.

NEED TO KNOW

❯ **Vodcast** Alternative term for vidcast (both short for video-on-demand broadcasts)

❯ **Rich site summary (RSS)** Format used for frequently updating text, audio, and video content online

❯ **Mobcast** Podcast that is created and published on a cell phone

Podcasting/vidcasting process

In order to get commercial results from a podcast or vidcast, a company needs to create and publish interesting and informative content.

Capture content
Decide on topic, and create an outline, then film video for vidcasts or record audio material for podcasts.

Process content
Edit video footage or audio track for background noise, mistakes, repetitions; test and edit further, if necessary.

Select correct format
Save podcasts in MP3 format; save video in small-screen format; compress file size for optimal download speed.

Publish content
Embed and publish content on new post. Use app to generate feed address; submit to iTunes or other platform.

Tracking
Count number of subscribers; use web feed services to access user location, level of interaction, and other statistics.

1 billion+ users subscribe to Apple's podcast app

BUSINESS BLOGGING AND PODCASTING ETHICS

Independent online reviewers often collaborate with businesses, which is beneficial to both. However, business promotion on blogs/podcasts is not regulated like advertising, and ethical boundaries can become blurred.

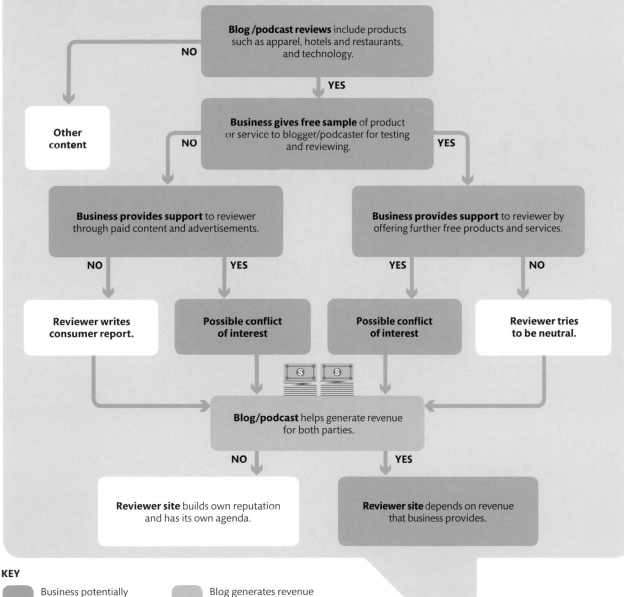

Blog /podcast reviews include products such as apparel, hotels and restaurants, and technology.

NO → Other content

YES

Business gives free sample of product or service to blogger/podcaster for testing and reviewing.

NO

YES

Business provides support to reviewer through paid content and advertisements.

Business provides support to reviewer by offering further free products and services.

NO — Reviewer writes consumer report.

YES — Possible conflict of interest

YES — Possible conflict of interest

NO — Reviewer tries to be neutral.

Blog/podcast helps generate revenue for both parties.

NO — **Reviewer site** builds own reputation and has its own agenda.

YES — **Reviewer site** depends on revenue that business provides.

KEY

Business potentially influences blogger

Blog generates revenue for blogger/business

Blogger operates independently of business

Social media marketing

By posting content on social media, marketers try to attract website traffic and draw attention to their products and services. Occasionally, interest in the posted content can multiply rapidly across these channels.

How it works

Social media marketers are responsible for generating engaging content. Typically, the content provides entertainment or offers useful information that social media users actively look for. If the content is compelling enough it will attract followers, who will share it with their audiences. As the content continues to be shared, liked, and commented upon, it will eventually get picked up by Google and other search engines, helping to generate more interest.

Social media process

The makers of a new health supplement for repairing sun-damaged skin generate video content showing the dramatic results of the product, and launch it across two social media channels. Video footage, an image, or a story that is spread quickly and widely via the internet is said to have gone "viral".

CONVERTING SEEKERS TO JOINERS

The goal of content marketers is to convert "seekers," who have arrived on a website, blog, or social media page, into "joiners," who subscribe and allow two-way communication.

Stage 1 Marketers post content, such as a video, article, or special offer, to draw consumers (seekers and joiners).

Stage 2 They rely on "amplifiers"—social media users who share content with their friends—to spread their post to a wider audience.

Stage 3 They monitor response rates from seekers, joiners, and amplifiers, and audit their posts.

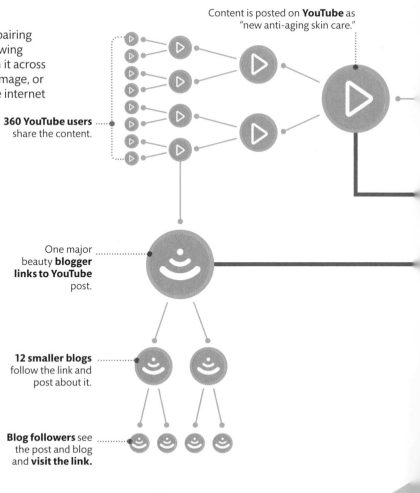

Content is posted on **YouTube** as "new anti-aging skin care."

360 YouTube users share the content.

One major beauty **blogger links to YouTube** post.

12 smaller blogs follow the link and post about it.

Blog followers see the post and blog and **visit the link.**

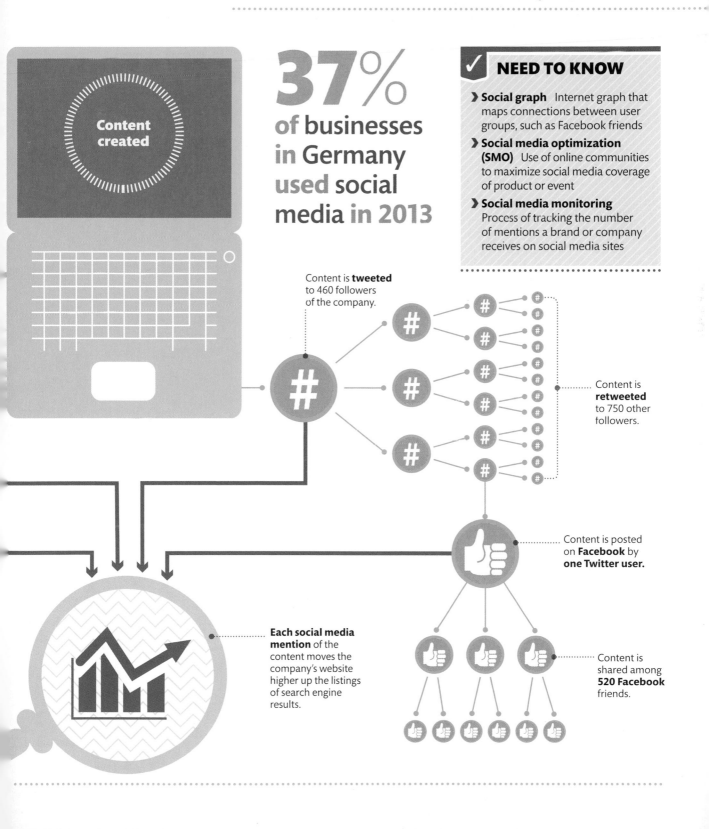

Content created

37%
of businesses in Germany used social media in 2013

Content is **tweeted** to 460 followers of the company.

Content is **retweeted** to 750 other followers.

Content is posted on **Facebook** by **one Twitter user.**

Content is shared among **520 Facebook** friends.

Each social media mention of the content moves the company's website higher up the listings of search engine results.

Search engine optimization (SEO)

SEO is a process marketers use to acquire traffic from search results on search engine sites. SEO software tools are available to help the user create web pages that will appear at the top of search engine listings.

How it works

Companies that have a web presence must ensure that their website has a high ranking on search engine listings. To achieve this, they frequently use SEO tools to monitor where their website appears when keywords are searched for, and take steps to keep it moving up the search results page. Some of the important measures marketers take include coming up with the right keywords, linking to other websites, and generating content that includes frequently searched keywords or phrases, so that their website remains relevant to a wide variety of search queries.

Search engines offer pay-per-click, a service that places a company's listing at the top of a search results page. Every click generates a fee payable to the search engine.

92%
of all Google traffic goes to entries on the first page of results

SEO process

These tools can be used regularly in a continuous attempt to move a website higher up the listings.

Keyword selection
Use a combination of intuition and analysis to choose words.
> Think of key phrases
> Avoid overused words
> Try variations of a word

Keyword research
Use SEO tools to research the most popular keywords.
> Brainstorm keywords
> Find words in top engines
> Test traffic using words

Competition analysis
Check competitors' rankings to ascertain how to rise above them.
> See ranking with SEO tool
> View rival web links
> Find top-ranked domain

✓ NEED TO KNOW

❯ **Robot.txt** Text file that stops web crawler software, such as Googlebot, from crawling certain web pages

❯ **Search algorithm** Step-by-step calculation that looks for clues to decide on search rankings

❯ **Metadata** Information that describes stored data – data about data

❯ **Cloaking** Technique for improving SEO by making some web content invisible

❯ **Panda and Penguin** Two updates to how Google calculates its website rankings, preventing unfair rankings from SEO tools

SEO TIPS

Avoid single words because multiple-word phrases rank higher.

Add blog to offer content that search engines will pick up.

Use reputable sites with relevant content to link back to your site.

Monitor search statistics using Google Keyword Tool, for example.

Prioritize good content and update it regularly with keywords.

Give headings keywords that relate to content on page.

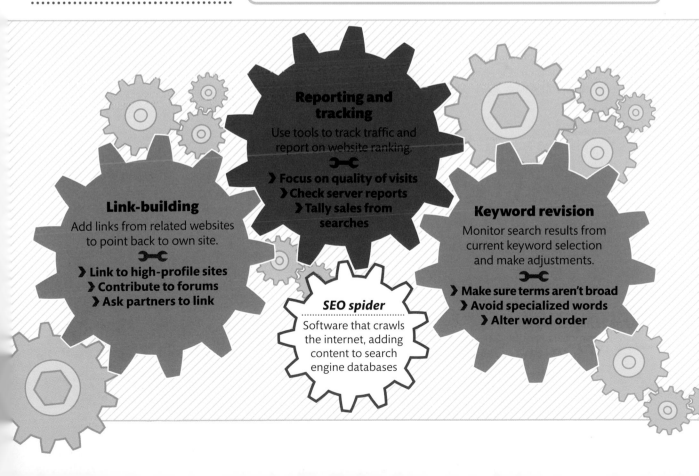

Reporting and tracking
Use tools to track traffic and report on website ranking.
❯ **Focus on quality of visits**
❯ **Check server reports**
❯ **Tally sales from searches**

Link-building
Add links from related websites to point back to own site.
❯ **Link to high-profile sites**
❯ **Contribute to forums**
❯ **Ask partners to link**

Keyword revision
Monitor search results from current keyword selection and make adjustments.
❯ **Make sure terms aren't broad**
❯ **Avoid specialized words**
❯ **Alter word order**

SEO spider
Software that crawls the internet, adding content to search engine databases

Business development

The overall goal of sales and marketing teams is to generate customer contact and convert it into revenue. This is the core of business development, and it involves a continual process of drawing in potential customers, enticing them to purchase, and keeping them engaged. During this process, marketers and sales people use a range of strategies and channels to attract customers and to earn their long-term commitment to a brand and product.

Collaborative process

Marketing departments generate brand identity while sales teams do the selling. Working together, they aim to take potential customers on a journey from brand awareness to repeat sales, communicating the message through various channels.

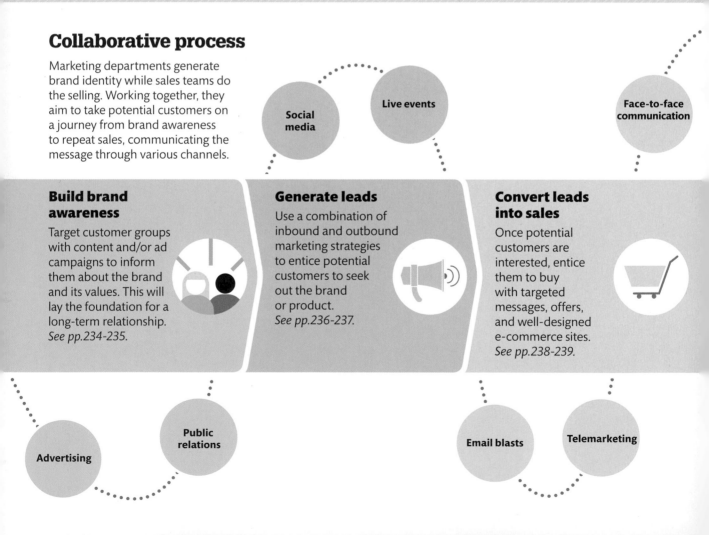

Social media

Live events

Face-to-face communication

Build brand awareness

Target customer groups with content and/or ad campaigns to inform them about the brand and its values. This will lay the foundation for a long-term relationship.
See pp.234-235.

Generate leads

Use a combination of inbound and outbound marketing strategies to entice potential customers to seek out the brand or product.
See pp.236-237.

Convert leads into sales

Once potential customers are interested, entice them to buy with targeted messages, offers, and well-designed e-commerce sites.
See pp.238-239.

Advertising

Public relations

Email blasts

Telemarketing

15%
of companies have specialized business development staff who are not involved in sales

BUSINESS DEVELOPMENT STRATEGIES

Business development is reliant on growth. Sales and marketing teams can increase long-term profitability by building up a customer base and then trying to retain it. There are several ways to ensure that the customer base remains buoyant.

> **Chart customer journey** from before to after sale
> **Think of ways to reduce cost of sale** and increase customer satisfaction
> **Integrate sales processes** with marketing to gain and retain customers; think about ideal customer
> **Monitor and evaluate** these processes regularly

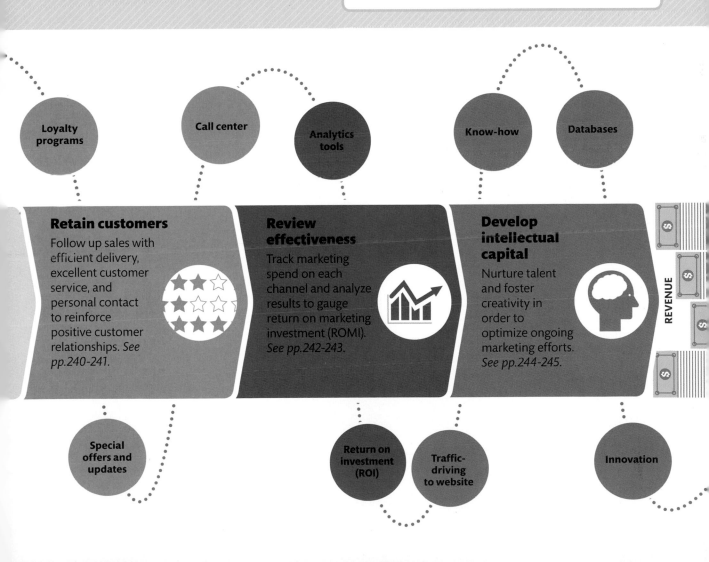

Loyalty programs

Call center

Analytics tools

Know-how

Databases

Retain customers

Follow up sales with efficient delivery, excellent customer service, and personal contact to reinforce positive customer relationships. *See pp.240-241.*

Review effectiveness

Track marketing spend on each channel and analyze results to gauge return on marketing investment (ROMI). *See pp.242-243.*

Develop intellectual capital

Nurture talent and foster creativity in order to optimize ongoing marketing efforts. *See pp.244-245.*

REVENUE

Special offers and updates

Return on investment (ROI)

Traffic-driving to website

Innovation

Branding and rebranding

A brand is defined by the characteristics that mark a particular product. Branding is used to communicate a product's qualities to a consumer, and create a lasting bond between supplier and customer.

How it works

When a supplier develops a brand, it creates a defined set of values, expressed in product imagery, colors, logo, slogan, jingles, promotional imagery, and association with high-profile individuals or characters. The brand works for both the supplier and the customer, aiming to eliminate uncertainty and risk and to convey key attributes. Social media helps to promote brands—for example, 29 percent of Facebook users follow a brand and 58 percent have "liked" a brand.

The branding cycle

There are typical stages to branding a product. In order to rebrand (redevelop) a product, the supplier starts over at the beginning.

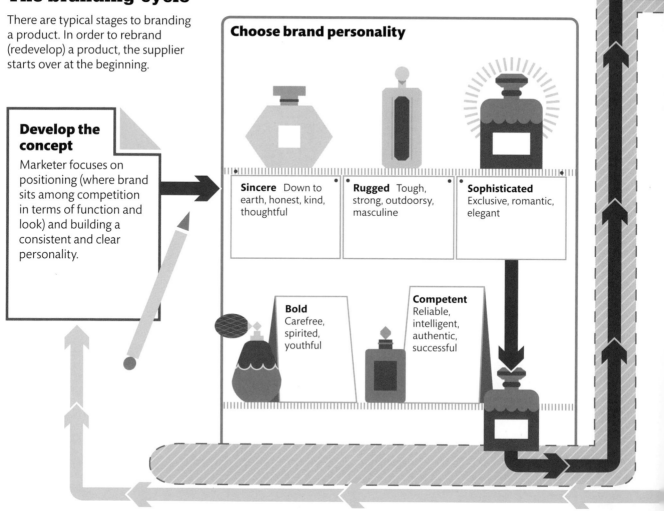

Develop the concept

Marketer focuses on positioning (where brand sits among competition in terms of function and look) and building a consistent and clear personality.

Choose brand personality

Sincere Down to earth, honest, kind, thoughtful

Rugged Tough, strong, outdoorsy, masculine

Sophisticated Exclusive, romantic, elegant

Bold Carefree, spirited, youthful

Competent Reliable, intelligent, authentic, successful

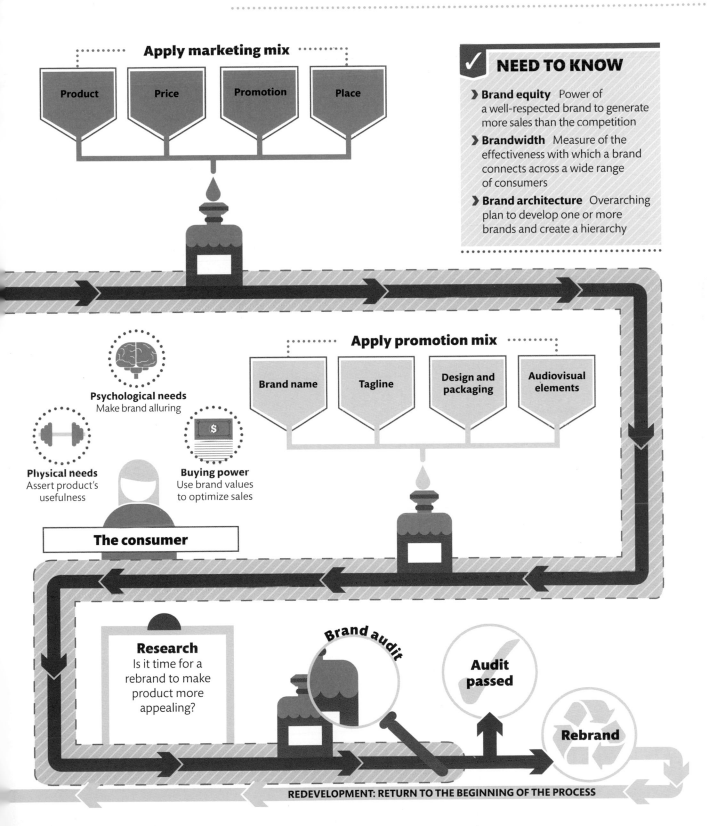

Apply marketing mix

- Product
- Price
- Promotion
- Place

Psychological needs
Make brand alluring

Physical needs
Assert product's usefulness

Buying power
Use brand values to optimize sales

The consumer

Apply promotion mix

- Brand name
- Tagline
- Design and packaging
- Audiovisual elements

Research
Is it time for a rebrand to make product more appealing?

Brand audit

Audit passed

Rebrand

REDEVELOPMENT: RETURN TO THE BEGINNING OF THE PROCESS

Lead generation

For a business to grow, one of its basic goals is to acquire new customers. Lead generation is the strategy it uses to locate, target, and nurture leads (potential customers).

How it works

The purpose of generating leads is to find consumers who may need or want to buy the product a business is selling. Sales teams do not want to waste resources on people who have no interest in the product in the first place, so the process of lead generation helps to define and capture the potential customers who seem most inclined to become actual customers—known as high-quality leads. To generate leads, marketing and sales departments typically collaborate on a campaign, offline or online, designed to identify and recruit promising customer prospects. Acquiring contact information is the first part of the process. Converting leads into sales is the next step (*see pp.238–239*).

Lead-generation process

Generating leads is a multi-step process that involves sales, marketing, and customer service teams working together to plan, design, produce, test, and refine a campaign.

Produce campaign
Create and deliver materials for each medium involved in the campaign.

Plan the approach
Set goals and parameters, including expected return on investment (ROI) and number and quality of leads.

RESEARCH
Ascertain which media and customer touchpoints are most effective.

SEO/PPC
Integrate search engine optimization (SEO) efforts and pay-per-click spend (*see pp.230–231*).

EMAIL BLASTS
Include a benefit for the recipient and a call to action (*see pp.216–217*).

REVIEW OBJECTIVES
Check that they are realistic; compare with previous efforts.

PLANNING
Ensure that sales, marketing, and customer service are working together.

BIG IDEA
Devise a compelling message to engage and entice leads.

AUDIT
Assess current lead generation.

SYSTEMATIZE
Integrate customer relationship management (CRM) software to manage the leads.

TRADE SHOW
Invite potential leads to visit the company's stand and meet face to face.

TELEMARKETING
Review key message and call script with customer service team.

ADVERTISING
Generate broad interest with ads on selected media.

Identify target customer
Define the characteristics of the customer the business is aiming to capture in as much detail as possible.

Design campaign
Craft a multi-channel message to entice the lead to opt in and give contact information.

TOP FIVE STRATEGIES FOR LEAD GENERATION

> **Create content** such as a viral video or a newsworthy business report that takes leads to a sign-up page.

> **Use both online and offline channels**, as most customers will respond to just one channel.

> **Trace the customer touchpoint—** the point at which a customer comes into contact with the product—before, during, and after purchase. Touchpoints may range from online reviews to billing.

> **Tailor the call to action** to the channel, such as inviting trade show visitors to enter a competition.

> **Design effective opt-in web forms** to capture data, such as asking customers to sign up for updates.

✓ NEED TO KNOW

> **Owned media** Channel owned by a business, such as a website, blog, or social media profile

> **Attention, interest, desire, action (AIDA)** Model for effective marketing messages

> **Cost per lead (CPL)** The amount it costs the company to acquire one potential customer

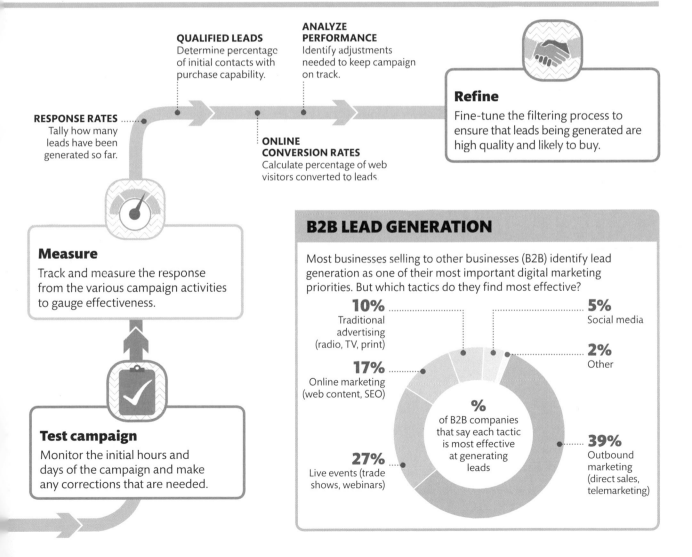

RESPONSE RATES
Tally how many leads have been generated so far.

QUALIFIED LEADS
Determine percentage of initial contacts with purchase capability.

ANALYZE PERFORMANCE
Identify adjustments needed to keep campaign on track.

ONLINE CONVERSION RATES
Calculate percentage of web visitors converted to leads.

Refine
Fine-tune the filtering process to ensure that leads being generated are high quality and likely to buy.

Measure
Track and measure the response from the various campaign activities to gauge effectiveness.

Test campaign
Monitor the initial hours and days of the campaign and make any corrections that are needed.

B2B LEAD GENERATION

Most businesses selling to other businesses (B2B) identify lead generation as one of their most important digital marketing priorities. But which tactics do they find most effective?

10%
Traditional advertising (radio, TV, print)

17%
Online marketing (web content, SEO)

27%
Live events (trade shows, webinars)

5%
Social media

2%
Other

39%
Outbound marketing (direct sales, telemarketing)

%
of B2B companies that say each tactic is most effective at generating leads

Lead conversion

The process of turning a customer's interest into a sale is called lead conversion. The task requires not only a sales pitch to promote the product or service, but also an approach tailored to the customer.

How it works

Sales and marketing departments are responsible for generating sales income for a company. The first step is to locate or identify potential customers—lead generation. The second step is to make contact with those potential customers and entice or persuade them to buy—lead conversion.

A sales pitch is used to convert leads into customers. However, nowadays the stereotypical spiel delivered by an overzealous salesperson has been largely replaced by more sophisticated tactics, such as live chat on shopping websites, which inform customers and invite them to participate in a dialogue, rather than simply pestering them.

✓ NEED TO KNOW

- **Lead scoring** System used to measure the readiness of leads for conversion
- **Sales pipeline** Visual tracking of the number of leads, suspects, and prospects at each stage in order to monitor sales process
- **Lead nurturing** Informal contact with a lead designed to gradually win them over as a customer
- **Cost per touch** Measurement of the cost of sales labor each time a lead is "touched" (contacted)

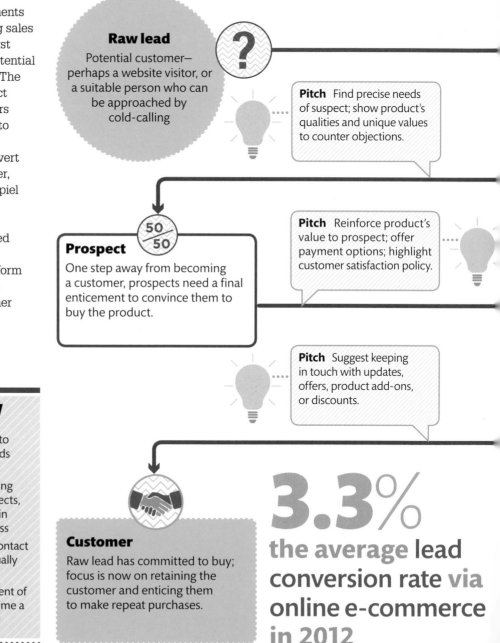

Raw lead
Potential customer— perhaps a website visitor, or a suitable person who can be approached by cold-calling

Pitch Find precise needs of suspect; show product's qualities and unique values to counter objections.

50 / 50

Prospect
One step away from becoming a customer, prospects need a final enticement to convince them to buy the product.

Pitch Reinforce product's value to prospect; offer payment options; highlight customer satisfaction policy.

Pitch Suggest keeping in touch with updates, offers, product add-ons, or discounts.

Customer
Raw lead has committed to buy; focus is now on retaining the customer and enticing them to make repeat purchases.

3.3%
the average lead conversion rate via online e-commerce in 2012

Online lead conversion

A strategy is required for steering website visitors through every step of the lead-converting process. It is often presented as a funnel. Once visitors have arrived at a website, they are enticed to click on a "call to action" (CTA) button, which takes them farther into the funnel.

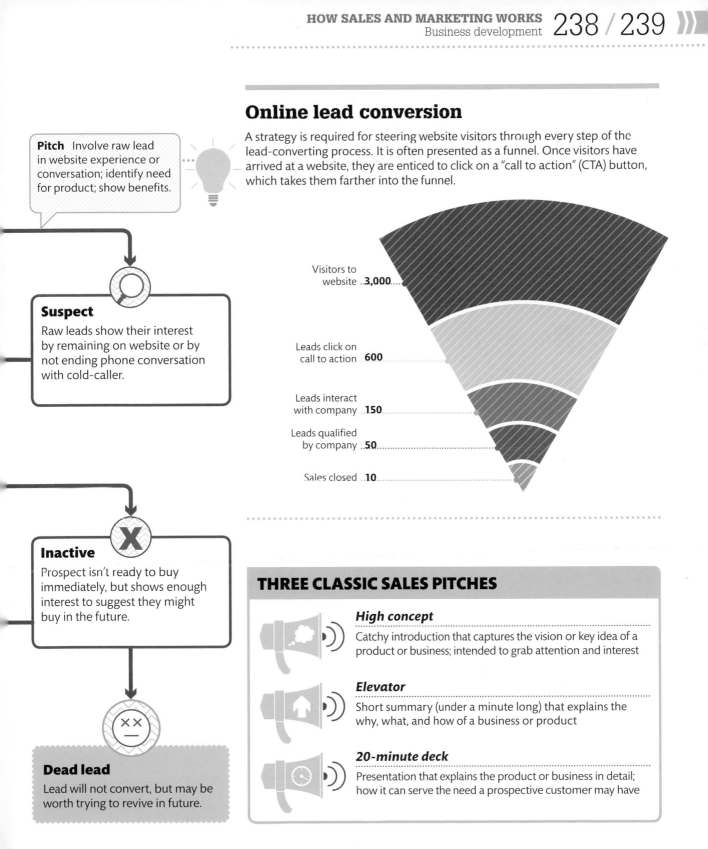

Pitch Involve raw lead in website experience or conversation; identify need for product; show benefits.

Suspect
Raw leads show their interest by remaining on website or by not ending phone conversation with cold-caller.

Inactive
Prospect isn't ready to buy immediately, but shows enough interest to suggest they might buy in the future.

Dead lead
Lead will not convert, but may be worth trying to revive in future.

Visitors to website ..**3,000**....

Leads click on call to action **600**

Leads interact with company ..**150**

Leads qualified by company ..**50**

Sales closed ..**10**

THREE CLASSIC SALES PITCHES

High concept
Catchy introduction that captures the vision or key idea of a product or business; intended to grab attention and interest

Elevator
Short summary (under a minute long) that explains the why, what, and how of a business or product

20-minute deck
Presentation that explains the product or business in detail; how it can serve the need a prospective customer may have

Customer retention

Existing customers help businesses generate the majority of profit and growth through making additional sales and referrals, and so retaining these customers is a high priority for marketers.

Measure customer retention level

Track how many customers repeat purchase or buy more products.

Identify satisfied customers

Customer referral
Measure the number of referrals an individual customer generates.

Loyalty
Pinpoint customers who are active in the brand's loyalty program.

Identify the dissatisfied

Defection
Find out why certain customers have left and which competitor they have gone to.

Complaint analysis
Examine written customer complaints and call-center records.

Introduce retention improvement strategy

Early warning systems
Anticipate any problems and alert customers in advance.

Recovery programs
Apologize for any mistakes and make amends to woo dissatisfied customers back.

Customer feed-back surveys
Listen to customers and identify people at risk of defecting.

Loyalty programs
Reward customers with improved incentives for staying loyal.

Boost customer service
Offer employees incentives to build customer relations.

Monitor and measure by analyzing

Customer satisfaction
Assess rate of customer complaints and recommendations.

EXISTING CUSTOMERS → **EXITING CUSTOMERS**

Attrition rate
Calculate the number of customers retained (existing), lost (exiting), or gained in a given period.

Revenue targets
Measure revenue targets against cost of customer retention efforts.

How it works

There are two stages to the process of customer retention: measuring the current rate of retention, and applying strategies to manage and improve it.

Practices include identifying the most valuable customers and nurturing relationships with them. The least valuable or most costly customers may be dropped if they show little development potential.

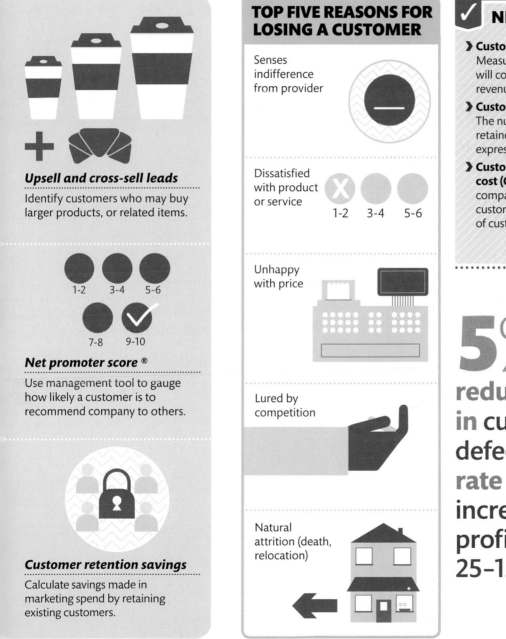

Upsell and cross-sell leads
Identify customers who may buy larger products, or related items.

| 1-2 | 3-4 | 5-6 |
| 7-8 | 9-10 |

Net promoter score ®
Use management tool to gauge how likely a customer is to recommend company to others.

Customer retention savings
Calculate savings made in marketing spend by retaining existing customers.

TOP FIVE REASONS FOR LOSING A CUSTOMER

Senses indifference from provider

Dissatisfied with product or service

1-2 3-4 5-6

Unhappy with price

Lured by competition

Natural attrition (death, relocation)

✓ NEED TO KNOW

❯ **Customer lifetime value (CLV)** Measure of the amount customer will contribute to company revenue in the long term

❯ **Customer retention rate (CRR)** The number of customers retained over a given period, expressed as a percentage

❯ **Customer acquisition cost (CAC)** The amount company spends to gain a customer; also called cost of customer acquisition (COCA)

5%
reduction in customer defection rate can increase profits by 25–125%

Return on marketing investment (ROMI)

Many organizations gauge the effectiveness of the amount they spend on marketing campaigns by measuring the return they make on marketing investment, which is commonly known as ROMI.

How it works

A subset of ROI (return on investment), ROMI is one of the key calculations businesses use to work out the effectiveness of the money they spend on marketing.

ROMI is measured by comparing the revenue gained against the investment made in marketing, and is used to assess online campaigns, in particular. This calculation, however, only reflects the direct impact of marketing investment on a business's revenue and fails to take into account other gains, such as the word-of-mouth effect on social media, which is more difficult to quantify than the more clear-cut response received from advertising or direct mail.

As a result, many digital marketers now factor lag time or brand awareness into their ROMI calculations in order to quantify less tangible benefits and target future campaigns more effectively.

✓ **NEED TO KNOW**

❯ **4P3C1E framework** Method that uses several variables to calculate effectiveness of marketing campaign

❯ **Success metrics** Use of standard measure (metric) to help manage marketing process and to assess its performance

---

ROMI in practice

The diagram shows how a commercial air-conditioning company might use ROMI to measure the performance of a marketing campaign. The company spends $2,100 on a direct-mail promotion, which it aims at offices in three major cities to generate sales leads and secure new contracts. The direct-mail brochure contains a contact form offering a 10 percent discount to new clients who respond to the promotion within a specified period of time.

Marketing sends 4,000 direct mails

120 leads respond to offer

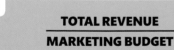

$$\frac{\text{TOTAL REVENUE}}{\text{MARKETING BUDGET}} = \text{ROMI}$$

63%

of chief marketing officers believe ROI will become the leading measure of success during 2011–2016

LONG-TERM BENEFITS OF MARKETING INVESTMENT

Some aspects of marketing investment are difficult to measure immediately. The benefits of providing excellent customer service, for example, or investing in research to help marketers retain customers, may not be evident right away but will reap long-term profits.

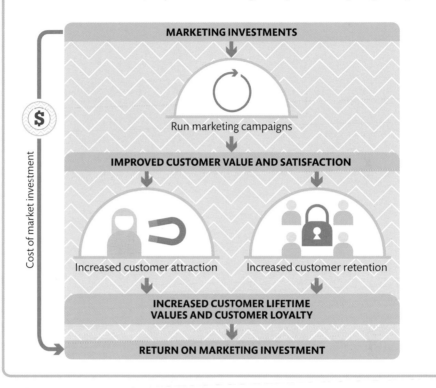

Cost of market investment

MARKETING INVESTMENTS

Run marketing campaigns

IMPROVED CUSTOMER VALUE AND SATISFACTION

Increased customer attraction

Increased customer retention

INCREASED CUSTOMER LIFETIME VALUES AND CUSTOMER LOYALTY

RETURN ON MARKETING INVESTMENT

14 qualified leads (who are a good fit for the product) become sales opportunities

3 of these become customers

Results

Total new customers = 3
Average customer spend = $6,500 (after 10% discount deducted from average $7,222 total spend)
Revenue from marketing = $19,500 (3 x $6,500)
Campaign spend = $2,100 + $2,167 (3 x $722) cost to company of promotional discount = $4,267 total
ROMI = $4.57 per customer / per $ spent on campaign

$$\frac{\$19,500}{\$4,267} = \$4.57$$

Intellectual capital

The knowledge within a company that is used to improve business performance is known as its intellectual capital.

How it works

Every business has capital, which refers to the physical, tangible assets that appear on the balance sheet of its financial statements.

A business also has intellectual capital—the knowledge and skills inside the company. This collective know-how is hard to quantify and measure, but it is essential to a company's ability to generate revenue. For instance, management must provide training and a handover period for new staff so that human capital does not go down when people leave the company, taking their expertise with them. Management academics have identified three main kinds of intellectual capital: human, structural, and customer.

✓ NEED TO KNOW

❯ **Strategic capital** A company's knowledge of its market and the business model needed for success

❯ **Intellectual property** Creations or inventions that are legally recognized as belonging to a particular entity or individual on a balance sheet

❯ **Intangible capital** All knowledge assets belonging to a business or organization; can be audited under various systems (*see far right*)

HUMAN INTELLECT

TOP TALENT

No. 1

VOLUME OF PRACTICAL EXPERIENCE

Difficulty

Human capital

The combined talents of the staff and executives employed by the business. It includes skills and abilities, drive, creativity, and innovativeness, all of which can be quite hard to measure.

EXTERNAL LINKS

Difficulty

Customer capital

Goodwill developed between a company and its customers, reflected in customer loyalty to the business and its products. This relational capital can be extended to suppliers, but is very hard to quantify.

MARKET RELATIONSHIPS

HOW LONG RELATIONSHIPS LAST

ORGANIZATIONAL ROUTINES

INTERNAL LINKS

Difficulty

INNOVATION

Structural capital

The support structures developed and held by the company, including its own software, databases and other information systems, patents, copyrights, and trademarks. Structural capital is non-physical, so it can be hard to assess.

"The only irreplaceable capital an organization possesses is the knowledge and ability of its people."

Andrew Carnegie

MEASURING INTELLECTUAL CAPITAL

Various different methods have been developed to quantify and measure a company's intellectual capital.

Watson Wyatt index

A survey conducted every two years in public companies to assess the value of human capital and HR practices.

Intellectual capital monitor

Matrix that measures the past effects, present power, and future potential of the intellectual capital in a company.

FIVA

Framework of intangible value areas (FIVA): an eight-step system used to calculate the worth of a company's intellectual capital.

Knowledge capital scorecard

Method developed by New York University professor Baruch Lev to rate a company's intellectual capital and assess its contribution to a company's success.

Information management

Monitoring the marketplace and making sense of the vast quantities of data available has become a priority for businesses; the data is crucial for digital marketing, which is taking on increasingly sophisticated forms. Most businesses have a system in place for managing information—and the most successful ones use data not only to monitor day-to-day performance at every level, but to predict future outcomes and plan accordingly.

External

Outside the business, data flows in from production, supply chain, sales outlets, partners, and customers.

Internal

Within the business itself, data feeds into the marketing and IT teams from operations, finance, and human resources.

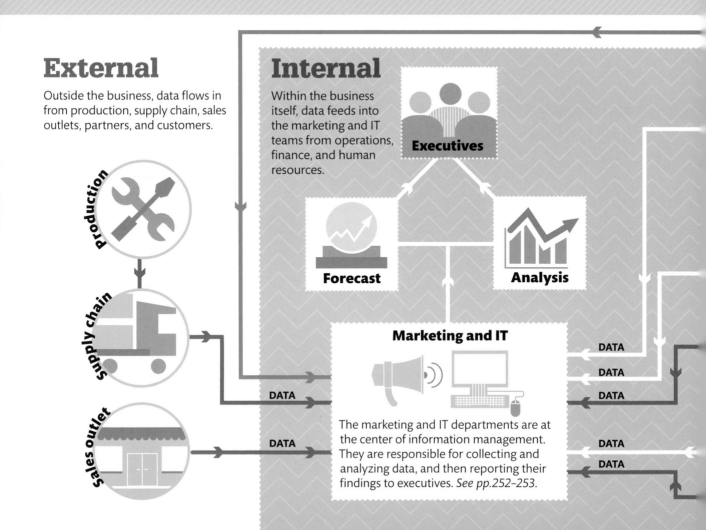

production

supply chain

sales outlet

DATA

DATA

Executives

Forecast

Analysis

Marketing and IT

The marketing and IT departments are at the center of information management. They are responsible for collecting and analyzing data, and then reporting their findings to executives. *See pp.252–253.*

DATA

DATA

DATA

DATA

DATA

7%
of organizations employ a chief digital officer

LEGAL COMPLIANCE

Operations

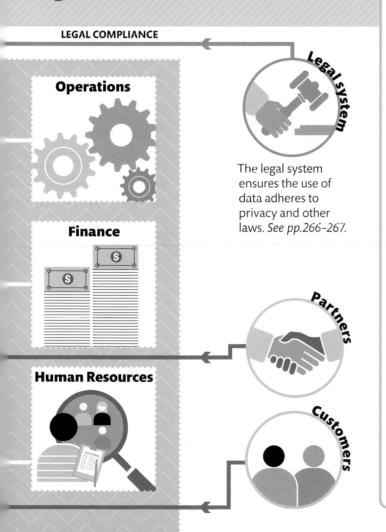

Finance

Human Resources

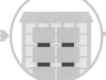

Legal system

The legal system ensures the use of data adheres to privacy and other laws. *See pp.266–267.*

Partners

Customers

TRANSFORMING DATA INTO DECISIONS

With relevant data easily accessible (*see pp.262–263*) a business can identify its strengths and weaknesses in order to improve its processes and operations, as well as customer relationships (*see pp.264–265*).

Source raw data
Gather customer data
See pp.254–255,
pp.258–261

Store information
Store data via data warehousing
See pp.256–257

Gain insight
Examine data using business analytics
See pp.250–251

Access knowledge
Retrieve data with business intelligence tool
See pp.248–249

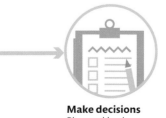

Make decisions
Plan and budget for future outcome

Business intelligence

Business intelligence (BI) is an umbrella term referring to the variety of software applications companies use to access and analyze the massive amounts of raw data they have at their fingertips.

How it works

BI relies on software programs and computerized systems for collecting and integrating data in order that a business can report on its activities, both past and present. The tools allow staff to pull relevant data from the company database. The marketer then views the information on a computer screen using a data visualization tool known as a dashboard, which can also be used for real-time monitoring of business operations.

Business intelligence process

BI tools allow retrieval of specific relevant data by specifying the terms of the intelligence they need (such as real-time sales compared to previous year's sales).

Collect source data

Company gathers raw data via several operation systems.

SUPPLY CHAIN MANAGEMENT (SCM)
Data from SCM sources

ENTERPRISE RESOURCE PLANNING (ERP)
Manages company data

WEB LOGS
Data relating to activity on corporate or e-commerce sites

TRANSACTIONAL DATABASE
Data of current commercial transactions

CUSTOMER RELATIONSHIP MANAGEMENT (CRM)
Data from CRM sources

EXTERNAL DATABASE
Information gathered from sources outside the company

Extract, transform, load: ETL process

ETL system pulls raw data from the source, formats it, and loads it for use.

ETL SYSTEM
Migrates raw data to data warehouse

Translates data codes

Transposes data columns and rows

Splits and separates information

Creates data archives

Store data

Business uses data warehousing to integrate and bank data in a readily accessible form.

DATA WAREHOUSE
Flexible access to data

Data from across organization

Data from outside organization

Current data

Historical data

14%

the increase in sales per employee if data usability is improved by 10%

Retrieve and analyze
Staff can fetch data to answer specific questions about what is happening in the company.

SPREADSHEETS
Form primary BI tool to display data (basic or advanced)

OLAP CUBES
Online analytical processing cubes enable 3-D analysis of three variables on spreadsheet

DATA MINING
Allows the sifting of data to find patterns and relationships

REPORTING TOOLS
Help users develop and produce reports

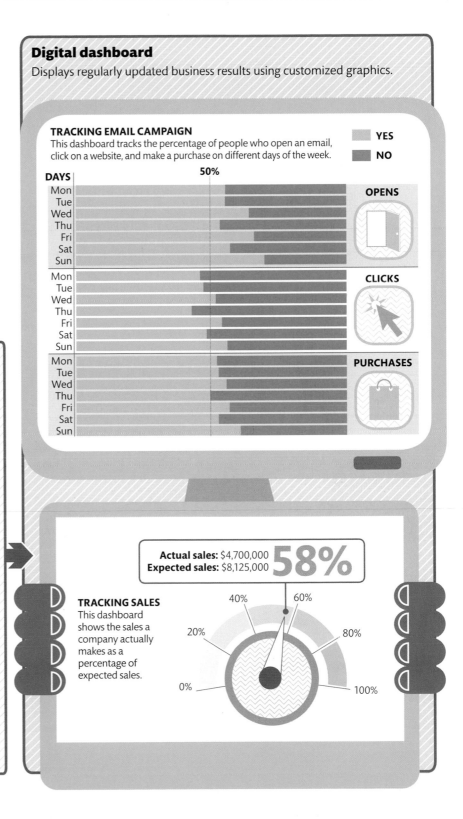

Digital dashboard
Displays regularly updated business results using customized graphics.

TRACKING EMAIL CAMPAIGN
This dashboard tracks the percentage of people who open an email, click on a website, and make a purchase on different days of the week.

YES
NO

50%

DAYS
Mon Tue Wed Thu Fri Sat Sun — **OPENS**
Mon Tue Wed Thu Fri Sat Sun — **CLICKS**
Mon Tue Wed Thu Fri Sat Sun — **PURCHASES**

Actual sales: $4,700,000
Expected sales: $8,125,000
58%

TRACKING SALES
This dashboard shows the sales a company actually makes as a percentage of expected sales.

0% 20% 40% 60% 80% 100%

Business analytics

More cutting-edge than business intelligence (BI), business analytics (BA) allows advanced statistical analysis of data, which is used to help make future business decisions.

How it works

BA takes a scientific approach to interpreting information. Businesses use BA's advanced software tools to analyze information about past or current trends and behavior to predict a future scenario. Unlike business intelligence or predictive analytics that analyze current and past data, BA allows businesses to forecast with a high degree of confidence. BA can be applied on a macro level to get a broad view of future business performance and on a micro level to assess, for example, the likelihood of individuals in niche markets making purchases.

Predictive modeling

Software program that predicts patterns of behavior and the likelihood of specific sets of customers, or even individuals, making a purchase.

Business analytics process

A skilled analyst interprets the raw data using BA tools. The results influence the business actions that will be taken in the future.

BUSINESS INTELLIGENCE AND BUSINESS ANALYTICS

The example of a 5 percent sales dip shows how BI and BA can be used to examine and understand the situation.

Business intelligence

> **Type of data investigation** Results reveal past and current event in the business.

> **Questions answered** What has happened in the business in the past and what is happening currently?

> **Tools used** Reporting, dashboards, scorecards, online analytical processing (OLAP)

Business analytics

> **Type of data investigation** Examines past event in the business, and applies the patterns discovered to a future scenario.

> **Questions answered** Why did it happen? Will it happen again? What can we do to stop it from happening again?

> **Tools used** Statistical analysis, data mining, pattern matching, predictive modeling

93% of IT executives in Brazil say that their business could be improved by using big data analytics or intelligence

Data visualization

Formulation of graphs depicting the results of data analysis; graphs may rank data, group common attributes, and compare relationships.

DATA USEFULNESS

Some data is more useful than other data; value is determined by the extent to which marketers can use it to make confident forecasts. Methods of interpreting data are increasingly sophisticated.

Pattern matching

Process of trawling through large quantities of data to find patterns between variables, which can be applied to other sets of data.

Predictive analytics

Program that conducts advanced analysis of data to forecast future outcome

Data mining

Use of computerized processes and software programs to find relevant patterns in large sets of data.

Monitoring

Process that uses software to show what is currently happening in a business, providing real-time results to help key operations make decisions

Statistical analysis

Software that organizes and investigates every piece of relevant data and interprets it to show trends and patterns

In

Out

Raw data

This includes company records (past and current customer data and transaction histories) and external data (economic, trade, and industry reports).

Analysis

Software tools are used to process and study raw data. Analysts interpret results and make forecasts that help future business decisions.

Reporting

Method that draws on historical data to provide a general overview, revealing, for example, how the business performed in a given year

Marketing and IT

The rise of digital marketing strategies means that marketers are working more closely with IT specialists to develop the best ways of launching and managing online publicity campaigns.

Convergence of marketing and IT

Communicating with customers online has become a vital part of many businesses. As a result, marketing relies so much on IT that in some companies marketing teams spend more money on technology than their IT departments do.

Marketer
Must grasp technology required to execute and track online campaigns.

Areas of overlap

◄ Digital marketing ►

Developing a technology program for publicity campaigns

Real-time transactions ►

Installing a system for recording and tracking online sales as they happen

◄ Big data ►

Locating key statistics from vast amounts of online information to improve marketing

◄ Data analytics

Using advanced tools to gather and analyze data for developing future marketing strategy

◄ Mobile technology ►

Understanding and keeping up to date with advances in mobile applications and e-commerce potential

◄ Data storage

Building infrastructure and software for storing and retrieving sales, campaign, and customer history

Social media ►

Developing the best methods for increasing online traffic via social media channels

Tracking ►

Following a customer through the online engagement and sales process

How it works

Marketers need to know how to use technology to increase revenue. At the same time, chief information officers (CIOs) are adapting to changes in external technology. This has led to an increasing overlap between the marketing and IT departments, and to the emergence of a new hybrid professional role—the marketing technologist (*see below*).

78%
of marketing executives believe that digital strategies will transform marketing by 2020

✓ NEED TO KNOW

> **MarTech** Annual business conference that focuses on overlap of marketing strategy and technology

> **Actionable metrics** Measurement of campaign results which enable businesses to make informed decisions

> **Vanity metrics** Measurements of campaign results that appear positive but are not meaningful

> **Growth hacking** Low-cost online marketing techniques, such as using social media to improve sales

IT person
Must find or develop software tools to implement and manage online campaigns.

RISE OF THE MARKETING TECHNOLOGIST

Online marketers rely on software to monitor and analyze campaigns, generate content, and extract data. The job of the marketing technologist, who has knowledge of both marketing and IT, requires a broad knowledge base.

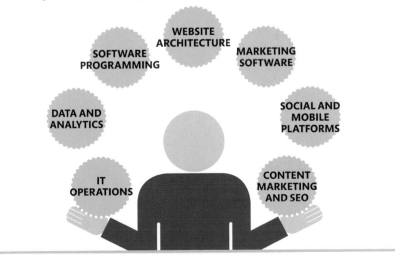

- WEBSITE ARCHITECTURE
- SOFTWARE PROGRAMMING
- MARKETING SOFTWARE
- DATA AND ANALYTICS
- SOCIAL AND MOBILE PLATFORMS
- IT OPERATIONS
- CONTENT MARKETING AND SEO

Collecting consumer data

Capturing key data is a priority for any business seeking to understand the marketplace. However, the task requires the use of innovative strategies to circumvent consumer sensitivity about privacy issues.

How it works

There are a number of methods companies use to collect customer data. When there is contact between a customer and the company, marketers can use the opportunity to gather as much information as possible. This might happen at the point of sale in a store or online, where marketers are able to observe customer behavior.

Marketers may also choose to solicit information directly by asking their customers to fill in registration forms and conducting telemarketing calls or customer surveys.

Collecting data to create consumer profile

Digital marketing and e-commerce have accelerated the rate at which customer information is gathered. Some methods require the customer's input, such as questionnaires that appear online. Others, such as website tracking, are possible without the need to contact the customer.

Surveys
Gather customer feedback via email, text, or mail, and face-to-face questionnaires.

Observations
Study customer's behavior while they shop in a store or online.

Customer research
Conduct research on existing customers or on those who fit the customer profile.

Contact center
Monitor customer calls and store data on preferences and purchase history.

! WARNING

Data collection errors

> **Barraging** Using a customer's data to bombard them with information on products viewed or sites visited

> **Overlooking technical flaws** Failing to integrate apps properly, leading to inconsistency (and errors) in collecting customer data

> **Using only automated systems** Neglecting the opportunity to strengthen relationships with customers by communicating with them personally

Social media

View customer's profile information on social media.

58%
of marketers could link data to an individual customer by 2012

Website trackers

Track website visitor's movement around a site and see what attracts interest.

Competitions

Use competitions to collect information, from opinions to demographic data.

Transactions

Ask questions at checkout—in the store, online, or on the phone.

TECHNOLOGY AT THE CHECKOUT

In this technological age, businesses have the means to learn about their customers without bombarding them with questions. Retailers, for example, typically use three methods in stores to capture information about the customer.

loyalty card

loyalty card

Loyalty program

A company may collect information by inviting customers to register for a loyalty program that offers an incentive. A loyalty program also helps track customer preferences.

Point of sale software

Computer software programs that track a customer's purchases are available, allowing marketers to tailor offers to their spending habits.

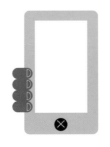

Mobile technology

The use of smartphones enables marketers to compile data, for example the frequency of customer visits and the amount of time they spend in the store.

Data warehousing

The process of data warehousing involves information from a company's internal system, such as invoices and sales logs, as well as data from outside sources, being filed away in an electronic vault.

How it works

The data warehouse is a repository that holds the company's sales and operational history, as well as relevant economic and trade information from other sources. The data goes through three stages before it is stored in the warehouse, which makes it usable for analytical purposes. Once stored, the data may be accessed by all areas of a company—from accounts and operations to sales and marketing.

The data is often used to assess beliefs and intuitions about the business. For example, the marketing manager of a power tools company might presume that 25–35-year-old men are more likely to purchase their products than women in the same age bracket. The manager would test this belief by analyzing sales data and customer records accessed from the data warehouse.

50%
of companies surveyed in 2011 were not sure their data warehouses were future-proof

Warehousing process

The data stored is regularly updated. When the business requires information from the warehouse, it is transformed into an accessible format and analyzed using software tools.

Tapping data sources

The information a company collects includes online transaction processing (OLTP) data, historical data, and data from external sources.

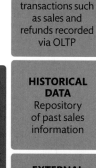

OLTP
Includes transactions such as sales and refunds recorded via OLTP

HISTORICAL DATA
Repository of past sales information

EXTERNAL DATA
Includes government statistics on business

Staging data

The ELT process converts raw data into a usable format.

EXTRACT, LOAD, TRANSFORM (ELT)

USABLE FORMAT

USABLE FORMAT

WHO USES THE DATA WAREHOUSE?

The key departments of a company can access the data warehouse to find out how they are performing. The method in which the data is formatted and stored makes it possible for them to seek answers to questions relevant to them. Typical questions various departments might ask include:

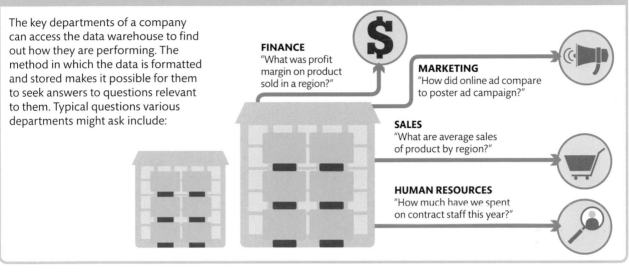

FINANCE
"What was profit margin on product sold in a region?"

MARKETING
"How did online ad compare to poster ad campaign?"

SALES
"What are average sales of product by region?"

HUMAN RESOURCES
"How much have we spent on contract staff this year?"

Storing data

The data is stored in three sections: metadata, summary data, and raw data.

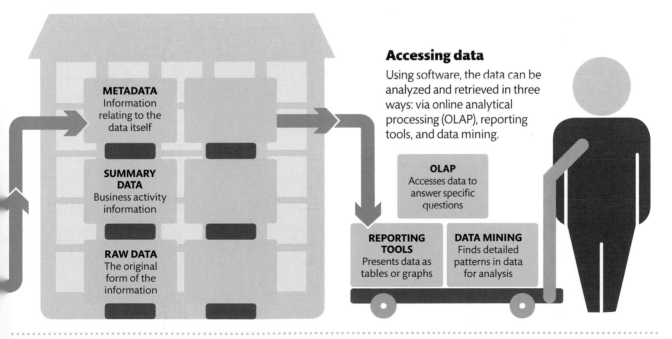

METADATA
Information relating to the data itself

SUMMARY DATA
Business activity information

RAW DATA
The original form of the information

Accessing data

Using software, the data can be analyzed and retrieved in three ways: via online analytical processing (OLAP), reporting tools, and data mining.

OLAP
Accesses data to answer specific questions

REPORTING TOOLS
Presents data as tables or graphs

DATA MINING
Finds detailed patterns in data for analysis

Customer profiling

Marketers can create detailed portraits of customers using internal company data on their purchase habits, preferences, and lifestyle, and cite external data sources to learn about attitudes and social trends.

How it works

In order to best understand their audience, marketing departments define their ideal customer by developing a customer profile. They build this profile by gathering information about the kind of person who usually buys the type of product they wish to introduce to the marketplace. The information they look at includes basic data about a person, such as gender, age, occupation, and salary, as well as more detailed ideas concerning the person's typical spending habits, such as the places where they like to shop and the amount they tend to spend.

Psychographic view

> **Personality** Outspoken; likes to stand out from the crowd
> **Attitude** Positive outlook and enjoys the good things in life
> **Ethic** Works hard and believes in contributing to social causes

Segmentation model

By constructing a segmentation model, layered with a number of variables (different levels of information) about consumers, marketers can gradually build up a clear picture of their ideal target customer—in this case, for a travel company.

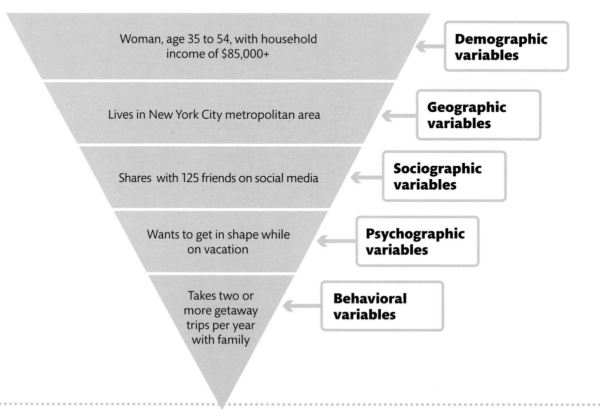

Woman, age 35 to 54, with household income of $85,000+ ← **Demographic variables**

Lives in New York City metropolitan area ← **Geographic variables**

Shares with 125 friends on social media ← **Sociographic variables**

Wants to get in shape while on vacation ← **Psychographic variables**

Takes two or more getaway trips per year with family ← **Behavioral variables**

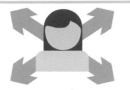

Behavioral view

> **Shopping location** Prefers to shop in smaller stores

> **Purchasing habits** Buys in bulk to save money, responds to discounts

> **Degree of loyalty** Faithful to a brand, but open to better offers

Sociographic view

> **Social media** Actively shares interests with connections

> **Community** Influential member who socializes and contributes to neighborhood

> **Groups and clubs** Member of bird-watching and hiking groups

75%
of marketers say personalization could have a significant effect on customer retention

Geographic view

> **Continent** North America

> **City** Booming metropolis with work and social opportunities

> **Climate** Varies from below freezing in winter to hot and humid in summer

Customer profile dimensions

What does the ideal customer look like? Where do they live? What do they spend their money on?

Demographic view

> **Age group** 35–54 (helps gauge family priorities and income)

> **Status** Married (children affect spending choices)

> **Occupation and salary** Teacher, $65,000

Creating a customer profile

By constructing a profile of an existing customer using data from within the company, marketers have a clearer view of the buying patterns and habits of an individual. They can then make projections about the long-term value of that individual as a customer.

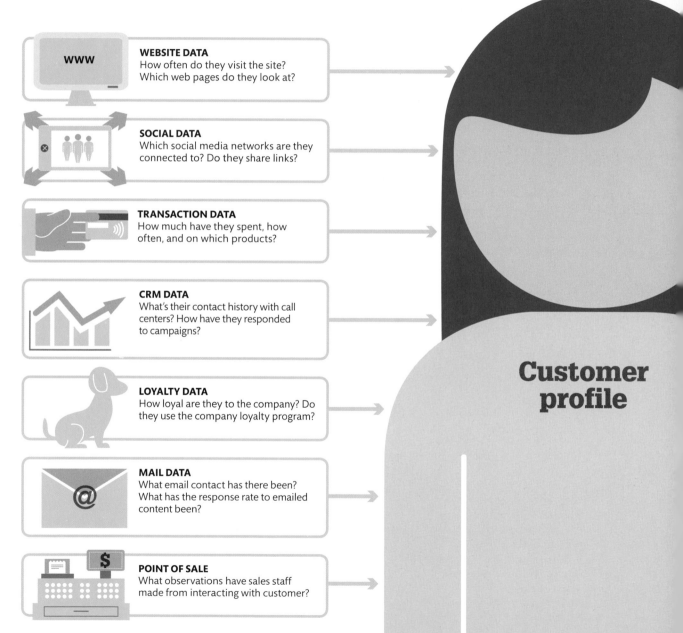

WEBSITE DATA
How often do they visit the site?
Which web pages do they look at?

SOCIAL DATA
Which social media networks are they
connected to? Do they share links?

TRANSACTION DATA
How much have they spent, how
often, and on which products?

CRM DATA
What's their contact history with call
centers? How have they responded
to campaigns?

LOYALTY DATA
How loyal are they to the company? Do
they use the company loyalty program?

MAIL DATA
What email contact has there been?
What has the response rate to emailed
content been?

POINT OF SALE
What observations have sales staff
made from interacting with customer?

Customer profile

"Once you understand customer behavior, everything else falls into place."

Thomas G. Stemberg

Assessing customer profile

Good customer

> Returns frequently to make repeat purchases

> Responds to marketing and in-store promotions

> Shares favorite products on social media networks

> Signs up for newsletters and special offers

Bad customer

> Bombards call center with complaints

> Frequently returns products for full refund

> Never joins loyalty programs or signs up for newsletters

> Spends less money than the cost of courting them

Three ways to use a customer profile

1 **Tailor content to suit customer** By sending out personalized messages and experiences, businesses engage customers and build a long-term relationship.

2 **Sell more to existing customer** Mining customer profiles to see their spending habits, likes, and interests enables marketers to make personalized offers.

3 **Reward loyal customers** Identifying good customers and offering gifts and incentives tailored to their tastes increases customer lifetime value.

SEGMENTATION SYSTEMS

Once marketers have gathered data and identified their ideal customer profile, they can compare their customer to a number of commonly used systems of segmenting, or characterizing, consumers. In the US, there are many systems, but one of those most well-known is that of the Nielsen company, which uses more than 60 segments that have names like "Boomtown singles" and "Up-and-comers."

In the UK, customers may be compared to the simple system of socioeconomic class:

A **Managerial and professional**

B **Middle management**

C1 **Clerical and junior management**

C2 **Skilled manual workers**

D **Working class**

E **Non-working and low-paid workers**

✓ NEED TO KNOW

> **Omnichannel customer** Consumer who shops using multiple channels, including store visits, mobile apps, and websites

> **Loyads** Customers who are loyal to a provider and champion them, bringing in other customers in the process

> **360-view** Profile that gives marketer a complete picture of a customer, making it possible to predict their needs and behavior

Big data

Business is trying to harness the huge amount of consumer data now available online. This information can be analyzed and used to create detailed profiles to target customers more precisely.

How it works

Big data is the huge amount of digital information transmitted via the internet every day. It is streamed at high speed and in many different formats, from database statistics to video, audio, and email documents. The challenge for most organizations is to sift through big data to find information that has the potential to add value to their business. Software tools are now available that can analyze the masses of external data generated on the internet.

Internally and externally mined big data

Businesses are now able to access data from sources such as mobile communications, social media networks, and commercial transactions, which show the activity of billions of people.

External data source

An ever-expanding amount of data is being generated by outside organizations, which will prove increasingly valuable to businesses.

Social media
Data monitors what people are saying about the organization and its products.

Audio
Data includes news broadcasts, interviews, call center recordings, and podcasts.

Photos and video
Data comprises blogs, images, video recordings from entertainment media, and surveillance.

Public data
Information shared outside the company, such as press releases, job descriptions, and marketing materials.

Big data store

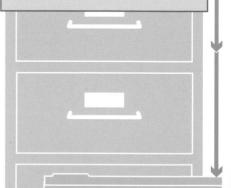

Big data
The volume of data is potentially so vast it cannot easily be moved and may overwhelm most organizations.

Big data vendor
Provides services, systems, and tools enabling companies to store, access, and analyze data. Vendor offers applications to suit individual business needs.

38%

of marketers had a centralized database for customer data by 2014

Internal data source

Internal data sent to the big data vault where it is traced and recorded is drawn from all parts of the organization and forms a unified database.

Transactions
> Spend per customer
> Foot traffic in stores
> Time spent per visit

Log data
> Customer reviews
> Customer service
> Audio files of customer service calls, for example

Emails
> Internal communications
> Customer contacts
> Email campaigns

✓ NEED TO KNOW

> **Apache Hadoop** Open-source software library for storing and processing big data
> **Terabyte** One trillion bytes
> **Petabyte** Unit of digital data equivalent to 1,024 terabytes
> **Exabyte** Unit of digital data equivalent to 1,024 petabytes (five exabytes equates to all words ever spoken by human beings)

INFORMATION OVERLOAD

The volume of data typically generated online every second:
> **Emails** 2,314,084 sent
> **Tweets** 7,231 sent
> **Instagram** 1,129 images uploaded
> **Tumblr** 1,362 posts
> **Skype** 1,473 calls
> **Internet** 22,148 GB of traffic
> **Google** 44,490 searches
> **YouTube** 84,841 videos watched
> **Facebook** 30,000 likes; 5 new profiles

DATA MANAGEMENT

Organizations can choose either offline or online options to store big data and various software for access and analysis.

> **Big storage hardware** Servers; storage and network equipment capable of supporting many terabytes of data
> **Software** Includes programs for research and analysis, storage and access, and graphic visualization of data
> **Cloud services** Third-party providers that offer storage networks for big data management and access

Customer relationship management (CRM)

CRM (customer relationship management) is a computerized system used for managing and coordinating marketing, sales, and customer-support data to maintain good customer relations and improve profitability.

How it works

CRM is a software tool in the company's IT system that records all interactions the business has with customers. The information can be used in a number of ways: the sales team may use it to find new business leads and improve relationships with existing customers, the marketing team may use it to reward loyalty, and customer service may use it to deal with problems.

✓ NEED TO KNOW

> **Technology-enabled relationship management (TERM)** Use of automated processes to manage customer relationships

> **Enterprise resource planning (ERP)** Precursor to CRM

> **Cloud-based CRM** Computerized CRM system that exists in the cloud (online)

CRM system

The system uses reliable processes that allow companies to connect more efficiently with customers and ultimately offer better service, resulting in long-term gains for the company.

Customer

Customer data flows into the CRM system through their transactions.

AUTOMATION

CRM can use automation as a tool to respond to customers who visit and use a website.

Customer segmentation

The market can be segmented into groups relevant to the product the company sells.

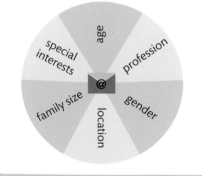

Email campaign management

Different emails are sent automatically to the relevant groups.

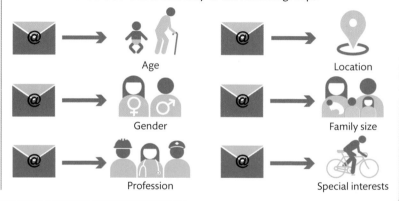

Age

Location

Gender

Family size

Profession

Special interests

871%
the average return on investment delivered by CRM

Marketing
Target groups for special campaigns; monitor and reward loyalty; generate leads

Sales
Convert new leads; find new prospects; cross-sell and upsell opportunities; customize pitches

Customer contact form
CRM uses the information to group customers according to their buying behavior.

Price quote
The company sends a price quote in response to the customer's interest in their product.

Customer feedback
The company asks questions to glean information about the customer's views.

E-commerce transaction
The customer pays for the product via the internet.

Support ticket
An automated ticket allows the customer to track delivery of the product.

Operations
Improve efficiency of manufacturing, product delivery, ordering, and tracking

Customer service
Respond to service issues immediately; manage customer cases; gather feedback

Finance
Generate invoices in a timely manner; manage payment process

Compliance

In most countries, companies have to adhere to laws and industry regulations that govern how they can sell and market their products. The rules are there to make sure that businesses operate fairly.

How it works

Governments impose rules on marketers to prevent any unscrupulous, misleading, or unwelcome practices, such as false advertising, the failure to disclose all terms and conditions, and spam marketing (sending unsolicited emails). The regulatory body is able to investigate any company accused of breaking the rules and impose penalties if it finds the company guilty.

Marketing regulations

To protect the consumer, regulatory bodies produce guidelines instructing companies on how they should market their products.

Business areas subject to regulation	Example of marketing practice
Comparative claims	"Our model is much better than our competitors' models!"
Endorsements	"I owe my success to their product!"
Special offers	"Buy one, get one free!"
Sweepstakes and contests	"Enter the prize drawing for the chance to win the vacation of a lifetime!"
Telemarketing	"Good evening. Would you like to save money on your energy bills?"
Marketing to children	"Step right up and enter the House of Toys..."
Customer data	"Please fill in the registration form."
Email marketing	"Today only—24-hour online sale!"
Use of spam	"Congratulations! You have been selected..."
Negative-option billing	"Please uncheck the box if you do not wish to..."

66% of all email traffic in 2014 was spam

Typical regulations to protect consumer

- ☑ A marketer making a claim that its product is superior to a rival's must be able to substantiate it with proof.

- ☑ A marketer must be able to prove that a person they have used to endorse a product has used the goods or service they are promoting.

- ☑ A marketer promoting a product with a special offer must set out the terms and conditions in writing. In the UK, use of the word "free" is subject to regulation.

- ☑ All competitions and prize draws must adhere to government guidelines to ensure that they are fair and impartial.

- ☑ Telemarketers must promptly disclose key facts of the proposed sale, including cost and quantity, restrictions and conditions, and refund policy.

- ☑ Marketers must stick to specific guidelines governing how they advertise and promote products to children.

- ☑ Customer information must be stored, managed, and used in accordance with privacy laws.

- ☑ It is illegal to use contact lists from external sources. Emails must disclose their commercial nature to the recipient.

- ☑ Marketers must refrain from sending bulk unsolicited emails, the most common form of spam, or other types of unrequested messages.

- ☑ Any item offered alongside the main product purchased must be presented as an option to buy, not an item the consumer must take action to refuse.

HOW
OPERATIONS
AND
PRODUCTION
WORK

Manufacturing and production ❯ Management
Product ❯ Control ❯ Supply chain

Manufacturing and production

Once a firm has decided what goods or services to make, its directors have to choose the method of production that best suits consumer demand, the product, and the market, as well as one that will be the most profitable. Companies work in three general areas of industry, which together form a production chain to provide consumers with finished goods or services.

Production methods

Before the Industrial Revolution, products were made by craftsmen. Then factories brought people together to work on machines. Typically, this was job production, with one person making one item. Economist Adam Smith first introduced the concept of division of labor, which led to mass production, with car-maker Henry Ford bringing in the moving assembly line at the start of the 20th century. Today, manufacturers can combine the best of all methods, with large-scale production of personalized products. Production typically involves three stages—here, from navy bean to canned beans sold in supermarkets.

Primary production

The acquisition and processing of raw materials—in this case, navy beans, as well as tomatoes for the sauce

Native to South America, navy beans are grown either for the immature green pods, eaten fresh as green beans, or for the beans themselves. These are dried and used most commonly in baked beans, a dish that originally came from Boston, MA.

CHOOSING THE BEST METHOD

> **Job production** Items are made individually (see pp.272–273).

> **Batch production** A number of items are all made together at the same time (see pp.274–275).

> **Flow production** Suitable for mass-producing identical items on an assembly line (see pp.276–277).

> **Mass customization** Mass product is customized by buyer (see pp.278–279).

> **Continuous production** 24/7 line of production, for products with consistent demand (see pp.280–281).

> **Hybrid processes** Mixing batch and flow production or combining other processes (see pp.282–283).

$2.33 trillion

the value of China's annual manufacturing output in 2011—the largest in the world

KEY PRODUCTION FACTORS

To make products, businesses need several resources

- **Capital** Money invested in business, including money spent on production tools, such as equipment, machinery, and buildings
- **Land** Natural resources used to create goods and services—for example, physical land or extractable resources such as minerals, lumber, oil, or gas
- **Labor** People employed in a business to produce the goods and services
- **Enterprise** Entrepreneurs and/or leaders who bring the factors of production together to make the whole process happen

Secondary production

The manufacture and assembly of raw materials to turn them into a product or service; in this instance, canned beans

Tertiary production

Services that support the production and distribution of the baked beans, such as transportation, advertising, warehousing, and insurance

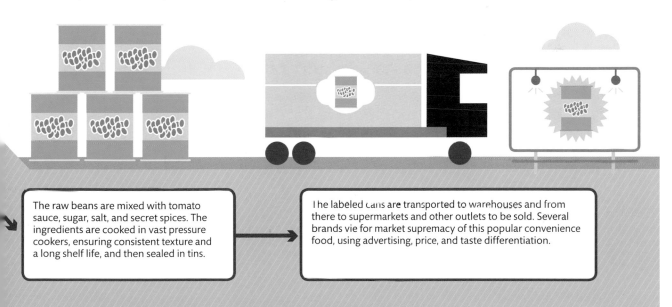

The raw beans are mixed with tomato sauce, sugar, salt, and secret spices. The ingredients are cooked in vast pressure cookers, ensuring consistent texture and a long shelf life, and then sealed in tins.

The labeled cans are transported to warehouses and from there to supermarkets and other outlets to be sold. Several brands vie for market supremacy of this popular convenience food, using advertising, price, and taste differentiation.

Job production

In job production, items are made individually. Each item is one job, which is usually finished before another is started. This method is typically used for small-scale production or for large one-time projects.

How it works

Job production is best suited to a business that has to meet specific customer requirements. Typically, these are unique requests, which an individual or a team handles from start to finish. Made-to-measure suits, or custom-made furniture are examples. The scale may be small, and firms often start with job production because it is simple and little investment is required. Job production can also be used for complex projects and those involving leading-edge technology, including film production, major constructions such as ships for the navy, architect-designed buildings, and structural engineering projects including bridges and tunnels.

SERVICES

Job production can also apply to services, such as hairdressing or processing an order for pickup. Airline flights come under the same umbrella—flight attendants tailor their services to passengers' dietary requirements and special needs for items such as wheelchairs.

Wedding dress production

A bride-to-be can choose to buy a dress off the rack (typically made by batch production) or have one specially designed and made for her, which costs significantly more.

Bride-to-be at the store

The bride cannot find the dress of her dreams and opts to pay for a custom garment.

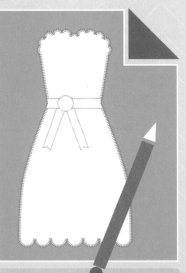

Dressmaker commissioned

A dressmaker is engaged to design a wedding dress to the bride-to-be's specifications.

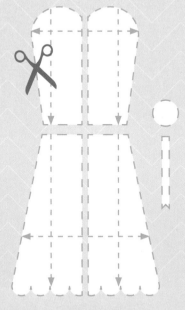

Cutting out the dress

The dressmaker makes a pattern and cuts one dress from the bride-to-be's chosen fabric.

JOB PRODUCTION PROS AND CONS

Pros	Cons
❯ Products generally of high quality	❯ Does not allow for economies of scale, so high production costs
❯ Great job satisfaction and pride in work followed through from start to finish	❯ Labor-intensive
❯ Producer can satisfy individual customer needs	❯ Special materials and investment in skills may be required
❯ Can make a profit with only a few customers	❯ High price may put off customers, especially in times of recession
❯ For small jobs, word-of-mouth recommendations reduce marketing costs	❯ Heavy reliance on just a handful of customers

$1,211

the average cost of a wedding dress in the US, in 2014

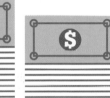

Sewing the dress
The dressmaker focuses on stitching and finishing the one garment.

Dress fitting
After any alterations, the dressmaker is satisfied that the dress fits the bride-to-be and meets her requirements.

Completing the dress
The price is high, but the dress is exactly what the bride-to-be wants. Now the dressmaker can start on another dress.

Batch production

When a number of the same items are made together, it is called batch production. One batch finishes each stage of the production process before the next batch starts, using the same equipment and steps.

How it works

Batch production allows a firm to make a quantity of items in one production run. Factory equipment is geared up in terms of scale and special tools that can be changed for each batch. For example, equipment is set up to make 200 size 8 dresses in red fabric and then adjusted to produce 400 size 10 dresses in blue fabric. Quantities can vary from as few as four identical items for a local supplier to thousands for a department store, and batches can be made as often as required. Batch production is common in the food, clothing, footwear, paints, adhesive, and pharmaceutical ingredients industries. Each batch must be traceable, with clear date stamping, in order to comply with laws and standards.

Bread by the batch

Bread is commonly made in batches. A baker might make 100 white rolls, then 50 large brown loaves.

Mix bulk ingredients

Ingredients for the batch of white rolls are mixed to form a dough.

Divide dough

After machine-mixing, the bulk dough is divided into small pans.

Proof dough

The dough is left to rise (proof) in pans.

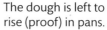

Batch 1

Adjust for second batch

The equipment is recalibrated to make 50 large brown loaves. Bulk ingredients for the batch of brown bread are mixed to form a dough.

Divide dough

After machine-mixing, the bulk dough is divided into large pans.

Proof dough

The dough is left to rise (proof) in pans.

Batch 2

12 million

loaves of bread **were** sold every day **in the UK, in** 2014

BATCH PRODUCTION PROS AND CONS

Pros
- Economies of scale: low unit costs, as large number is made
- Customer offered choice of, for example, size, weight, and flavor
- Output and productivity increases with use of specialty/dedicated machinery

Cons
- Repetitive work, so workers may be less motivated
- Costly because may require storage of raw materials, work in progress, and finished items (*see p.139*)
- Requires detailed planning and scheduling

Bake rolls
The whole batch is baked at the same time at the same temperature.

De-pan and cool rolls
The rolls are removed from their pans.

Bag up to complete
All the rolls finish the production process together.

Bake loaves
Baking time is longer than for Batch 1, as the units are larger.

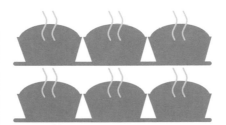

De-pan and cool bread
The large brown loaves are removed from their pans.

Slice and bag loaves
The loaves are sliced and packed for sale.

Flow production

The purpose of flow (mass) production is to produce a large number of identical, standardized items. This usually happens on a moving line, which can be interrupted when the product is changed.

How it works

Flow production typically involves large factories equipped with conveyor belts and expensive machinery, the assembly of individual components, which may be bought in from other companies, and the automation of tasks. Car manufacturing is an example where elements of the car are put together along a line; robot arms may install wheels and workers may perform specialized jobs. Significant output is possible with even a small number of workers. Newspaper printers, oil refineries, and chemical plants also use flow production.

The production line

In flow production, the item being made, such as a car, moves on a conveyor belt through different stages until completion. Components to build the car may have been outsourced or produced in another of the company's factories. They are all ready to be used along the line.

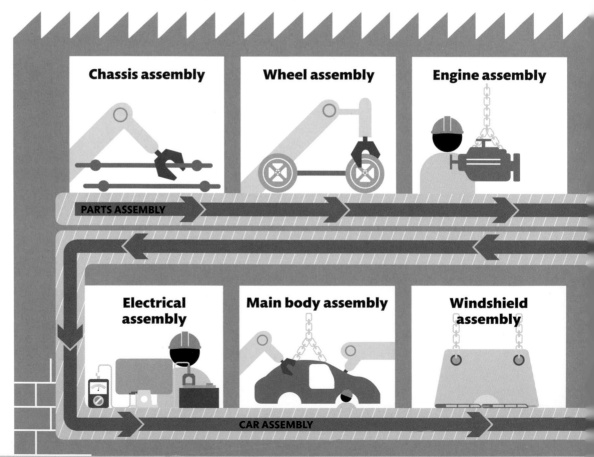

Chassis assembly

Wheel assembly

Engine assembly

PARTS ASSEMBLY

Electrical assembly

Main body assembly

Windshield assembly

CAR ASSEMBLY

FLOW PRODUCTION PROS AND CONS

Pros	*Cons*
❯ Economies of scale: can produce large number of goods cheaply	❯ Expensive machinery requires significant investment
❯ Unskilled labor keeps costs low	❯ Repetitive work means workers may be less motivated
❯ Materials bought in large quantities, so low cost	❯ Reliant on equipment: if line breaks, production is halted

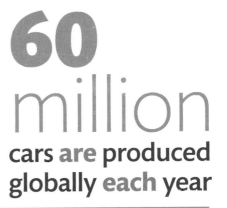

60
million
cars **are** produced globally **each** year

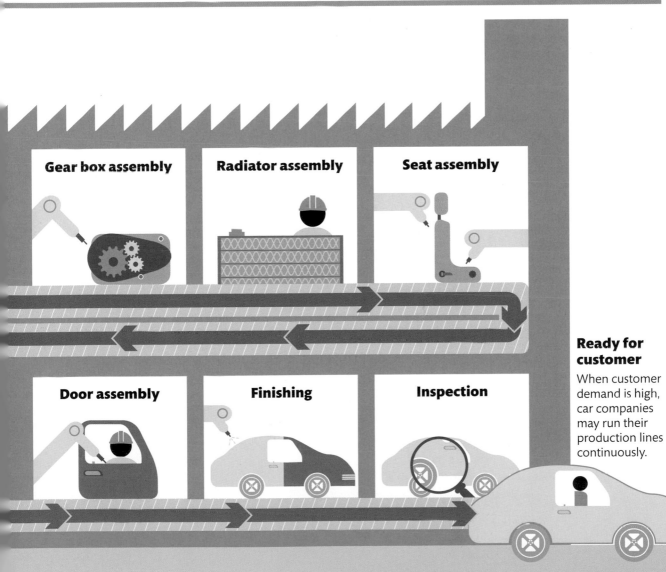

Gear box assembly

Radiator assembly

Seat assembly

Door assembly

Finishing

Inspection

Ready for customer

When customer demand is high, car companies may run their production lines continuously.

Mass customization

Sophisticated technology and manufacturing developments allow mass products to be personalized. The low unit costs of mass production combine with the marketing opportunities of custom-made.

How it works

Mass customization offers new opportunities for the manufacturing and service industries. Social media, online technology, 3-D modeling tools, e-commerce software, and flexible production systems and processes are allowing customers to configure products to match their own tastes and needs. Industries such as footwear (particularly athletic shoes), clothing, cars, jewelry, and computers already allow consumers to customize their purchases. The price is generally higher than for standardized goods.

Revolutionary new technologies are expected to further extend customization, allowing individuals to, for example, scan their body contours and use augmented reality to design and order unique clothing.

FOOD MIXES

The generation raised on social media expects to personalize every aspect of their lives, and food and drink is set to be a growth area for mass customization. Websites allow consumers to make their own cereal mixes, which is especially useful for those with allergies, and to create their own blends of tea and coffee.

Customers design own products

Mass customization has enormous potential to change consumerism. For example, consumers can buy shoes designed to their own specification via the internet. This is a high-status commodity among certain groups.

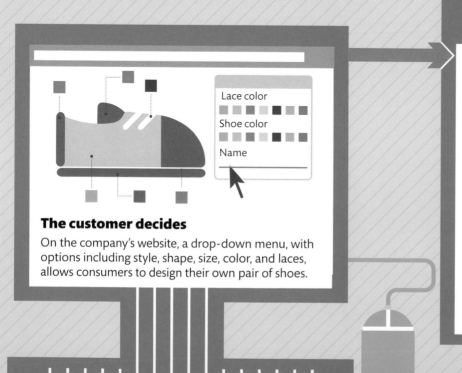

The customer decides

On the company's website, a drop-down menu, with options including style, shape, size, color, and laces, allows consumers to design their own pair of shoes.

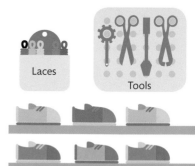

Sends order to factory

The firm holds no finished stock but manufactures to order from a range of parts, getting paid by the customer before production.

$10 million

the total value of customized sweets sold by Mars by 2007, including coloured M&M's

FOUR TYPES OF MASS CUSTOMIZATION

In his book *Mass Customization: The New Frontier in Business Competition*, B. Joseph Pine II outlines four distinct types:

❯ **Collaborative customization**
Work with individual customer to develop specific product to suit their needs. Technology firm Dell, for example, assembles computers to customer's specification.

❯ **Adaptive customization**
Produce standardized products that are customizable by end-user. For instance, US company Lutron produces a lighting system that lets customers choose own setting from programmed settings.

❯ **Transparent customization**
Provide unique products to individuals without overtly stating items are customized: the Ritz-Carlton hotel group keeps a database of preferences for pillows and newspapers to personalize a guest's stay.

❯ **Cosmetic customization** Make a standardized product but market it differently: Hertz distinguishes its standard rental car from its #1 Club Gold program.

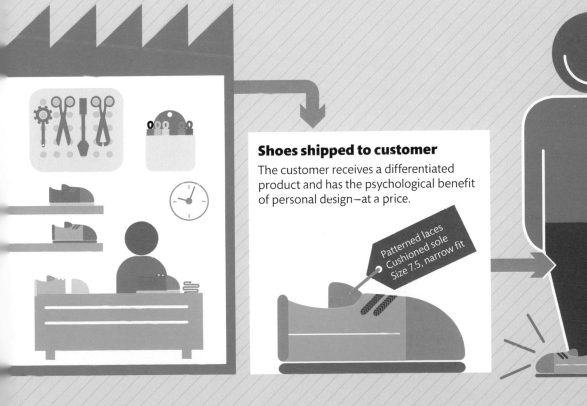

Shoes shipped to customer
The customer receives a differentiated product and has the psychological benefit of personal design—at a price.

Patterned laces
Cushioned sole
Size 7.5, narrow fit

Continuous production

During continuous production, a product is made 24 hours a day, seven days a week. The production line runs continuously to cope with demand, and staff work around the clock in shifts.

How it works

With flow or mass production, the line is stopped to change products or models. Continuous production uses the same concept, but it runs throughout the year so output is nonstop. This method is used for identical commodities with high, consistent demand, including paper, cardboard, packaging, laundry detergent, electronic components, and oil products. As with mass production, processes are automated, staffing levels are kept to a minimum, and quality control is essential.

There is high competition in industries using continuous production. Margins may be low, but demand is often relatively stable, encouraging investment in capital equipment.

The paper trail

Paper is used throughout the world, and factories operate 365 days a year to satisfy constant demand. Lumber is the raw material for papermaking. Once the lumber has been debarked, chipped, and pulped, the fibers are washed and dyed. At the end of its life cycle, some paper is recycled.

Wood

Lumber is a renewable resource and logs are stockpiled. Trucks make constant deliveries to processors for pulping.

Papermaking

In this continuous process, automated machinery runs 24 hours a day, 365 days a year.

Paper recycling

Recycled paper is an important resource for the paper industry.

HEADBOX
Fiber and water are fed onto a moving wire mesh.

WIRE SECTION
Some of the water is sucked away to leave wet fibers that form paper.

4 billion
trees are cut down every year to make paper

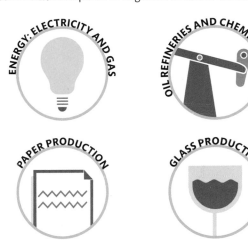

TYPICAL USES

Continuous production is used for undifferentiated commodities required in large and constant amounts.

ENERGY: ELECTRICITY AND GAS

OIL REFINERIES AND CHEMICAL PLANTS

PAPER PRODUCTION

GLASS PRODUCTION

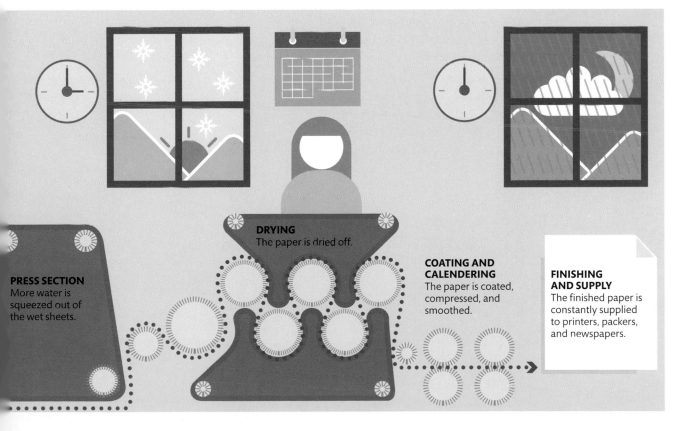

PRESS SECTION
More water is squeezed out of the wet sheets.

DRYING
The paper is dried off.

COATING AND CALENDERING
The paper is coated, compressed, and smoothed.

FINISHING AND SUPPLY
The finished paper is constantly supplied to printers, packers, and newspapers.

Hybrid processes

Manufacturing firms may adapt existing processes or combine two production methods for optimal performance, particularly if they make a wide range of products.

How it works

There are many examples of hybrid processes. One is linked batch flow production, where only two or three pieces of equipment are required and a batch flows from one process to another. This is common in the chemicals and pharmaceuticals industries. For instance, a company may make headache medication and a hay fever remedy in tablet, capsule, and liquid form, and in varying doses; each batch flows through a series of steps, depending on composition and form, from bulk processing to packaging. Another example is cell manufacturing, which combines job production with flow (mass) production.

✓ **NEED TO KNOW**

❯ **Increments** Small steps of gradual improvement over a period of time, rather than breakthrough or transformational change
❯ **Hybridization** Replacing several separate processes with one single hybrid process

Combining methods

On the classic assembly line, each worker is skilled at producing one type or part of an item. At the other end of the scale, one person completes all stages, creating the finished product from beginning to end. Cell manufacturing combines flow production with job production to create autonomous units. A number of workers are dedicated to production, or part-production, of a set of goods.

Flow production

One process is handled by one or more workers and that job is completed before the product or part moves on to the next workstation. Worker 1 uses only one set of tools for the process, before the product moves on to Worker 2, and so on down the line. (See pp.276–277.)

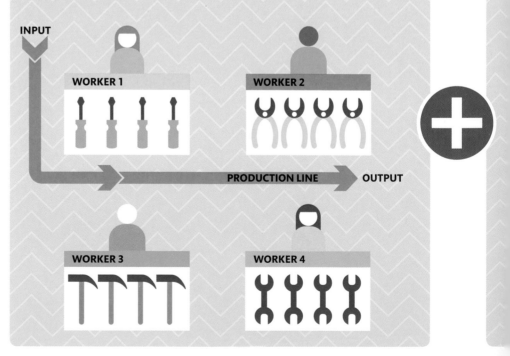

INPUT

WORKER 1

WORKER 2

PRODUCTION LINE → OUTPUT

WORKER 3

WORKER 4

HYBRID PROCESSES FOR INNOVATION

By combining manufacturing processes, companies can create products with new and original qualities. For instance, a food company that makes bread and french fries may speed up production of the fries by baking them in the bread oven first. This has the unintended but beneficial consequence of making the fries healthier. A new product is created, which may now be marketed as a new proposition to a different set of consumers.

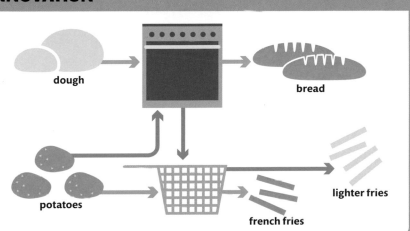

dough

bread

potatoes

french fries

lighter fries

Job production

One worker creates a one-of-a-kind product, such as a custom kitchen, from start to finish. This way of working can be more rewarding for the worker, who uses a range of skills, but it tends to be costly for the customer. (*See pp.272–273.*)

Cell manufacturing

Combining the best of flow and job production, here a group of products or parts is produced in separate small units (cells) made up of a number of workers in the factory. Workers are trained to produce all the items in the set. Dissimilar items can be produced without slowing the production line. The idea is to improve performance by giving each cell a degree of autonomy.

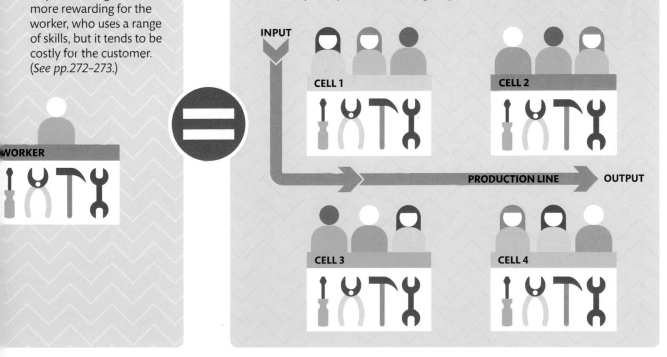

WORKER

INPUT

CELL 1

CELL 2

PRODUCTION LINE

OUTPUT

CELL 3

CELL 4

Management

Every manager in a business, particularly in manufacturing, has to ensure that all resources—from materials to equipment and staff—are used efficiently, while keeping the customer continually in mind. Managers make key decisions to lay down procedures and set standards and then work continuously to improve processes to ensure that the company remains profitable.

Which approach?

How people and processes are organized in making and delivering the product to the customer is critical if a company is to survive fierce competition and rapidly shifting consumer demands in a global market. In making decisions about how a business can meet its goals, managers may combine a number of approaches as many are interlinked and achieve similar outcomes.

MANAGER OR LEADER?

Management and leadership are not the same, but are closely linked:

> Managers **plan**, **organize**, and **coordinate**; leaders also **galvanize** and **motivate**.

> Managers organize workers to **maximize efficiency**; leaders also **nurture skills** and **develop talent**.

> Managers focus on the **bottom line**; leaders also **look to the horizon**.

> Managers **tell people** what to do; leaders also **ask questions**.

> Managers make sure workers are doing everything that **needs to be done**; leaders also inspire workers to **want to do more** than needs to be done.

The following classic distinction has been attributed to two different business leaders and writers, Peter Drucker and Warren Bennis: management is doing things right; leadership is doing the right things.

Agile production

How can we be more responsive to shifts in customer demand?
See pp.296–297.

Time-based management

How can we use time effectively?
See pp.294–295.

No.1
country for innovation in 2014: South Korea

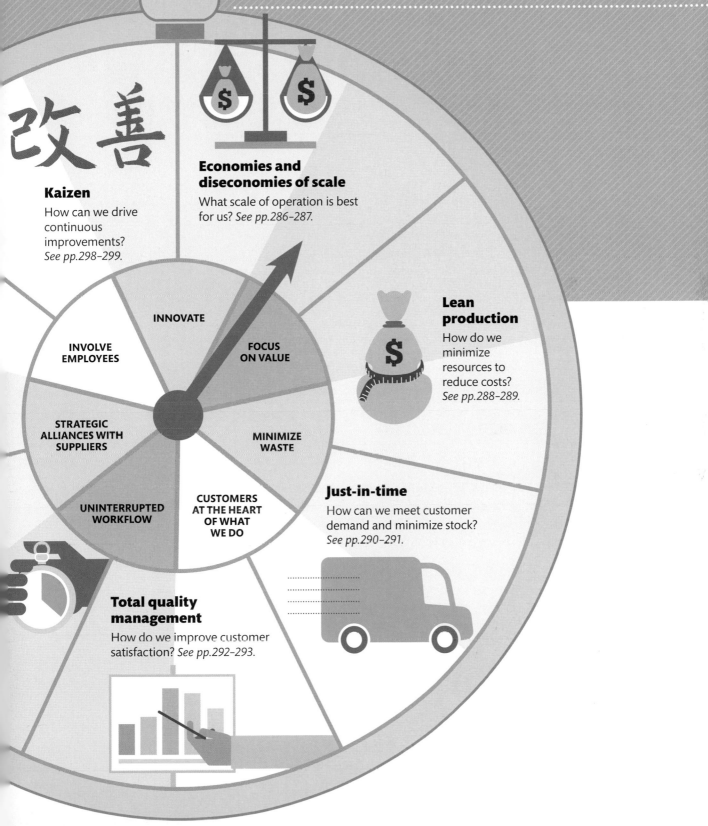

改善

Kaizen

How can we drive continuous improvements? *See pp.298–299.*

Economies and diseconomies of scale

What scale of operation is best for us? *See pp.286–287.*

Lean production

How do we minimize resources to reduce costs? *See pp.288–289.*

Just-in-time

How can we meet customer demand and minimize stock? *See pp.290–291.*

Total quality management

How do we improve customer satisfaction? *See pp.292–293.*

INNOVATE

INVOLVE EMPLOYEES

FOCUS ON VALUE

STRATEGIC ALLIANCES WITH SUPPLIERS

MINIMIZE WASTE

UNINTERRUPTED WORKFLOW

CUSTOMERS AT THE HEART OF WHAT WE DO

Economies and diseconomies of scale

Economies of scale are one of the advantages of large-scale production and result in a lower unit cost of each item produced. However, costs can also go up as the operation grows, resulting in diseconomies of scale.

How it works

Economies of scale is a simple concept: the more items produced or handled, the cheaper the average (unit) cost, as efficiencies and fixed costs are shared across all items. This gives a business a competitive advantage.

Supermarkets, for example, buy food in bulk at low unit costs, which they pass on to consumers. However, diseconomies of scale may occur when the operation grows because of high administration costs, wastage from lack of control, or lack of employee productivity.

Economies of scale

While it may be inefficient for a small dairy to supply milk to a supermarket, it is cost-effective for a large dairy operation producing thousands of bottles. If a delivery is too large, though, wastage can creep in due to associated costs.

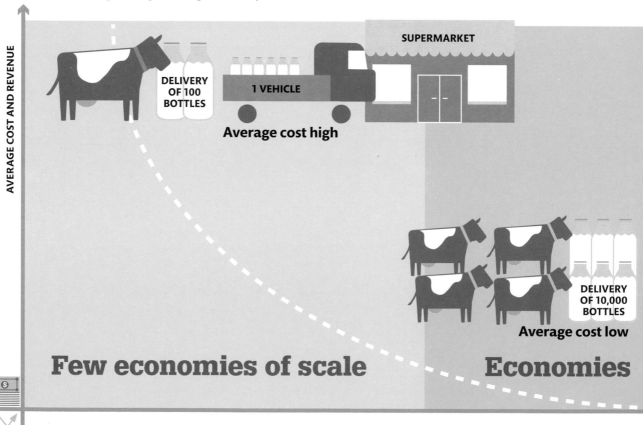

AVERAGE COST AND REVENUE

SUPERMARKET

DELIVERY OF 100 BOTTLES

1 VEHICLE

Average cost high

DELIVERY OF 10,000 BOTTLES

Average cost low

Few economies of scale

Economies

NETWORK ECONOMY

Online networks, such as eBay and Facebook, rarely stray into diseconomies of scale. They can deliver economies of scale even at an international level: the cost of adding one more user to a network is almost zero. However, the resulting benefits may be huge, because each new user in the network can interact or trade with other members of the network.

150 million

the number of eBay users worldwide in 2014

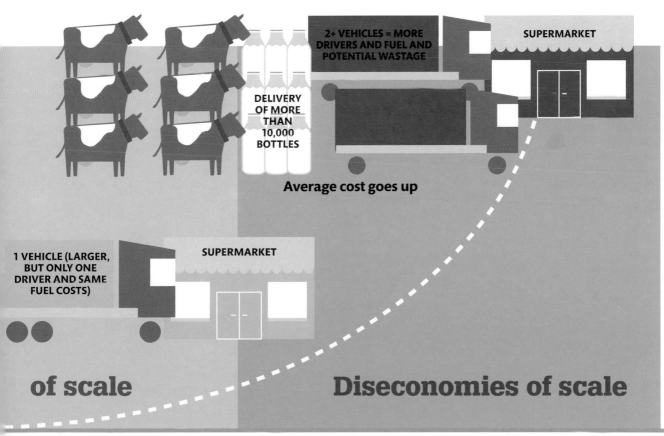

2+ VEHICLES = MORE DRIVERS AND FUEL AND POTENTIAL WASTAGE

SUPERMARKET

DELIVERY OF MORE THAN 10,000 BOTTLES

Average cost goes up

1 VEHICLE (LARGER, BUT ONLY ONE DRIVER AND SAME FUEL COSTS)

SUPERMARKET

of scale

Diseconomies of scale

OUTPUT

Lean production

The goal of lean production is to reduce the resources used to supply goods and services to consumers. By cutting down human effort, materials, space, capital, and time, lean production cuts costs.

How it works

The focus in lean production is on efficiency to maximize value for the customer, but without affecting quality. Lean seeks to eliminate all activities that do not add value to the production process, including holding inventory (stock), repairing faults, and unnecessary movement of people and products around a manufacturing plant.

Optimizing the flow of products and services through value streams—sequences of activity that flow horizontally across technologies, assets, and functions to customers—allows the business to respond more quickly to consumer demand. Efficiency also makes it simpler and more accurate to manage information.

Case study: how Toyota eliminates waste

Lean production is about getting rid of waste, sometimes called non-value-added activities. Car manufacturer Toyota has identified eight areas of waste and a lean approach to counter these.

Overproduction

Waste
Items produced surplus to customer demand

Lean solution
Manufacture based upon a pull system, producing products as customers order them

Waiting

Waste
Unproductive time spent waiting for material, information, equipment, tools

Lean solution
All resources provided on a just-in-time (JIT) basis—not too early, not too late (see pp.290–291)

Excess inventory

Waste
Extra, unwanted stock held in inventory

Lean solution
Kanban cards used to indicate material order points: how much, from where, and to where

Defects

Waste
Consumes materials and uses up labor; results in customer complaints

Lean solution
Total quality management (see pp.292–293) used to improve all areas

BENEFITS OF LEAN PRODUCTION

According to a US National Institute of Standards and Technology survey, 40 firms implementing lean production reported these benefits:

BENEFIT

- Amount of space required reduced by **75%**
- Quality improved by **80%**
- Work-in-process inventory reduced by **80%**
- Productivity increased by **50%**
- Lead time (taking product from start to finish) reduced by **90%**

PERCENTAGE

10 million
the number of cars Toyota expected to sell in 2014

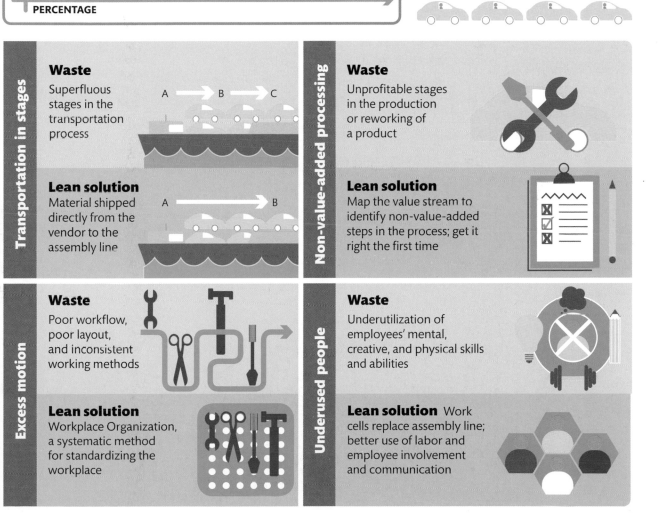

Transportation in stages

Waste
Superfluous stages in the transportation process

A → B → C

Lean solution
Material shipped directly from the vendor to the assembly line

A → B

Non-value-added processing

Waste
Unprofitable stages in the production or reworking of a product

Lean solution
Map the value stream to identify non-value-added steps in the process; get it right the first time

Excess motion

Waste
Poor workflow, poor layout, and inconsistent working methods

Lean solution
Workplace Organization, a systematic method for standardizing the workplace

Underused people

Waste
Underutilization of employees' mental, creative, and physical skills and abilities

Lean solution Work cells replace assembly line; better use of labor and employee involvement and communication

Just-in-time

The system of production in which an actual order is the trigger for an item to be manufactured is called just-in-time. It enables a firm to produce only the items required, in the right amount, at the right time.

How it works

Also called demand-pull production, just-in-time means that stock levels of raw materials, components, work in progress, and finished goods are kept as low as possible, reducing costs. The system requires detailed planning, scheduling, and flow of resources throughout the production process, now assisted by sophisticated production-scheduling software. Supplies have to be delivered directly to the production line when they are needed, requiring strong relationships and interconnected systems with suppliers. The benefits of reduced inventory are balanced against the cost of frequent deliveries and loss of purchasing economies of scale (discounts for bulk buying). The system dates back to 1953, the year Toyota brought in just-in-time manufacturing. The phrase is sometimes used in a more general sense today to mean eliminating waste of resources.

JUST-IN-TIME PROS AND CONS

Pros

- ❯ **Lower stock** so less storage space and less working capital needed
- ❯ **Demand-pull** avoids obsolete, out-of-date stock
- ❯ **Staff** spend less time checking and moving items

Cons

- ❯ **No room for error**—for instance, if there are any faults in the stock delivered, the whole day's production is halted
- ❯ **Operation** is reliant on suppliers
- ❯ **No cushion** for sudden upsurge in demand

5 NEW STOCK IS DELIVERED TO STORE TO REFILL SHELVES

4 SYSTEM TRIGGERS DELIVERY FROM SUPPLIER WHEN MINIMUM STOCK LEVEL REACHED

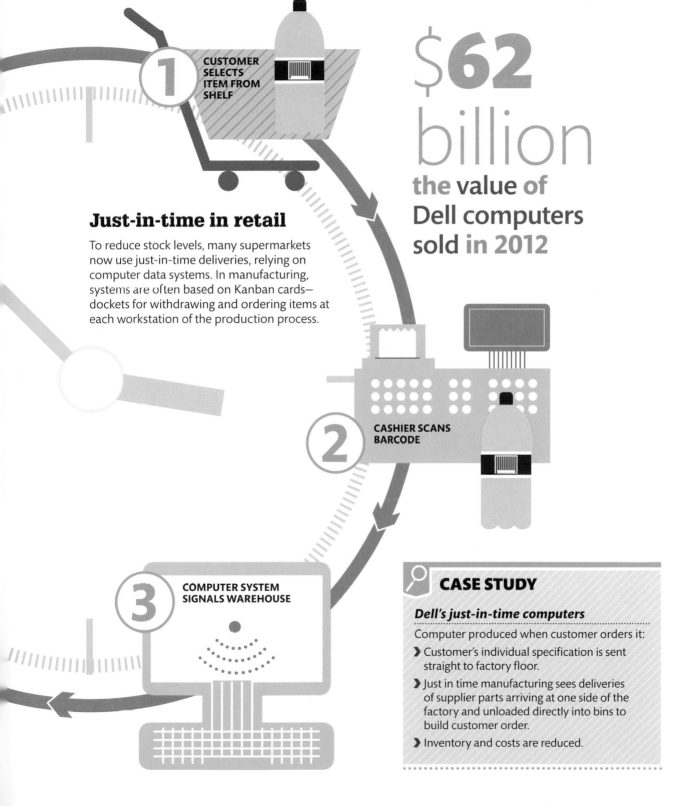

1 CUSTOMER SELECTS ITEM FROM SHELF

$62 billion
the value of Dell computers sold in 2012

Just-in-time in retail

To reduce stock levels, many supermarkets now use just-in-time deliveries, relying on computer data systems. In manufacturing, systems are often based on Kanban cards—dockets for withdrawing and ordering items at each workstation of the production process.

2 CASHIER SCANS BARCODE

3 COMPUTER SYSTEM SIGNALS WAREHOUSE

CASE STUDY

Dell's just-in-time computers

Computer produced when customer orders it:

❯ Customer's individual specification is sent straight to factory floor.

❯ Just in time manufacturing sees deliveries of supplier parts arriving at one side of the factory and unloaded directly into bins to build customer order.

❯ Inventory and costs are reduced.

Total quality management

Success though customer satisfaction is the ethos of total quality management (TQM). Everything a company does is relevant, and the focus is on managing and improving processes rather than outcomes.

How it works

Companies use TQM to create a customer-focused organization that involves all employees in continuous improvement. It is a strategic and systematic approach that puts quality at the heart of the organization's activities and culture. Customers determine the level of quality, measured through their satisfaction. The organization is viewed as a series of horizontal processes that take inputs from suppliers through to the outputs that are delivered to the customer. Recording and measuring performance data is critical, as is effective communication to maintain momentum.

WHAT TQM MEANS

> **Total** Involves everyone and all activities in the company
> **Quality** Conformity to meeting customer requirements
> **Management** Quality can and must be managed

Case study: The Walt Disney Company

Manufacturing companies, in which the focus is on meeting or exceeding customer expectations by making products within certain specifications, are often used as TQM examples. TQM can also be applied in service industries, of which Disney is a very good example.

"**TQM is a philosophy for managing an organization to meet stakeholder needs without compromising ethical values.**"
Chartered Quality Institute

The Walt Disney Company

Disney's goal is to maximize long-term shareholder value, and part of this involves delivering a magical customer experience at its theme parks.

Focus on the customer

Disney incorporated the TQM concept of quality into its approach to customer service. Its visitors are seen as guests and treated as VIPs and individuals.

Involve everyone in quality

Founder Walt Disney firmly believed in quality and saw it as everyone's job, something that could not be delegated.

Perfect processes

Walt Disney viewed the theme parks as factories producing delight. He built quality by designing processes and repeating them.

12,000

Disneyland "cast members" are employed to make guests happy

Employees

Disney calls its employees "cast members." They are trained in every aspect of delivery, including posture, gestures, facial expressions, and tone of voice.

Exceptional service

Cast members (employees) are focused on delighting the customer—their sole job is to make visitors happy.

Suppliers

Disney collaborates with suppliers—for example, it has partnerships with McDonald's and Coca-Cola—to ensure consistent quality.

Continuous improvement

Walt Disney saw the theme parks as an incomplete product; today, improvements come from the bottom up.

"When does the Three O'Clock Parade start?"

Cast members are trained to answer this common question by responding with the time the parade will be passing a particular point in the park.

Shared purpose

Walt Disney started by defining a company culture based entirely on creating a genuine shared purpose that people would be proud to support.

Integrated systems

Technology supports the experience: for example, the volume of ambient music is the same in all theme parks, delivered through thousands of perfectly placed speakers.

✓ NEED TO KNOW

❯ **American customer satisfaction index (ACSI)**
Cross-industry benchmarks for customer satisfaction in the US; NCSI is the UK equivalent

❯ **Net Promoter Score (NPS®)**
Metric for company performance from the perspective of customers, who are divided into promoters, passives, and detractors

Time-based management

The general approach that recognizes the importance and value of time and seeks to reduce the level of unproductive time in an organization is called time-based management.

How it works

The fast pace of competition means a business that can manage time efficiently will enjoy a significant competitive advantage. This applies to new product development, faster response times to meet changing market and customer needs, and reduced waste. For a business to operate a time-based management system, its people have to be multi-skilled and able to move swiftly between different tasks; its machinery has to be flexible so that production runs can be changed at short notice; and there has to be a culture of mutual trust between workers and managers. Time-based management is a key aspect of lean production.

Case study: managing time in Ford Electronics

Between 1988 and 1994, Ford Motor Company's electronics division implemented a number of change programs. One that used time-based management had a sustained and dramatic impact on the company's performance. A senior leader led the program with visits to the factory, where the focus was on the length of the production cycle and adding value at every stage. The factory worked with suppliers to improve shipment, reliability, and quality of raw materials used.

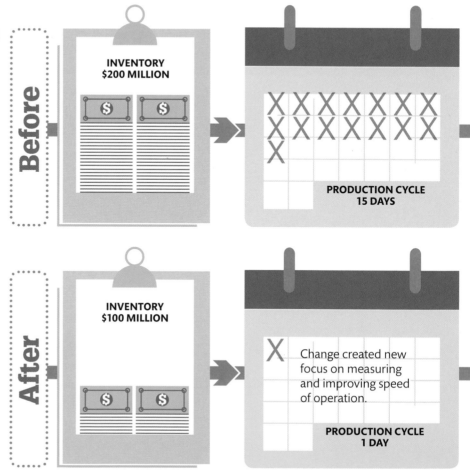

Before

INVENTORY
$200 MILLION

PRODUCTION CYCLE
15 DAYS

After

INVENTORY
$100 MILLION

Change created new focus on measuring and improving speed of operation.

PRODUCTION CYCLE
1 DAY

70%

of companies use formal project-management methodologies

PART OF PROJECT MANAGEMENT

Time-based management is a critical part of project management. Timing aids include:

❯ **Tools** such as Gantt charts show the project schedule as a bar chart, making it easy to plot and monitor daily progress and targets.

❯ **Project management systems** PRINCE2 (PRojects IN Controlled Environments) and similar methods help to structure projects step by step in logical, organized ways.

❯ **Methodologies** such as Agile help project managers working in software development respond to the unpredictable; they are often implemented via the Scrum framework, in which one person takes charge of constant reprioritizing. Based on the premise that software cannot be built up like a product on an assembly line, as it would be out of date before it was released, every area of development is constantly reappraised.

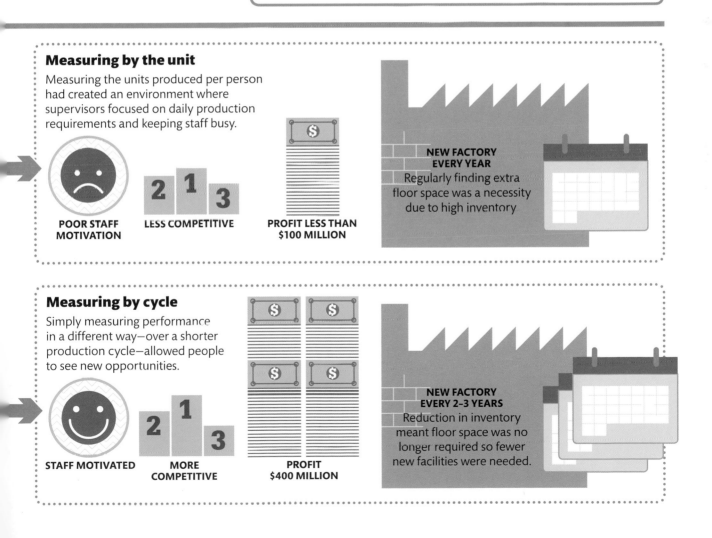

Measuring by the unit

Measuring the units produced per person had created an environment where supervisors focused on daily production requirements and keeping staff busy.

POOR STAFF MOTIVATION

LESS COMPETITIVE

PROFIT LESS THAN $100 MILLION

NEW FACTORY EVERY YEAR
Regularly finding extra floor space was a necessity due to high inventory

Measuring by cycle

Simply measuring performance in a different way—over a shorter production cycle—allowed people to see new opportunities.

STAFF MOTIVATED

MORE COMPETITIVE

PROFIT $400 MILLION

NEW FACTORY EVERY 2–3 YEARS
Reduction in inventory meant floor space was no longer required so fewer new facilities were needed.

Agile production

Speed and agility are the key competitive advantages of agile production: the focus is on rapid response to the customer, enabling the business to take advantage of short windows of opportunity.

How it works

The goal of agile production is to stay ahead of the competition. Often incorporating concepts of lean production (*see pp.288–289*), agile has an extra dimension: meeting customer demand rapidly and effectively. It relies on flexible and collaborative workers, who can deliver swiftly and effectively. The company has to be able to change or increase production quickly. Design of products might incorporate modular concepts, allowing for customization, and strong relationships with suppliers are essential.

Rapid response
Company setup allows it to respond quickly and effectively to customer and market demands

Customer

Customer demand is trigger to start production

Agile manufacturing

The organization has to create a position from which it can alter course as nimbly and swiftly as a cheetah. It needs to be able to retool facilities quickly, modify agreements with suppliers, and continually introduce new ideas and improvements.

Product reaches consumer

Integrated technology
Effective information systems, often linked to suppliers

Continuous innovation
Constant search for new and better ways to deliver for customer

Knowledge culture

Capturing experience, learning from mistakes

Modular products

Independently created parts used in different/customized products

LOCAL EDGE

Agile production is typically adopted by companies in extremely competitive environments with high labor costs, such as North America, where local manufacturing can provide a competitive advantage:

❯ Proximity to customers allows feedback and response.

❯ Small variations in performance and delivery can make a huge difference in customer satisfaction, company reputation, and financial results.

❯ Unprecedented levels of speed and personalization cannot be matched by offshore competitors.

3 months
the time it took **Wikispeed** to develop a revolutionary new car in 2012

Strategic partnerships

Supplier collaboration rather than contract negotiation

Transportation system

Systems, facilities, infrastructure to speed product to customer

Flexible workforce

Self-organizing, adaptable teams

Kaizen

Started in Japan, kaizen is a system of continuous improvement that involves all employees. From senior managers to people on the shop floor, everyone is encouraged to suggest improvements day to day.

How it works

The kaizen philosophy is "to do it better, make it better, improve it even if it isn't broken, because if we don't, we can't compete with those who do." Kaizen is rarely about ideas for major change but has more to do with ongoing, systematic, incremental improvement. A relentless attempt to eliminate unnecessary activities, delay, or waste (*muda*), Kaizen starts with setting high standards and then looking for ways to continually improve those standards. It is supported by a framework of training, communication, and supervision, and results in improved efficiency, productivity, quality, lead time, and customer loyalty.

Creating good change

Kaizen events are implemented through a cycle of activity, known as plan, do, check, act. Central to kaizen are quality, ongoing effort, involvement of every employee as part of their daily work, willingness to change, and communication.

BETTER AND BETTER

Kaizen was created in Japan after World War II. It comes from the Japanese words *kai*, which means "change" or "to correct," and *zen*, which means "good." Companies such as Toyota and Canon have seen significant improvements by involving their employees in recommendations for change.

KAI   ZEN

改 善

CHANGE   GOOD

70 suggestions per employee were implemented at Toyota in 1983

Quality

Innovate—find and implement better ways to meet requirements and increase productivity.

Effort

Gauge measurements against required standards.

Standardize operation and activities; make each improvement standard practice, enshrined in the five foundations, or 5S.

Standardize

Willingness to change

Communication

Measure

People involvement

Measure the operation—for example, the length of the production cycle and amount of in-process inventory.

FIVE FOUNDATIONS

The five steps of workplace organization, known as 5S, are the foundations for continuous improvement in kaizen.

Seiri (Sort)
Keep only essential items in the work area. Remove and store all unnecessary items.

Seiton (Streamline)
Retrieve ordered items swiftly and easily to create efficient workflow.

Seiso (Shine)
Keep the workspace clean, because cleanliness leads to efficiency.

Seiketsu (Standardize)
Keep consistent work practices, tools, and workstations, and make roles clear.

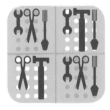

Shitsuke (Sustain)
The four cornerstones above become the standard way to operate all the time.

Product

The items that firms sell to satisfy a consumer need and to make a profit for the business are broadly termed product, whether they are something tangible like toothpaste or an intangible service such as an insurance policy. In a typical life cycle, a product is developed and launched, and a few customers take it up. The domino effect causes wider distribution. Growth eases as the market becomes saturated, and sales flatten and decline until the product is no longer viable.

Product evolution

From start to finish, every product, such as a tube of toothpaste, goes through a process of testing, innovation, and quality control to ensure that it will make the biggest impact on release and throughout its life span. Successful companies understand the limited life span of products and thus invest in the early stages to maximize growth later on.

"A lot of times, people don't know what they want until you show it to them."

Steve Jobs

New product idea

A company decides to release a tube of toothpaste with a new flavor. Its viability is evaluated and potential competition researched. The new toothpaste also requires other qualities, such as whitening and enamel protection, to capture its segment of the market (*see pp.304–305*).

Testing and development

A focus group is assembled to taste the new flavor, along with some variations (*see pp.302–303*). Their preferences and comments are noted, and the toothpaste is developed into a usable product.

$3.6 trillion

the value of goods traded between EU member states in 2013

PRODUCT LIFE SPAN

Home entertainment offers different products to consumers. These are four examples of products at different stages in their life cycle (*see pp.184–185*):

> **Introduction** 3-D televisions—only recently available for the home

> **Growth** Blu-ray players—steady increase in sales because of enhanced viewing experience

> **Maturity** DVD players—challenged by more sophisticated technology

> **Decline** Video recorders—cheaper and more modern viewing formats now available

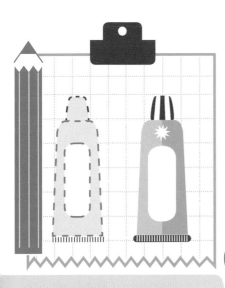

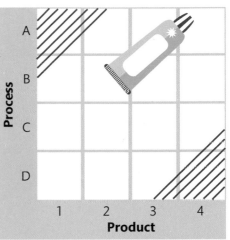

Packaging and design

The toothpaste tube is given a bright, clean, and attractive look. Design considerations include functionality, expense of materials, and an appeal to current trends (*see pp.306–307*).

Quality management

A period of quality control begins, in which standards of safety and comfort are thoroughly checked. It is far cheaper to correct defects in the design phase than later in production (*see pp.308–309*).

Product-process matrix

Using a product-process matrix, the company identifies the correct production method for the toothpaste. Because the company makes only a few products, each at a high volume, it decides to use assembly-line production (*see pp.310–311*).

New product development

Companies cannot stand still. In today's fiercely competitive marketplace, they have to budget for research into new ideas and identify new products to bring to market simply to stay in business.

How it works

New product development is a process with a number of critical stages to ensure that a business focuses its investment on products that will sell and, above all, make a profit. It starts with an idea, possibly to improve and relaunch an existing product. Some companies run sessions to encourage creativity and generate a pool of ideas, a few of which can be explored. They might work with potential customers and also with suppliers, if part of the manufacturing process is to be outsourced, to refine and develop ideas before finally bringing the product to market.

The development process

The nature of the idea and the size of the company affects each stage and how long the product takes to reach the market, but the process is generally the same.

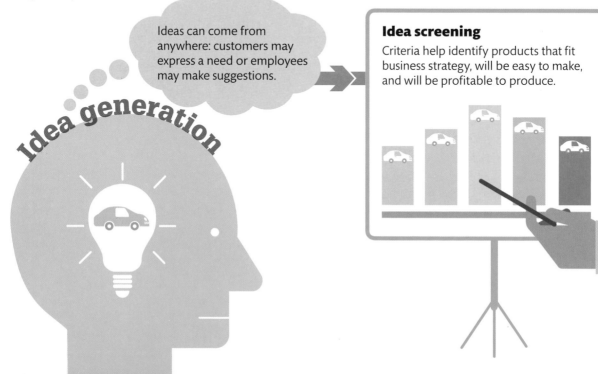

Ideas can come from anywhere: customers may express a need or employees may make suggestions.

Idea generation

Idea screening
Criteria help identify products that fit business strategy, will be easy to make, and will be profitable to produce.

Test concept
Feedback from consumers, using focus groups, interviews, or online evaluation, ensures that an idea is worth pursuing.

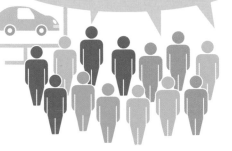

Analyze market
Analysis of opportunity, influenced by predicted growth and trends, helps build a picture of potential sales.

Test market
Product is tested on section of market, perhaps a selected geographic area with good representation of target audience.

Develop products
Features are confirmed, actual product designed—taking account of test-concept stage—and prototype developed.

Launch
Companies ensure distribution and tell customers about new product, through social media or advertising, to kick-start sales.

250,000
new products are launched globally each year

Innovation and invention

Innovating is more than just having a bright idea—it is the way inventions and ideas reach commercial success. It is the lifeblood of any company, because keeping ahead of the game is essential for survival.

How it works

Innovation needs a culture that encourages people to be inventive and explore ideas. It also requires processes that can take initial ideas and develop them. Successful businesses such as the 3M, Apple, and Google technology companies know how to do this. Innovation is not small, incremental changes, but transformational ones, such as solving an existing problem in a radically different way, or identifying an unknown problem and inventing a solution.

From idea to product

Innovation is stimulated by many triggers. The idea then requires people to be working in a conducive environment to ensure that it is implemented and makes a difference.

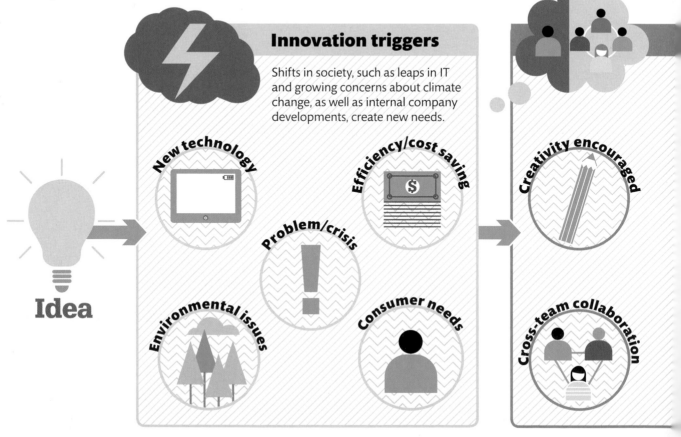

Innovation triggers

Shifts in society, such as leaps in IT and growing concerns about climate change, as well as internal company developments, create new needs.

Idea

New technology

Problem/crisis

Environmental issues

Efficiency/cost saving

Consumer needs

Creativity encouraged

Cross-team collaboration

DIFFERENT TYPES OF INNOVATION

Sustaining innovation Significantly improving existing products, typically through technology—for example, more pixels in cameras, smaller and more powerful laptops

Sustainable or eco-innovation New product that has minimal impact on the environment

Frugal innovation Low-cost product for emerging mass market

Breakthrough innovation Product or service that simultaneously shifts a market and has significant outcomes for the world at large, such as the Fairtrade initiative

Disruptive innovation Displaces established competitors or changes the norm—for instance, the internet or iPads

> "Genius is one per cent inspiration, and ninety-nine per cent perspiration."
> Thomas Edison

Intellectual property (IP) is the expression of an idea. IP might be a design, an invention, or another type of intellectual creation, and it can be protected by law—for example, with a patent.

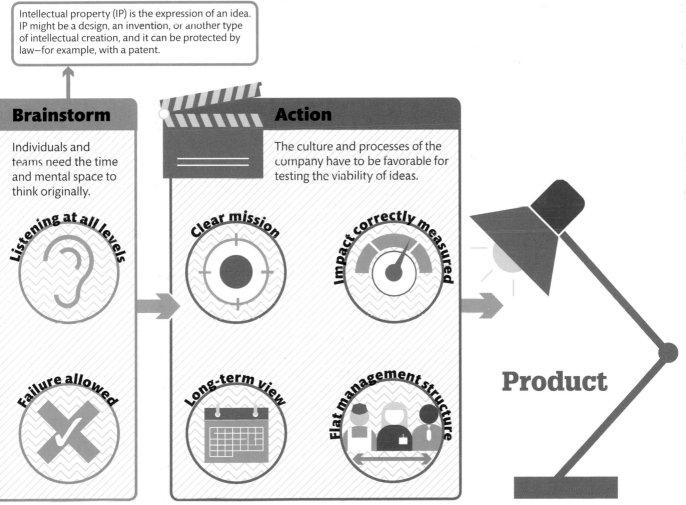

Brainstorm

Individuals and teams need the time and mental space to think originally.

Listening at all levels

Failure allowed

Action

The culture and processes of the company have to be favorable for testing the viability of ideas.

Clear mission

Impact correctly measured

Long-term view

Flat management structure

Product

Design

Any product has to be well designed to succeed. Excellent designs for everyday items—from the Anglepoise lamp to reflective road signs—have shaped our modern world.

How it works

The starting point for design is an idea for a product that fulfills a need, whether it is a specialty item or something in day-to-day use. The designer has to think of ways in which a product can serve its purpose and meet other criteria, including aesthetics, cost, durability, and environmental considerations. The design may be integral to the product, such as Apple's rectangular devices with rounded corners, for which it obtained a design patent. Some designs are iconic, such as the Coca-Cola bottle. Yet design is more than just shape. As well as functionality, it includes materials and color, and extends from the products to their packaging.

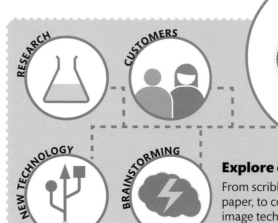

RESEARCH

CUSTOMERS

NEW TECHNOLOGY

BRAINSTORMING

IDEAS

Explore concept

From scribbles on a piece of paper, to computer-generated image technology, it may help to visualize options.

Product-design process

Designs for mass-produced items, such as furniture, lighting, domestic appliances, and communications technology, take a lot of hard work. The process of creating a functional design that looks good has several steps.

CONSIDERATIONS FOR DESIGN SUCCESS

> **Functional** Serves a purpose
> **Aesthetic** Enjoyable to use
> **Innovative** Different and new, possibly using innovative technology
> **Easy to use** Understandable and with useful features
> **Simple** Unobtrusive, subtle
> **Long-lasting** Sustainable, not too fashion-sensitive
> **Environmentally friendly** Minimizes resources and pollution

Redesign

Next year, the product may need revamping.

End product

The design of the final version that goes on sale may look very different from the initial concept.

Develop concept

The design can be broken into components, such as functional requirements and production options, and each evaluated independently.

Make prototype

This might be a single item or a series of prototypes, to test and refine the functionality.

10–18%
of the budget for bringing a new product to market is spent on design

Feedback

Now is the time to find out what people think of the product and how it could be improved.

Design decisions

Before full-scale production begins, all decisions have to be made and paperwork, such as intellectual property rights, finalized.

CUSTOMERS (EXTERNAL)

MANUFACTURING

MARKETING (INTERNAL)

Quality management

For businesses, quality is not a vague term but a philosophy of meeting or going beyond consumer expectations. Excellent quality management can give a company a key competitive edge.

How it works

Many consumers might find it hard to define quality, because it can be subjective, but they know it when they see it. However, companies need to define and measure it. They know that to build a good reputation and thrive, they have to exceed customers' expectations in terms of quality for both products and services. To do this, they have a number of standards or key performance indicators (KPIs) for the manufacturing process, and continually measure themselves against these. Quality does not apply just to the product or service itself; it ripples out to the associated people and processes, and across the organizational environment.

Cost of quality

Quality management is essential to ensure that any defects are nipped in the bud, the earlier the better, and definitely before they become apparent to the consumer.

CUSTOMER FIRST

Before the 1970s, quality was seen as something to be inspected and corrected. Then US businesses began to lose out to Japanese companies—for example, Toyota and Honda were able to produce cars at lower cost and with a much higher quality. The difference was that quality had a strategic meaning for Japanese firms—they made the customer their priority and were the first companies to define quality as meeting or exceeding customer expectations.

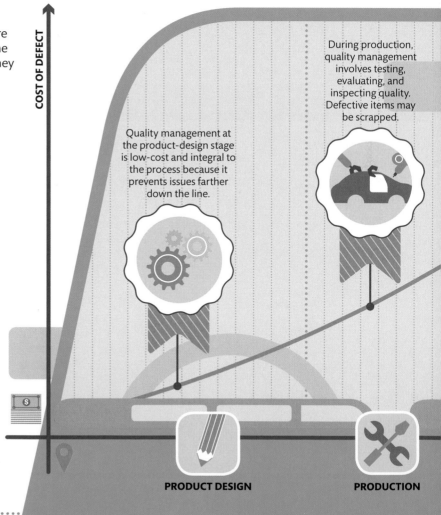

COST OF DEFECT

Quality management at the product-design stage is low-cost and integral to the process because it prevents issues farther down the line.

During production, quality management involves testing, evaluating, and inspecting quality. Defective items may be scrapped.

PRODUCT DESIGN

PRODUCTION

$3.6 million

the annual saving Singapore supermarket NTUC FairPrice made by implementing ISO quality standards, 1999–2009

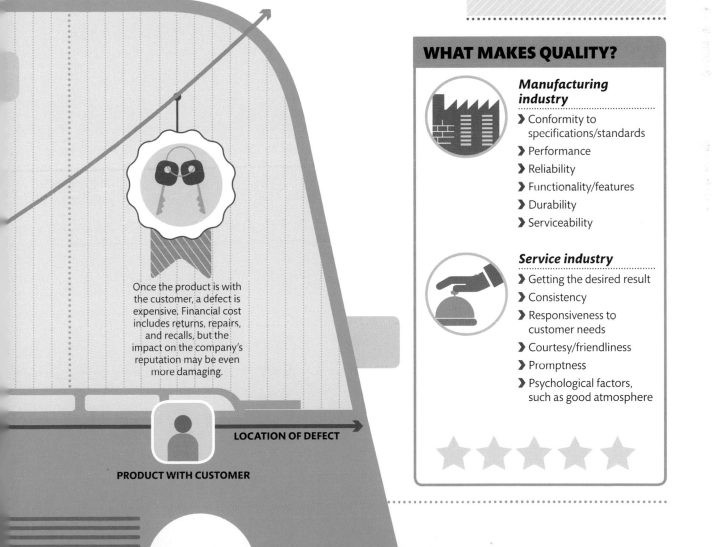

Once the product is with the customer, a defect is expensive. Financial cost includes returns, repairs, and recalls, but the impact on the company's reputation may be even more damaging.

LOCATION OF DEFECT

PRODUCT WITH CUSTOMER

WHAT MAKES QUALITY?

Manufacturing industry

❯ Conformity to specifications/standards
❯ Performance
❯ Reliability
❯ Functionality/features
❯ Durability
❯ Serviceability

Service industry

❯ Getting the desired result
❯ Consistency
❯ Responsiveness to customer needs
❯ Courtesy/friendliness
❯ Promptness
❯ Psychological factors, such as good atmosphere

Product-process matrix

A product-process matrix is a tool that can help a business to identify the best way to make a product, based on volume and the level of customization.

How it works

Products pass through different stages and so does the production process. Businesses typically start with low volume and are highly flexible but not very cost-efficient. A print shop or dressmaker is an example of a company positioned in the bottom left-hand corner of the product-process matrix, where each job is unique and job production is most effective. Production stages then progress through increasing standardization and mechanization to full automation. Companies in the top right-hand corner have high-volume products and a small range so continuous flow production is the best option.

Choosing the best method

A business, or business unit in a large company, occupies a particular region in the matrix. Different processes suit different products, depending on the stage of their life cycle and the scale of the business.

EVOLVING PROCESS

The product-process matrix was first introduced by Harvard academics Robert H. Hayes and Steven C. Wheelwright in the *Harvard Business Review* in 1979. Since then, some companies have worked out the apparent contradiction of how to customize high-volume products (mass customization). Nevertheless, the product-process matrix remains relevant in many industries.

NOT VIABLE

Product

Low volume
Low standardization; unique, one-off products

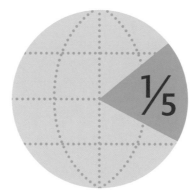

China **accounts for** one-fifth **of** global manufacturing

Dressmaker

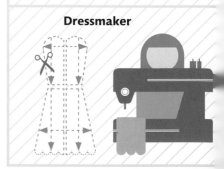

Process

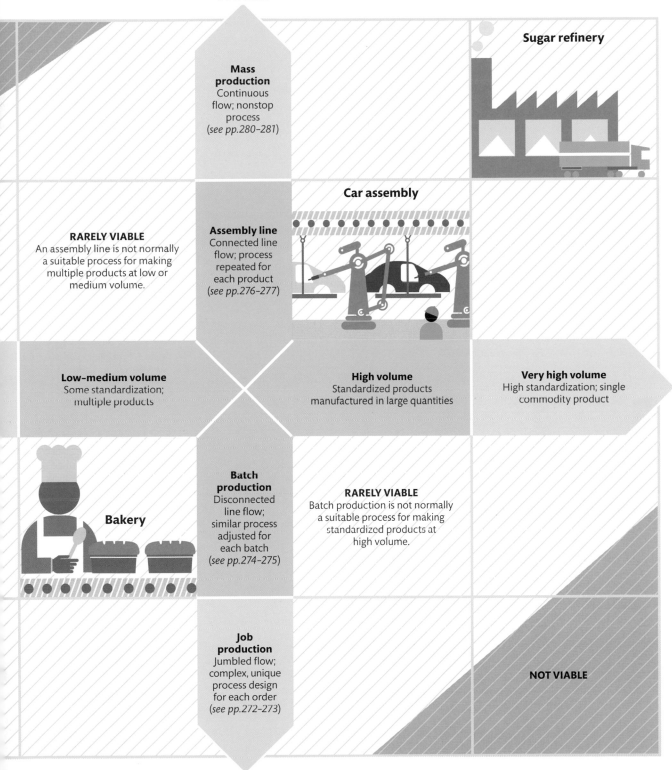

Mass production
Continuous flow; nonstop process
(*see pp.280–281*)

Sugar refinery

Car assembly

RARELY VIABLE
An assembly line is not normally a suitable process for making multiple products at low or medium volume.

Assembly line
Connected line flow; process repeated for each product
(*see pp.276–277*)

Low-medium volume
Some standardization; multiple products

High volume
Standardized products manufactured in large quantities

Very high volume
High standardization; single commodity product

Batch production
Disconnected line flow; similar process adjusted for each batch
(*see pp.274–275*)

Bakery

RARELY VIABLE
Batch production is not normally a suitable process for making standardized products at high volume.

Job production
Jumbled flow; complex, unique process design for each order
(*see pp.272–273*)

NOT VIABLE

Control

Essential in any type of organization, control is fundamental when the primary goal is to generate profits. Control needs to cover costs, resources, and quality of the product or service to ensure that the operation runs smoothly. As well as crossing departments, control has to run from top to bottom, with directors formulating strategy while managers allocate resources, people, materials, and equipment and oversee the work of individuals and teams.

The chain of control

It is simplest to think of a business as an end-to-end chain. Leaders have to make decisions on business goals, strategy, and policies at the start of the chain. This is critical for control along the chain. If there is no clear direction from the start, problems become exacerbated as they travel farther along the line. Controls are put in place all the way along the chain to ensure that the organization is working toward its goals, that it meets the desired standards, and that individuals and teams are clear about what is involved in specific tasks.

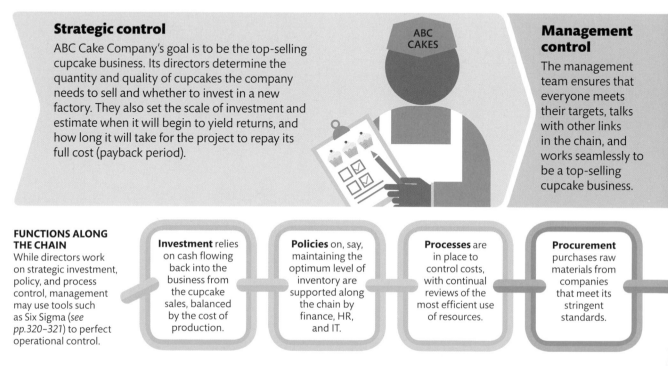

Strategic control

ABC Cake Company's goal is to be the top-selling cupcake business. Its directors determine the quantity and quality of cupcakes the company needs to sell and whether to invest in a new factory. They also set the scale of investment and estimate when it will begin to yield returns, and how long it will take for the project to repay its full cost (payback period).

ABC CAKES

Management control

The management team ensures that everyone meets their targets, talks with other links in the chain, and works seamlessly to be a top-selling cupcake business.

FUNCTIONS ALONG THE CHAIN
While directors work on strategic investment, policy, and process control, management may use tools such as Six Sigma (see pp.320–321) to perfect operational control.

Investment relies on cash flowing back into the business from the cupcake sales, balanced by the cost of production.

Policies on, say, maintaining the optimum level of inventory are supported along the chain by finance, HR, and IT.

Processes are in place to control costs, with continual reviews of the most efficient use of resources.

Procurement purchases raw materials from companies that meet its stringent standards.

130:1

the average ratio of CEO
to employee pay of FTSE 100
companies in 2014—compared
with a ratio of 47:1 in 1998

LEGALLY IMPOSED CONTROL

Many industries are subject to
external controls as well as their own:

❯ **Financial institutions** National and
international regulatory controls

❯ **Advertising industry** National
regulation to protect public interest

❯ **Health and social care** National
laws to protect vulnerable members
of the public

❯ **Manufacturing** National
regulations on health and safety

"Drive thy business
or it will drive thee."

Benjamin Franklin

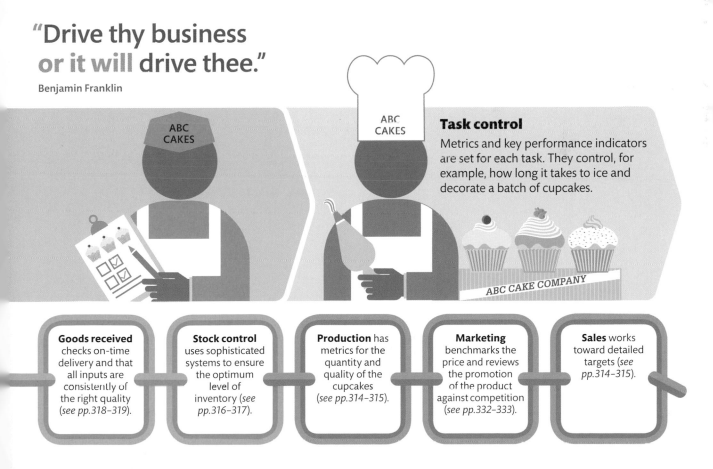

ABC CAKES

ABC CAKES

ABC CAKE COMPANY

Task control

Metrics and key performance indicators
are set for each task. They control, for
example, how long it takes to ice and
decorate a batch of cupcakes.

Goods received
checks on-time
delivery and that
all inputs are
consistently of
the right quality
(see pp.318–319).

Stock control
uses sophisticated
systems to ensure
the optimum
level of
inventory (see
pp.316–317).

Production has
metrics for the
quantity and
quality of the
cupcakes
(see pp.314–315).

Marketing
benchmarks the
price and reviews
the promotion
of the product
against competition
(see pp.332–333).

Sales works
toward detailed
targets (see
pp.314–315).

Managing capacity

In terms of production, capacity means how much work can be achieved in a given time. Ideally, a business matches its capacity to customer demand, using its resources with maximum efficiency.

How it works

Every business has to consider how much capacity it needs for its operation, and how to manage this capacity both day-to-day and in the future. Management has to choose a priority: whether to deliver excellent customer service by having extra capacity, and thus price its products or services high; or to manage its resources efficiently for a better return on investment, at the risk of disappointing customers if and when demand goes beyond capacity. Businesses may offer consumers incentives to help manage capacity—for instance, cheaper late-morning train fares encourage passengers to travel after rush hour, easing overcrowding on trains that are full to capacity in the early morning. Likewise, many hotel chains do not charge a fixed price for rooms, pricing them according to demand to maintain capacity.

Capacity decisions

The fundamental decision is whether to compromise on demand or capacity—whether to put customers or the streamlining of operational costs first.

Customer focus

The company, in this case a car dealer, keeps more cars in stock than required so it can always satisfy customer demand.

Manage capacity— raise prices

Customers are happy to have a product immediately but must pay a higher price to cover the cost of holding excess stock.

Increase demand

To use up stock, pricing policies increase demand by encouraging customers to buy fast—for example, offering on-site deals for older car models.

SALE

HOW CAPACITY AFFECTS A COMPANY

Capacity management is critical to ensure, for example, that a manufacturing operation has the right level of resources to work to a production schedule. It affects many areas of the business, as all are interlinked and cost the company money:

❯ Factory or office size
❯ What and how much equipment is needed

❯ Staffing levels
❯ Use of labor—for example, shift work
❯ Which materials to use, how much/how often to order
❯ Inventory (stock) levels
❯ Production scheduling
❯ Speed and ease of processes
❯ Type of information technology used

✓ NEED TO KNOW

❯ **Potential capacity** The capacity that can be made available long-term, a factor that affects investment decisions and business growth
❯ **Immediate capacity** The maximum potential capacity available in the short term
❯ **Effective capacity** The total capacity that is realistically achievable when all resources are being used optimally

Resource focus

The company uses resources as efficiently as possible. Wastage is kept to a minimum, but satisfying demand is hard because work is at full capacity and output cannot rise.

90 million
the number of iPhone 6 units made by one manufacturer to meet demand in 2014

Manage capacity—keep stock low

It produces stock according to demand and holds low inventory to minimize unnecessary spending and storage costs.

Demand not satisfied

Company is unable to meet surges in demand; customers may have to wait while production catches up, and business may be lost to competitors.

Inventory

Companies have to manage inventory (stock) to meet customer demand, even if they trade online and have no physical storefront. Successful inventory management is a complex process.

How it works

Stock may include finished goods, work in progress, and raw materials. Getting the right level is a balance between having enough to meet customer demand and having too much, which is costly in terms of finished goods, storage space, and warehouse staff. Stock may also lose value if it perishes or become unsalable because of changes in fashion or obsolete technology.

Effective inventory management involves systems and programs for sales forecasts, production targets, and actual inventory status, plus the physical tracking and handling of the different items. Bar codes and radio-frequency identification (RFID) tags have revolutionized inventory management, making it much easier to monitor stock levels.

Inventory management

Successful inventory management is a fine balance between satisfied customers and minimizing the risk of holding too much stock. In this example, the clothing company is managing the supply of T-shirts for a range of sites and for direct delivery to customers.

Make sales forecasts

The company sets production targets based on prediction of demand.

Order from suppliers

Decisions on the level of raw materials to hold are based on lead times and reliability of suppliers.

Production

The quality of raw materials and finished goods is checked at every stage of production.

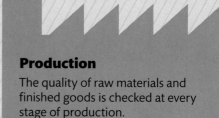

Smaller storage

Firm may use smaller facilities to hold buffer stock—for example, to meet seasonal demand.

✓ NEED TO KNOW

> **First in, first out (FIFO)** Oldest inventory items sold first (or recorded as sold for accounting purposes rather than physically moving goods)

> **Last in, first out (LIFO)** Most recently produced items sold first (or recorded as sold)

> **Stock-keeping unit (SKU)** A distinct item that has its own stock code

> **RFID tag** A chip that enables remote tracking of an item by radio sensors

142,000
different items were handled by Walmart Supercenters in any one store in 2005

Main warehouse

Company may have one main warehouse or a number of warehouses as hubs for smaller storage facilities.

Delivery to customers

Efficient and timely delivery is part of the overall customer experience, especially as online shopping grows. Stock is checked in by scanning bar codes or RFID tags.

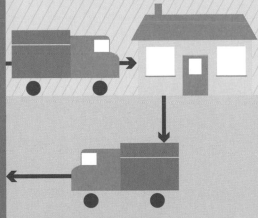

Customer returns

Returns are checked out by scanning bar codes or RFID tags. Batch number and other data can be monitored.

Quality control

There is a series of processes to ensure that a business maintains a prescribed level of quality in its products or services. Quality control is particularly important in industries where safety is an issue.

How it works

Businesses measure and manage the quality of their output against national legal standards and/or internal standards. For example, the manufacturing industry sets its own standards. Checking takes place against these and any national standards at various points along the production process, such as when raw materials arrive in the factory, during production, and before shipment of finished goods to the customer.

Quality control relies on a predetermined percentage of products for inspection, agreed corrective action, and remedial efforts to minimize future defects. Industries in which safety is paramount, including food, clothing, pharmaceuticals, construction, and car, train, and aircraft manufacture, are subject to extremely strict standards of quality control. Some are there to protect workers—for instance, if they are handling chemicals—while others safeguard the consumer.

The bread and butter of quality control

Hygiene and safety are essential in the food industry, as in this example of quality control in a factory making prepacked sandwiches. Samples are tested all along the line. Any lapses in quality are not only a dangerous health hazard but would also be extremely damaging to the company's reputation.

Delivery to factory

Before assembly, weight, chemicals, bacteria, taste, and interaction of individual ingredients are tested.

Assembly line

During assembly, weight, temperature, hygiene, and visual appearance are assessed.

THE CONSTRUCTION INDUSTRY

Standard safety procedures are mandatory in developed countries, including site organization with suitable work gear, limited access, materials storage, and traffic flow; working at heights using appropriate ladders and scaffolds; and avoidance of slips and trips with awareness of obstacles, trailing cables, and uneven or wet surfaces.

$4.4 billion

the value of the prepacked sandwich market in the UK

Packaging station

Samples are tested to check that sealing is accurate, labels are correctly applied, and overall presentation is good.

Storage

The temperature is checked for accuracy and safety, and samples are tested for taste, texture, and contamination by foreign objects.

Transportation

The temperature in the vehicles and their delivery time are checked to ensure product freshness.

Six Sigma

Used in organizations to strive for near-perfect products and services, Six Sigma is a disciplined, data-driven approach for eliminating defects in any process.

How it works

The idea is that measuring the number of defects in any process makes it possible to systematically work out how to eliminate them and get as close to zero defects as possible. Individuals are trained to become experts in the different methods, creating a cadre of black belts, green belts, and champions.

Every Six Sigma project is carefully documented, follows a defined sequence of steps, and has quantified value targets, such as increasing customer satisfaction or reducing costs. To achieve Six Sigma quality, a manufacturing process must have 99.99966 percent of output free of defects (3.4 defective parts per million).

SIX SIGMA ROLES

Six Sigma professionals are experts at improving processes. They drive the implementation of change.

 Master black belt Trains and coaches black belts and green belts; works at highest level, developing key measures and the strategic direction

 Black belt Leads problem-solving projects; coaches project teams, assigning roles and responsibilities; trains green belts

 Green belt Leads green-belt projects; helps with data collection and analysis for black-belt projects

 Champions Translate the company's vision, mission, and goals to create an organizational deployment (OD) plan and identify individual projects

 Executives Provide overall alignment by establishing strategic focus of the Six Sigma program within the context of the organization's culture and its vision of what the customer sees and feels

5 Control

Perform before-and-after analysis; monitor systems; document results; work out recommendations for next steps.

4 Improve

Implement improvements and so address the root causes of major problems.

$320 million

the sum saved by General Electric with Six Sigma in 1997

1

Define

Define the project's purpose and scope; identify processes that need improvement; determine customer needs and benefits.

Striving for perfection

The DMAIC methodology (standing for Define, Measure, Analyze, Improve, Control) is an integral part of Six Sigma. It is used for improving existing business processes that are falling below targets and where step-by-step improvements can be made.

2

Measure

Use data on current processes as a baseline; pinpoint problem locations and occurrences; identify potential areas for improvement.

3

Analyze

Identify root causes of problems and check them against data; determine precise improvements that need to be made.

CHAMPIONS

Mobile-phone maker Motorola used Six Sigma quality as a goal for its manufacturing operations; CEO and chairman Jack Welch made it central to his business strategy at General Electric in the 1990s; tech company Dell has used a form of Six Sigma since 2000 and is now the model for many other businesses.

2/3

of Fortune 500 US organizations were running Six Sigma initiatives by the late 1990s, with the goal of improving quality and reducing costs

Supply chain

Along the journey from raw material to finished item in the hands of a consumer, every business needs an efficient supply chain. Supply chain management involves different organizations, people, activities, and resources to take, for example, grains of corn from a field to a finished box of cornflakes on the consumer's breakfast table. The company may outsource parts of the chain to other firms. It may also send some activities, typically administrative functions, offshore.

Supply chain management

The traditional supply chain takes raw materials and resources through to a finished product for the consumer. The company has to manage costs and ensure standards, being particularly careful that it does not harm people or the environment along the way, from fair wages for labor at the source to recyclable packaging after consumption. Supply chain is big business—in the US, 4.2 million people are employed in warehousing and transport alone.

Raw materials and resources
Whether from a field or a mine, raw materials start somewhere.

Supplier and processor
The raw materials are processed, often near their source.

Manufacturer
Organizations bring resources together to manufacture goods, often near the customer.

$688 billion

the cost of supply chain transportation in the US, in 2009

EXTENDING THE CHAIN

- **Adding value** Companies may try to add value along the chain, rather than just seeing it as a way to transport a product from A to B (*see pp.324–325*).
- **Delegating functions** To save money and use specialized expertise, the business can outsource activities and/or have them done by local companies or a branch of its own company offshore (*see pp.326–329*).
- **Returning goods** Part of the supply chain involves an efficient system for dealing with goods returned by the consumer (*see pp.330–331*).
- **Competitive edge** At every stage, the company compares its performance with its competitors to see how it can improve (*see pp.332–333*).
- **Ethics and the environment** Taking responsibility for avoiding pollution and protecting workers' rights is part of the package (*see pp.334–335*).

Distribution
Finished goods are transported to storage depots or retailers.

Retailer
The store displays the products for maximum appeal to the consumer.

Consumer
The consumer enjoys the finished product, and ideally recycles the packaging.

Value chain

Rather than looking at the supply chain as merely a series of activities, organizations are increasingly looking at how value is created by each stage of the process. Lowering costs or raising performance are key.

How it works

Harvard Business School professor Michael Porter first introduced the concept of a value chain in his book *Competitive Advantage*. Most organizations have dozens—possibly hundreds—of activities along the supply chain in the process of converting raw materials (inputs) to products or services (outputs). These can be classified generally as either primary or support activities that all businesses must undertake. The idea of the value chain is that how activities are organized and carried out determines a company's costs and thus its margin (profit). Each link of the chain must communicate to other departments clearly and promptly. For example, marketing and sales must make accurate sales forecasts and pass them on in time for procurement to buy the correct type and quantity of raw materials, who in turn must connect with inbound logistics so they can organize receipt of goods.

Porter's value chain

Primary activities work directly to create or deliver a product or service, while support activities help to improve their efficiency. To apply the value chain, a company has to identify each activity and either lower its cost or differentiate it from its competitors to add value in the customer's eye.

CASE STUDY

Pizza Hut's value chain

Pizza Hut's greatest asset is breaking down complex pizza-making into simple steps unskilled chefs can do.

> **Inbound logistics** Vast global purchase orders for ingredients

> **Operations** Target countries with a liking for Italian food, on a franchise model with local staff

> **Outbound logistics** In-house meals and home delivery service

> **Marketing** Differentiate from other pizza chains

> **Service** Delicious, convenient pizzas at a fair price

PRIMARY ACTIVITIES Each department must cooperate and provide necessary information between value-chain activities to make a profit.

Inbound logistics
Involves relationships with suppliers, including all activities to receive, store, and allocate inputs

Operations
Activities required to transform inputs into outputs

SUPPORT ACTIVITIES Although not directly involved in outputs, these support primary activities, improving their efficiency and successful function.

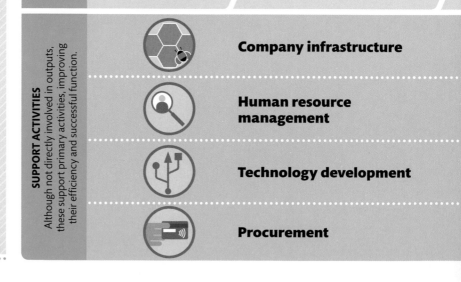

Company infrastructure

Human resource management

Technology development

Procurement

ONLINE VALUE CHAIN

More than a quarter of the world's population uses the internet for everyday activities, from shopping and banking to sharing photos and watching TV. To handle this volume, a complex value chain delivers internet services, made up of global and local firms with assets as diverse as content rights, communications and IT infrastructure, proprietary software, and global brands.

$1.93 trillion

the internet value chain revenue in the US, in 2008

Outbound logistics
Activities required to collect, store, and distribute the output

Marketing and sales
Activities that inform buyers, encourage purchase, and facilitate transaction

Service
Activities to keep product working effectively for buyer after it is received

PROFIT MARGIN
Profit equals the customer's willingness to pay more than the sum of all the activities in the value chain.

Functions such as accounting, legal, finance, planning, public affairs, and quality assurance

People activities: recruiting, hiring, training, developing, compensating, and terminating

Equipment, hardware, software, procedures, and technical knowledge used in transformation of inputs into outputs

Acquisition of inputs (raw materials) for the company

Outsourcing

Firms may choose to pay outside suppliers to do work rather than complete the tasks internally. Handing over part or all of production or a service to a third party increases flexibility.

How it works

Outsourcing grew in the 1980s because firms looked to save costs by contracting peripheral business activities to third parties. But outsourcing today is no longer just about cost savings. It is a strategic tool that is increasingly important in the global economy in the 21st century. Firms may choose outsourcing for elements of the production process, for support functions such as accounting, or because they do not have the specialized knowledge or skills within the organization. Outsourcing may be to a firm in the same country or it may be to an organization in another country. Rapid expansion of logistics networks and information technology has made it easier to outsource, thus accelerating the growth of outsourcing over the last decade.

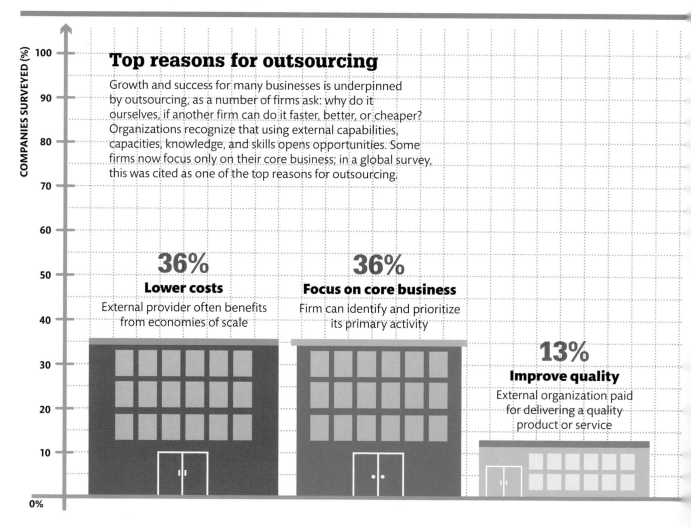

COMPANIES SURVEYED (%)

100 — 90 — 80 — 70 — 60 — 50 — 40 — 30 — 20 — 10 — 0%

Top reasons for outsourcing

Growth and success for many businesses is underpinned by outsourcing, as a number of firms ask: why do it ourselves, if another firm can do it faster, better, or cheaper? Organizations recognize that using external capabilities, capacities, knowledge, and skills opens opportunities. Some firms now focus only on their core business; in a global survey, this was cited as one of the top reasons for outsourcing.

36%
Lower costs
External provider often benefits from economies of scale

36%
Focus on core business
Firm can identify and prioritize its primary activity

13%
Improve quality
External organization paid for delivering a quality product or service

✓ NEED TO KNOW

❯ **Outsource** To subcontract work to another company or to buy in components for a product rather than manufacture them

❯ **Offshore** The practice of moving a company's operating base to a foreign country where labor costs are cheaper

❯ **Network structure** The task or operation is performed by another firm—which may be in the same country, a neighboring country, or overseas—within a network structure of organizations

90%
of firms worldwide **say outsourcing is crucial to** growth strategies

EXAMPLES OF BUSINESS TASKS THAT CAN BE OUTSOURCED

Outsourcing certain tasks within a business enables focus to remain on core business activities, which helps generate growth as well as income. Some tasks are better suited to outsourcing than others due to factors including expertise, how time consuming a task is, and how much face-to-face time it requires. IT operations, for example, can be highly expensive, requiring expert knowledge and can easily be managed remotely. Human resources, however, is more employee focussed, so better suited to in-house.

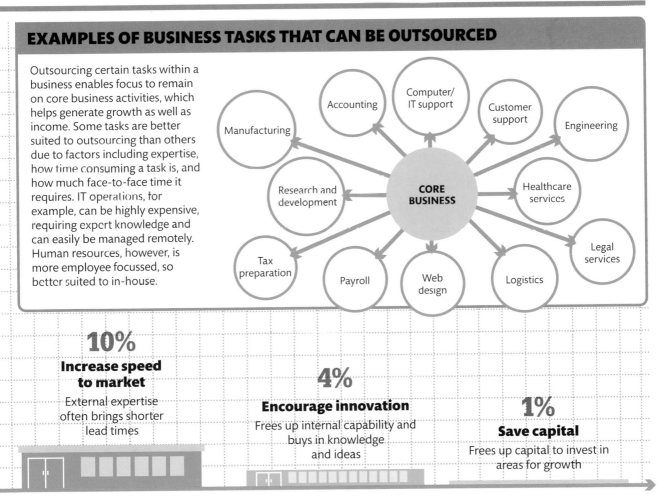

10%
Increase speed to market
External expertise often brings shorter lead times

4%
Encourage innovation
Frees up internal capability and buys in knowledge and ideas

1%
Save capital
Frees up capital to invest in areas for growth

REASON

Offshoring

Moving jobs outside the country where a company is based is called offshoring. Either the company employs people overseas to perform some functions, or work is outsourced to a third party overseas.

How it works

Offshoring grew in the 1980s as Western companies with high labor costs realized they could make significant savings by manufacturing in countries with lower wages. Information technology (IT) services followed, enabled by the internet and global communications. However, companies are now rethinking this strategy, driven by factors including the need to be close to customers, consumer dislike of overseas call centers, high unemployment in Western countries after the 2008 financial crisis, global wage equalization, and growing transportation costs. Some firms are now nearshoring—for instance, US firms placing operations in Canada—or reshoring, bringing activities back to their home country.

Case study: global expertise

Offshoring started in India and today it still leads the way. The country's IT and business processing outsourcing export industries employ more than 2.2 million people and are worth more than $100 billion. Other regions have different areas of expertise—for example, Eastern Europe specializes in IT services.

Examples of offshoring

KEY

- Banking
- IT
- Technology
- Technical support
- Financial services
- Design
- Back-office functions
- Software
- Insurance
- Call centers
- Engineering
- Manufacturing
- Research and development
- Business processes
- Customer support

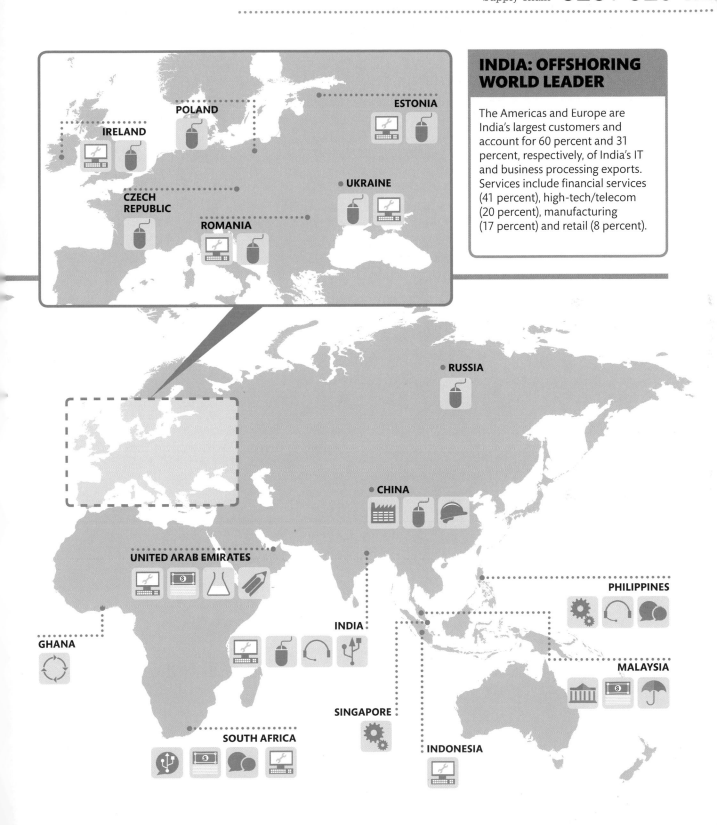

INDIA: OFFSHORING WORLD LEADER

The Americas and Europe are India's largest customers and account for 60 percent and 31 percent, respectively, of India's IT and business processing exports. Services include financial services (41 percent), high-tech/telecom (20 percent), manufacturing (17 percent) and retail (8 percent).

ESTONIA

POLAND

IRELAND

CZECH REPUBLIC

ROMANIA

UKRAINE

RUSSIA

CHINA

UNITED ARAB EMIRATES

GHANA

INDIA

PHILIPPINES

MALAYSIA

SINGAPORE

INDONESIA

SOUTH AFRICA

Reverse supply chain

Supply chain takes a product to a customer. Reverse supply chain is the series of activities it takes to retrieve an unwanted or used product from a customer and dispose of it, recycle, or resell it.

How it works

Companies have to focus on more than simply bringing a product to a customer. Now an efficient reverse supply chain is essential to satisfy consumers, especially for the growing number of online retailers. Manufacturers, too, in industries from carpets to computers, may need reverse supply to recycle products to meet environmental regulations.
For example, companies have to manage products that are returned from consumers for a refund; products that do not sell and are returned to producers from retailers; or products near the end of their life, where disposal may be subject to environmental legislation.

Reverse logistics

The cost to companies of reverse supply is enormous. For example, in the US, statistics from the Reverse Logistics Association suggest that the annual volume of consumer returns is estimated to cost $150–200 billion. This represents about 0.7 percent of gross national product (GNP) and 6 percent of the US's total annual retail sales of $3.5 trillion.

CUSTOMER RETURNS

US retailers Sears and JCPenney were the first stores to allow consumers to return goods with no penalty. This pioneering move in the late 19th century encouraged people to shop with them and helped build a loyal following. British retailer Marks & Spencer at one time had the most lenient returns policy in the retail word—until 2005 they had no time limit on returns, as long as the customer could produce a receipt.

Please return
within 28 days

Retrieve

Companies may have processes in place to collect used or unwanted items, whether from the customer or a retailer.

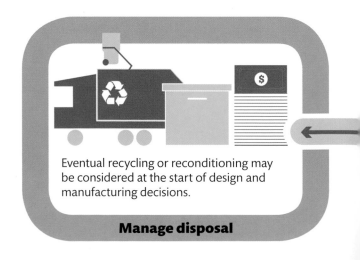

Eventual recycling or reconditioning may be considered at the start of design and manufacturing decisions.

Manage disposal

✓ NEED TO KNOW

❯ **Electronic waste (e-waste)**
Electrical or electronic devices that are unwanted, do not work, or are obsolete

❯ **Warehousing** Administrative and physical functions necessary for storage of goods, either for selling or retrieval

32%
of an item's original product value **could be reclaimed as a result of a well-managed reverse logistics system**

Transport

Customers expect items to be transported back to the seller in a straightforward system, in person or by a delivery service.

Receive

Effective inventory management is critical to ensure that inbound items are recorded so the company can keep track of returns.

Sort

Items and components are sorted and separated, ready for reselling, recycling, or disposal.

Inspect

Items are carefully checked on return. If they are to be resold, they must be in pristine condition.

Benchmarking

Businesses use benchmarking to improve efficiency by comparing their performance with that of other organizations. The goal is to identify and learn from best practices within or outside the industry.

How it works

To improve results, a business may look outside the organization, industry, or country to explore others' levels of performance and identify how they achieve it. Benchmark areas include unit cost, customer ratings, and pay and benefits. The evaluation takes into account a range of factors, including training, technology platforms, and manufacturing equipment. For example, Formula 1 is often used as a benchmark for teamwork as pit-stop crews have perfected the changing of four tires in less than seven seconds.

The process of benchmarking

There are several stages to benchmarking performance before a company can start to see cost savings and increased efficiency.

Identify need to benchmark

In this example, a company wants to improve its energy efficiency.

Company owns a commercial building

Compare to competition

The company gathers information on others' energy systems and costs.

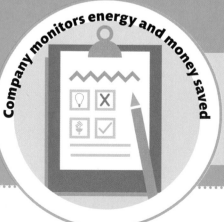

Company monitors energy and money saved

Company replaces lighting

Monitor value

It measures how much its energy costs have gone down and how well the new lighting system works.

SOCIAL MEDIA MAKES IT EASY

It is now easier than ever before for organizations to gather data about their competitors. Social media can provide data on customer preferences, brands, and campaigns of other organizations. Analytical tools are available to simplify benchmarking across many different channels.

49%

of companies across 44 countries used performance benchmarking in 2008

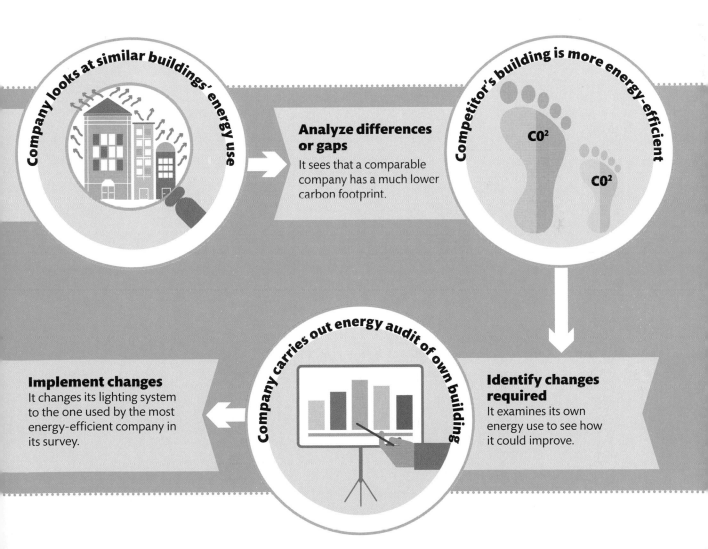

Company looks at similar buildings' energy use

Analyze differences or gaps
It sees that a comparable company has a much lower carbon footprint.

Competitor's building is more energy-efficient

CO_2

CO_2

Identify changes required
It examines its own energy use to see how it could improve.

Company carries out energy audit of own building

Implement changes
It changes its lighting system to the one used by the most energy-efficient company in its survey.

Corporate social responsibility

Businesses today must aim not only to do no harm to the environment, people, or communities, but also to show commitment to building a better society. This is termed corporate social responsibility (CSR).

How it works

For a business, CSR goes further than aiming to be compliant with national or international regulations, managing risks, or corporate philanthropy—it has to be an integral part of every aspect of operations, helping to create a sustainable business. A company still has to be competitive and profitable, but must avoid making decisions merely for short-term gain. Instead, it has to consider the future impact on society, the environment, and a wide range of stakeholders. Companies now report annually on how they have met their CSR and are benchmarked and ranked against competitors.

Community
Housing; healthcare; infrastructure; partnering with local institutions; local supplier initiatives; education; training; local employment

97%
of UK FTSE 100 companies reported on CSR in 2011

Environment
Company's carbon footprint, including recycling; water and waste management; energy use; transportation

Workforce

Workplace safety, health, and well-being; diversity; equal opportunities; learning and development; ethical policies and practices

Suppliers

Fair trade, supply-chain ethics, and sustainability (including use of child labor); code of conduct; transportation policies

CSR stakeholders

A number of different business areas have to be considered in assessing a company's CSR, from how it affects people working in and for the company to wider environmental and community implications.

Operations

Ethical trading including marketing practices and pricing; managing customers; financial reporting; policies; values

 **CASE STUDY**

Fairtrade International

Many consumers expect the companies they buy their latte from to uphold ethical practices. A US campaign in 2000 pressurized Starbucks to serve Fairtrade coffee. The public wanted to understand the coffee giant's supply chain as there was concern for the livelihoods of coffee farmers, many of whom are indigenous people. Fairtrade International ensures that coffee farmers receive a fair price for their crop, plus a premium that is invested in improving farming practices. Coffee was one of the first products to carry the Fairtrade Mark.

How companies work

Businesses in the US are registered in the state in which they are domiciled. Most states and the federal government recognize four business structures: sole proprietorship; partnership; corporation; and nonprofit corporation.

Sole proprietorship

An individual (or married couple) may register their business as a sole proprietorship if they plan to conduct operations on their own. This is the simplest form of business structure. The owner is entitled to all revenues and profits, while maintaining personal responsibility for all debts and liabilities. Income from sole proprietorships is taxed as individual income.

Partnerships

Partnerships are business entities formed by two or more individuals. The most basic form is the general partnership. Partners in a general partnership contribute an agreed-upon share of money, skill, and labor to the enterprise, in exchange for a proportionate share of the profits. Liabilities are thusly divided as well. A limited partnership includes general partners and limited partners (also known as silent partners) who share in the profits but whose losses are generally limited to the size of their initial investment. Similar to a general partnership, a limited liability partnership indemnifies one partner from claims arising from other partners' negligence. Lawyers and doctors frequently operate under this structure.

Corporation

The federal government and states recognize corporations as business entities that are separate and apart from employees and shareholders in terms of income and liabilities. This structure protects management and workers in the case of litigation or other claims, but is more complex and subject to greater regulation than a partnership. Such entities must be registered through articles of incorporation. A corporation may be privately held, in which case equity is shared by a limited group of stock owners. A publicly held corporation makes shares available to the public through a stock exchange or through over-the-counter markets.

Nonprofit corporation

A nonprofit corporation engages in activities meant to further the public good, such as works in charitable, scientific, educational, or artistic fields. Such organizations, most frequently registered with the Internal Revenue Service (IRS) through form 501(c)(3), are generally tax-exempt at the federal and state level. They may in fact make profits and pay competitive salaries, but are prohibited from engaging in political activities.

In Canada

Businesses in Canada can also be sole proprietorships, partnerships, or corporations. They can also be run as cooperatives, a business that it is owned and controlled by its members. Co-ops are often used by agricultural enterprises. Canadian companies must register in the province or territory in which they are domiciled.

Reporting requirements

Businesses in the US are subject to a range of financial reporting requirements and regulations, depending on structure. Owners of sole proprietorships include income on their individual returns filed annually with the IRS. Corporations must also report income to the IRS, but are subject to additional requirements. Privately held corporations must, at a minimum, file charter documents, including name and address, with the Secretary of State in the state in which they are headquartered. Publicly traded corporations are subject to considerably greater disclosure requirements. They must file with the Securities and Exchange Commission quarterly (10-Q) and annual (10-K) reports detailing revenue, income, profits, and losses. They must also file interim reports (8-K) disclosing significant events, such as an acquisition or divestiture, as well as reports (Form 4) that disclose significant buying and selling of shares by company insiders.

Company law

The US Constitution vests in individual states the power to regulate commerce and administer and oversee companies that operate within their borders. States maintain a Department of State or equivalent (such as Massachusetts' Secretary of the Commonwealth) that act as registrar for commercial endeavors. Departments of State maintain publicly searchable databases of all registered companies, hold administrative hearings, and can take enforcement actions.

Taxation

The IRS collects taxes from businesses on behalf of both the federal and state governments. At the time of printing, the federal tax rate on corporations ranged from 15 percent to 35 percent. Tax rates vary widely among states, and six states impose no corporate income tax at all.

The federal government and states do not collect Value Added Taxes (VAT) from businesses, but many states impose sales tax on consumers that businesses collect at the point of sale. Several states have no sales tax. Sales taxes can also vary depending on the item purchased. For example, in New York state, groceries are tax-free, while takeout meals are taxed at the prevailing rate of 4 percent. New York City also applies an additional sales tax of 4.5 percent to most items. Other municipalities around the country are also free to establish their own sales tax rates.

ORGANIZATIONS AND RESOURCES

The Small Business Administration website has information on the corporate structures permitted under US law.
https://www.sba.gov

Taxation

The Internal Revenue Service provides a number of online services for business owners, including when and where to file tax returns and how to obtain tax credits.
http://www.irs.gov/Businesses

Startups

BusinessUSA is a central repository where entrepreneurs can access a range of services. Its website provides information on funding, taxation, hiring, growth strategies, and more. It also offers advice tailored to specific groups, such as women, veterans, and minorities.
http://business.usa.gov

The US Department of the Treasury also offers advice and services for would-be proprietors. In addition, it operates the Small Business Lending Fund, which secures loans made to business owners by private banks.
http://www.treasury.gov

Registering intellectual property

The main arbiter for determining whether a product or business method is worthy of exclusivity is the United States Patent and Trademark Office.
http://www.uspto.gov

Immigration

All employees must be authorized to work in the US through citizenship or some form of visa. US Citizenship and Immigration Services, part of the Department of Homeland Security, determines visa eligibility and enforces immigration rules.

In Canada

The Canada Business Network offers information about starting and operating a business.
http://www.canadabusiness.ca/eng/page/2853/
http://www.entreprisescanada.ca/fra/page/2853/

How finance works

For publicly traded companies, the Securities Exchange Act of 1934 is the framework for financial accounting and reporting. The Securities and Exchange Commission (SEC) enforces the Act.

The SEC has established reporting requirements for companies whose shares trade on public exchanges such as the New York Stock Exchange, the NASDAQ Stock Market, and the NYSE Market LLC. Privately held companies are subject to fewer requirements.

Tax reporting

Both private and public companies must file tax returns to the Internal Revenue Service on an annual basis. The due date varies based on the filer's status. Sole proprietorships follow the same schedule as individuals and must file by April 15 or request an extension. Partnerships must file by the 15th day of the fourth month after the end of their fiscal year. Public companies must file by the 15th of the third month.

Financial disclosure

Exchange-listed companies must make their financial records publicly available on a quarterly and annual basis, respectively. They must report unscheduled, material events (such as an acquisition or divestiture). Officers and insiders must declare significant purchases or sales of company stock, and the terms of issuance for corporate notes must be detailed.

Regulation Fair Disclosure (Reg FD) stipulates that companies must disseminate financial information simultaneously to all investors. The SEC amended Reg FD in 2013 to include disclosures through social-media channels such as Twitter and Facebook.

Public companies must retain a licensed auditing firm to verify the veracity of their financial records. Under SEC rule 3235-AI74 (2003), auditors must retain client records, including worksheets, financial data, meeting minutes, electronic correspondence, and other materials used to form an opinion for seven years.

Reporting standards

Companies must log and report financial transactions to the SEC according to Generally Accepted Accounting Standards (GAAP) as established by the Financial Accounting Standards Board, a private, nonprofit organization. Due to the increasingly global nature of business, there is a movement to adopt International Financial Reporting Standards (IFRS).

In the aftermath of several events in recent years, including the bursting of the so-called dot-com bubble, the increased use of controversial financial instruments like mortgage-backed securities (MBS) and collateralized debt obligations (CDO), and the 2007–2008 financial crisis, the FASB has adopted a number of new rules aimed at restoring order and clarity in the markets.

Accounting periods

For sole proprietorships, the reporting period for tax purposes runs simultaneous to the calendar year. Publicly traded companies may set their own fiscal years. Public companies must file a report for each fiscal quarter, as well as a report at the end of each fiscal year. Reports generally must be released within 45 days after the close of a quarter.

Corporate fraud

In addition to its regulatory functions, the SEC, through its Division of Enforcement, is also the US's chief watchdog when it comes to policing and prosecuting financial fraud. The SEC is mainly on the lookout for several types of misconduct:

False statements. Corporations must report financial information that, to the best of management's knowledge, is complete and accurate.

Insider trading. Corporate insiders, such as officers and executives, can legally buy and sell shares in their companies, but not on the basis of non-public information. For example, a CFO cannot unload shares on the basis of negative financial news that has not yet been released. Insiders are also barred from tipping off friends, family, and business associates.

Ponzi schemes. This is the practice whereby a money manager distributes returns to existing investors from funds acquired from new investors. These schemes generally collapse once a fund runs out of fresh capital. The most infamous Ponzi scheme to date was that orchestrated by fund manager Bernard Madoff, starting in the 1990s and continuing until his arrest in 2008.

Pump and dumps. A "pump and dump" occurs when a brokerage acquires a large amount of stock, spreads false news meant to increase the stock's value, then quickly sells its position before the fraud is uncovered.

Front running. This occurs when a brokerage acquires a block of shares in a particular company before executing a large, pending buy order from a client. The client's order, if large enough, will increase the value of the stock, allowing the firm to profit from its foreknowledge of the transaction.

In Canada

The Toronto Stock Exchange is Canada's largest and most commonly used stock market. It is overseen by the Ontario Securities Commission. Stock markets also operate in Vancouver and Montreal.

Businesses operating in Canada must file tax returns to the Canada Revenue Agency. Forms may be filed through the mail or electronically. Unlike the US, the federal government in Canada imposes a value-added tax known as the Goods and Services Tax (GST). The current rate is 5 percent. The tax is levied on manufacturers and producers throughout the chain of production. In some cases, companies can claim tax credits for VAT already paid. In some provinces, the GST is included in the Harmonized Sales Tax (HST).

ORGANIZATIONS AND RESOURCES

Financial reporting

The Securities and Exchange Commission provides information on financial reporting requirements for publicly listed companies.
http://www.sec.gov

The Financial Accounting Standards Board website features educational webcasts and seminars for finance and accounting professionals.
http://www.fasb.org

The Association of Chartered Accountants in the United States offers online training videos, while the CFA Institute maintains a glossary of finance and investment terms.
http://www.acaus.org
http://www.cfainstitute.org

Corporate fraud

Those who wish to report corporate fraud may approach the SEC directly through its Office of the Whistleblower.
http://www.sec.gov/whistleblower

Similarly, the Internal Revenue Service maintains an office through which the public can anonymously report suspected corporate tax cheats.
http://www.irs.gov

In Canada

The Canada Revenue Agency website has information on the GST and other taxation issues.
http://www.cra-arc.gc.ca

The Ontario Securities Commission offers a number of online resources for companies considering a listing on the Toronto Stock Exchange.
http://www.osc.gov.on.ca

How sales and marketing works

Advertising and marketing in the United States are regulated at both federal and state level. The Federal Trade Commission (FTC) sets national policies and enforces relevant laws passed by Congress.

The First Amendment to the US Constitution restricts the government's ability to limit or inhibit public speech or communication. However, courts over the years have ruled that commercial speech is subject to less protection than noncommercial speech.

The Federal Trade Commission (FTC) was established in 1914 through the Federal Trade Commission Act. Much of the FTC's work involves enforcing truth-in-advertising regulations, a legislative rubric that requires ads to be truthful, not misleading, and backed by scientific data if appropriate. In a case of suspected false advertising, the FTC can sue the perpetrator in federal court to obtain a cease-and-desist order, freeze assets, and obtain recompense for victims. A bill pending in Congress at the time of writing, the Truth In Advertising Act of 2014, would prevent marketers from using digital tools such as Adobe Photoshop to alter the appearance of models' bodies and faces in ads.

The FTC also enforces legislation aimed at electronic marketing communications, such as email campaigns and telemarketing. For example, the Commission can file suit against agencies suspected of violating the National Do Not Call Registry. Telemarketers are forbidden from calling consumers who have entered their numbers in the registry. Similarly, the FTC enforces the CAN-SPAM Act of 2003, which requires marketers to give consumers a means to opt out of receiving future messages.

The Federal Communications Commission (FCC) also has some authority to regulate commercial speech. For instance, the FCC enforces the CALM ACT of 2012, which stipulates that broadcasters and cable companies must air commercials at the same volume as regular programming.

Individual states can set marketing and advertising rules, particularly for highly regulated industries like health care, financial services, and real estate.

At the state level, the Better Business Bureau accepts and responds to complaints regarding companies doing business within state jurisdictions.

In Canada

Freedom of speech and expression in Canada is protected by Section Two of the Canadian Charter of Rights and Freedoms. As is the case in the US, commercial speech is afforded less protection than political or other types of expression. Still, the Charter places numerous limitations on the federal and provincial governments' ability to abridge marketing and advertising communications. For example, Canada's Supreme Court in Ford v. Quebec (1988) struck down a Quebec law that required all advertising signs to be in French.

Commercial speech in Canada is also governed by the Consumer Packaging and Labelling Act (1985). The law prohibits the use of misleading ads and claims on consumer goods.

Data protection

Unlike Europe, with its centralized Data Protection Directive, the US does not have a single, overarching law on data protection. Rather, Congress has passed a series of laws that together form a framework around the safeguarding of consumers' privacy and information. Many of these rules are directed at particular industries. For example, the Department of Health and Human Services enforces the Health Insurance Portability and Accountability Act of 1996 (HIPAA). The Act dictates the administrative, physical, and technical safeguards that health care insurers and providers must follow to protect patient records.

In financial services, the Gramm-Leach-Bliley Act of 1999 stipulates the steps that banks, credit unions, and other financial institutions must follow to safeguard customer data. The act is enforced by the FTC. Other industries are also subject to specific privacy and data protection rules.

Direct marketing

Direct marketing agencies are subject to laws enforced by the above-mentioned agencies, but are also supposed to adhere to self-imposed codes of conduct adopted by the Direct Marketing Association. The DMA is a lobby group for the industry that promotes "responsible, data-driven marketing." The DMA promulgates member policies on a number of issues, including privacy, the environment, e-commerce, and consumer protection.

E-commerce

For marketers that conduct campaigns through the internet and social media channels, the Interactive Advertising Bureau (IAB) publishes codes of conduct that members are expected to follow. For example, the IAB expects all members to be transparent about the data and personal information they collect from consumers on the web.

ORGANIZATIONS AND RESOURCES

Advertising

The Federal Trade Commission oversees truth-in-advertising laws and regulations and offers resources to advertisers and marketers to help keep them from running afoul of the rules. On its website, the FTC publishes advisory opinions on how changes to laws or court rulings may have an impact on future enforcement decisions.
http://www.ftc.gov/policy/advisory-opinions

The Bureau of Consumer Protection, an arm of the FTC, operates an online Business Center that advises businesses how to comply with Do Not Call, CAN-SPAM, and other rules. It also offers general guidelines on advertising and marketing basics, marketing to children, health claims, and "Made in the USA" claims.
http://business.ftc.gov/advertising-and-marketing

Data protection

Various federal agencies can provide information on rules, regulations, and methods concerning the protection of consumer data and privacy, depending on the industry.

The Department of Health & Human Services publishes an online FAQ for complying with HIPAA. It also posts guidelines for covered entities and their business partners and associates.
http://www.hhs.gov

For marketers and advertisers who work within the financial services industry, the SEC has a web page devoted to the topic of protecting consumers' financial data and personally identifiable information (PII).
http://www.sec.gov/about/privacy/secprivacyoffice.htm

In Canada

Canada's Competition Bureau maintains a website that provides in-depth information on the Consumer Packaging and Labelling Act, as well as on other relevant legislation.
http://www.competitionbureau.gc.ca

How operations and production work

In the US, practices concerning corporate governance, responsibility, fiduciary obligations, and social responsibility are broadly governed by the Sarbanes-Oxley Act, passed by Congress in 2002.

Also known as the Public Company Accounting Reform and Investor Protection Act, the Sarbanes-Oxley Act of 2002 (SOX) was passed by Congress in the wake of several high-profile corporate accounting scandals—most notably at Tyco International, WorldCom, Enron, and Enron's auditor, Arthur Andersen.

SOX established the Public Company Accounting Oversight Board (PCAOB), which regulates auditing of corporate financial statements. It prohibits auditing firms from operating consulting businesses and stipulates that a company may not engage an auditor if certain members of senior management worked for that company within the prior year.

SOX requires Chief Executive Officers and Chief Financial Officers to sign and attest to the veracity of their company's financial statements. Board audit committees must have at least one independent director.

In addition to government oversight, the auditing profession has stepped up self-regulation in the wake of the financial scandals. The American Institute of Certified Public Accountants (AICPA) has in recent years issued several key Statements on Auditing Standards (SAS). SAS 70 sets audit standards for the services industry, SAS 85 requires auditors to obtain written representations from management, and SAS 99 sets out steps to be taken to detect material misstatement and accounting fraud.

In Canada

Businesses in Canada are governed by the Competition Act. The Act prohibits misleading advertising and marketing practices, and requires truthful statements concerning warranties, guarantees, and prices. It enables wronged parties to sue defendants for fraud in civil court, usually at the provincial level.

Standards and quality control

In the US, numerous independent standards organizations play a role in ensuring adherence to standards and quality control in various industries, including manufacturing, services, and health care. Many of these standards are promulgated by the International Organization for Standardization (ISO), a nongovernmental organization based in Geneva, Switzerland. ISO 9000 sets out eight principles for achieving quality control and operational consistency. ISO 9001 establishes formal processes that companies must adhere to, including the establishment of formal quality-control committees, to achieve the designation. ISO 3100 stipulates procedures for controlling and managing risk, while ISO 22,000 concerns food safety.

There are other, privately sponsored quality-control initiatives in which many large US companies participate. Beyond ISO, one of the most widely adhered to is the Six Sigma program, which was developed by Motorola and widely deployed by General Electric under former CEO Jack Welch. Six Sigma seeks to build processes aimed at removing defects from the manufacturing process.

Health, safety, and the environment

Companies operating in the US are expected to operate in a socially responsible manner that attempts to minimize environmental impact while protecting worker health and safety. The federal Environmental Protection Agency (EPA) has broad authority to interpret, apply, and enforce federal laws concerning environmental impact. The EPA regulates greenhouse gas emissions, estuarial runoff, and wetlands protection, among other things.

To maintain worker safety, corporations and even small, privately held companies must adhere to standards set by the Occupational Safety & Health Administration (OSHA). OSHA regulations require a workplace that keeps workers safe from everything from slips and falls to major industrial hazards like exposure to toxic chemicals. OSHA has the power to halt production at job sites deemed unsafe.

Food production and processing are further subject to health and safety standards set by the Food and Drug Administration (FDA) and the US Department of Agriculture's Food Safety and Inspection Service.

Liabilities, warranties, and guarantees

Companies that sell goods and services in the United States must adhere to various consumer protection laws that are generally promulgated and enforced at the state level. For example, New York State maintains a Division of Consumer Protection, California has its Department of Consumer Affairs, and the Texas Attorney General maintains a Consumer Protection unit. These organizations enforce laws concerning the terms and conditions under which goods and services are sold to the public. New York State, for instance, requires stores to post their refund policies in open view, maintain transparent rebate policies, and limit restrictive provisions on gift card redemption.

Intellectual property law and patent protection

Intellectual property laws in the US are upheld and enforced mainly through the United States Patent and Trademark Office (USPTO) and the US Copyright Office.

The USPTO adjudicates the validity of patent claims and awards patents on new designs of products, services, and business methods. The USPTO also evaluates trademark claims.

The Copyright Office registers claims and issues certificates for copyrights on literary, artistic, and design works, such as a corporate logo.

ORGANIZATIONS AND RESOURCES

Compliance and corporate responsibility

The Securities and Exchange Commission enforces Sarbanes-Oxley compliance.
http://www.sec.gov

Standards and quality control

ISO's site provides full information on all of the standards overseen by the organization.
http://www.iso.org

Health, safety, and the environment

OSHA's website offers information on new regulations, compliance tips, and enforcement actions.
https://www.osha.gov

The EPA has online tools for checking compliance with federal environmental regulations.
http://www.epa.gov

Information on food safety laws and practices can be obtained from the FDA's site.
http://www.fda.gov

Liability, warranties, and guarantees

In the US, consumer protection generally falls to the state level. Individual state websites provide information on regulations concerning public sale of goods and services.

Intellectual property law

The USPTO is the main resource for all information concerning the filing of patent applications.
http://www.uspto.gov

The US Copyright Office website includes information about the copyright process and fees.
http://copyright.gov

In Canada

Information on corporate law and operations in Canada can be obtained from the federal government's Competition Bureau.
http://www.competitionbureau.gc.ca
http://www.bureaudelaconcurrence.gc.ca

Index

Acknowledgments

Dorling Kindersley would like to thank Douglas Bell and Debra Wolter for editorial assistance; Margaret McCormack for the index; and Nicola Gary, Vaibhav Rastogi, and Riti Sodhi for design assistance.

Credits

DK would like to thank Wessex Water for their kind permission to reproduce sections of their 2013 annual report and accounts on **pp.100–123**; the Radio Advertising Bureau for permission to reproduce the graph on **p.212**; and Upstream/YouGov for permission to reproduce the graph on **p.214**.

Sources of statistics and quotes:
p.13: Roach, B., "Corporate Power in a Global Economy," Global Development and Environment Institute, Tufts University, 2007; **p.15:** www.brusselsnetwork.be/eu-news-m/563-smes-contribution-to-a-dynamic-europe.html; **p.16:** UK government business population estimates 2013; **p.18:** Biery, M.E., "4 Things You Don't Know About Private Companies," forbes.com, May 26, 2013; **p.19:** www.nyse.com/why-nyse; **p.24:** The Nonprofit Almanac, 2012; **p.26:** Kauffman Index of Entrepreneurial Activity; **p.27:** France Digitale; **p.29:** Harvard Business School; **p.30:** IBISWorld; **p.32:** Panel Study of Entrepreneurial Dynamics, University of Michigan, 2008; **p.36:** Entrepreneurs Index report, 2013; **p.39:** National Business Incubation Association; **p.41:** Mergermarket M&A Trends Report, 2013; **p.43:** Humber, Y., "Japan Mergers Fall to Nine-Year Low as Yen Volatility Surges," bloomberg.com, July 8, 2013; **p.45:** Hashem, N., "Demerger Study: Analysing the value of demergers through share price performance," Deloitte & Touche, March 2002; **p.47:** Grant Thornton International Business Report, 2014; **p.49:** Craven, N., "KKR Agrees to Buy Alliance Boots, Beating Guy Hands," bloomberg.com, April 24, 2007; **p.51:** "Employee attitudes and the recession," Chartered Institute of Personnel and Development, 2009; **p.53:** Huang, S., "Zombie Boards: Board Tenure and Firm Performance," INSEAD—Finance;

Singapore Management University—School of Accountancy, July 29, 2013; **p.55:** Tribbett, C., "Splitting The CEO and Chairman Roles—Yes Or No?", *The Corporate Board*, Russell Reynolds Associates, Vol. XXXIII, no. 197, November/December 2012; **p.56:** "Born to be digital: How leading CIOs are preparing for a digital transformation," EY, 2014; **p.57:** Guadalupe, M., Li, H., Wulf, J., "Who Lives in the C-Suite? Organizational Structure and the Division of Labor in Top Management" Working Paper, Harvard Business School, June 18, 2013; **p.59:** National Bureau of Economic Research, 2003; **p.60:** Kappel, V., Schmidt, P., Ziegler, A., "Human rights abuse and corporate stock performance—an event study analysis," white paper, December 21, 2009; **p.63:** "The Sustainability Edge: Sustainability Update," Bloomberg LP, 2011; **p.65:** Booz & Company, 2013; **p.67 left and right:** Shaw, M., "Communication networks," in L. Berkowitz (ed.), *Advances in Experimental Social Psychology*, Academic Press, 1964, pp.111–147; **p.69:** Econsultancy; **p.71:** Bowman, H., Singh, H., Useem, M., Bhadury, R., "When Does Restructuring Improve Economic Performance?", *California Management Review*, 41:2, 1999, p.48; **p.73:** "The Rise of the Networked Enterprise: Web 2.0 finds its payday," *McKinsey Quarterly*, 2010; **p.77:** Hartman, C., "Managing the Journey: Interview with CEO Ralph Stayer," inc.com, November 1, 1990; **p.79:** International Labour Organization Global Employment Trends 2014; **p.80:** Society for Human Resources Management; **p.82:** 2013 Jobvite Social Recruiting Survey; **p.87:** Gallup State of the Global Workplace 2013; **p.93:** Ruddick, G., "John Lewis pays staff more than £200m in bonuses for first time," *The Telegraph*, March 7, 2013; **p.95:** "Insights and Trends: Current Portfolio, Programme, and Project Management Practices: The third global survey on the current state of project management," PwC, 2012; **p.97:** Barbara & Allan Pease, *The Definitive Book of Body Language*, 2006; **p.100:** Caux Round Table, "Lehman Brothers, Repo 105 Sales, Lawyers and Ethical Abuse," April 2, 2010; **p.103:** Occupational Outlook Handbook (2014–15

Edition), US Bureau of Labor Statistics; **p.107:** Wessex Water, *Striking the Balance: Annual Review and Accounts 2013*, p.7; **p.111:** www.accounting-degree.org/scandals; **p.125:** The AA; **p.131:** The Association of Accountants and Financial Professionals in Business; **p.135:** Pangburn, E., "Cash Flow Problems in Small Business Startups and How to Tackle Them," modestmoney.com, January 28, 2014; **p.136:** "Forecasting with confidence," KPMG, 2007; **p.141:** MasterCard, December 2005; **p.142:** Ernst & Young 2003 Survey of Management Accounting; **p.145:** "Management Barometer, Price Waterhouse Coopers and BSI Global Research Inc," 2002; **p.147:** Gartner Research "Predicts 2013: Business Process Reinvention is Vital to Digital Business Transformation"; **p.149:** www.inc.com/encyclopedia/financial-ratios.html; **p.151:** Gartner Research "Predicts 2013: Business Process Reinvention is Vital to Digital Business Transformation"; **p.152:** US Securities and Exchange Commission, cited in *Forbes*, 2010; **p.154:** Graham, J., Harvey, C., "The Theory and Practice of Corporate Finance: Evidence from the Field," *Journal of Financial Economics*, Vol. 60, 2001, pp.187–243; **p.157:** Credit Management Research Centre, Leeds University Business School, 2008; **p.158:** Domowitz, I., Glen, J., Madhavan, A., "International Evidence on Aggregate Corporate Financing Decisions," in A. Demirgüç-Kunt and R. Levine (eds.), *Financial Structure and Economic Growth: A Cross-Country Comparison of Banks, Markets and Development*, The MIT Press, 2004, p.274; **p.161:** The U.S. Small Business Administration; **p.163:** Index characteristics, NYSE Composite Index; **p.165:** Ewing, T., Gomes, L., Gasparino, C., "VA Linux Registers a 698% Price Pop," *The Wall Street Journal*, December 10, 1999; **p.171:** *Bank for International Settlements Quarterly Review*, March 2014; **p.181:** Adams, M., "Findings from the PDMA Research Foundation CPAS Benchmarking," 2004; **p.185:** The Federal Trade Commission; **p.186:** Marketing guru Peter Doyle; **p.187 graph:** Based on US hospitality industry guidelines; **p.188:** Columbus, L., "IDC: 87% Of Connected Devices Sales By 2017 Will Be

Tablets And Smartphones," forbes.com, September 12, 2013; **p.190:** Gartner Research, 2013; **p.193:** US Bureau of Labor Statistics 2012; **p.197:** she-conomy.com; **p.198:** The Pareto principle, suggested by management expert Joseph M. Juran and part of long-tail marketing theory; **p.201:** Rizen Creative 2012 Idaho Marketing Tactic Survey; **p.203 doughnut charts:** Barnard, J., "ZenithOptimedia Forecasts 4.1% Growth in Global Adspend in 2013," zenithoptimedia.com, December 3, 2012; **p.203:** Statista, 2014; **p.205:** Shaw, C., Ivens, J., *Building Great Customer Experiences*, Palgrave Macmillan, 2002; **p.206:** JWT Intelligence, "Data point: Constantly connected Millennials crave sensory experiences," 2013; **p.211:** Axonn Research Content Marketing Trends in 2013; **p.212:** Statista, 2013; **p.212 bar chart:** "Radio: The ROI Multiplier," Radio Advertising Bureau (www.rab.co.uk), 2013, p.23; **p.213:** YouGov for Deloitte, 2010; **p.214:** eMarketer, September 2014; **p.214 bar chart:** 2012 Digital Advertising Attitudes Report, Upstream/YouGov, p.8; **p.215:** eMarketer, January 2014; **p.216:** Direct Marketing Association 2010 Response Rate Trend Report; **p.218:** Holman, D., Batt. R., Holtgrewe, U., "The Global Call Center Report, International Perspectives on Management and Employment," 2007; **p.221:** Hubspot 2013 State of Inbound Marketing; **p.223:** HubSpot 2013 State of Inbound Marketing; **p.225:** comScore, 2011; **p.226:** "Apple: One billion iTunes podcast subscriptions and counting," macworld.com, 2013; **p.229:** Federal Statistical Office of Germany (Destatis), 2013; **p.230:** Chitika Insights, "The Value of Google Result Positioning," June 7, 2013; **p.233:** The Bloom Group LLC, "Integrating Marketing and Business Development in Professional Services Firms," 2007; **p.237 doughnut chart:** Content Marketing Institute/ MarketingProfs: 2014 B2B Content Marketing Trends—North America; **p.238:** MarketingSherpa 2012 Website Optimization Benchmark Report; **p.241:** Probstein, S., "Listen to the Voice of the Customer," destinationCRM.com, April 1, 2009; **p.243:** IBM research report 2011, "From Stretched to Strengthened: Insights From the Global Chief Marketing Officer Study"; **p.247:** Harvey Nash CIO survey 2014; **p.249:** Barua, A., Mani, D.,

Mukherjee, R., "Measuring the Business Impacts of Effective Data," The University of Texas at Austin/Sybase, 2010; **p.250:** Vanson Bourne Intelligent Market Research, 2013; **p.253:** Accenture, "CMOs: Time for digital transformation or risk being left on the sidelines," CMO Insights 2014; **p.255:** "Marketing ROI in the Era of Big Data: The 2012 BRITE/NYAMA Marketing in Transition Study," Columbia Business School's Center on Global Brand Leadership and the New York American Marketing Association; **p.256:** Independent Oracle Users Group, "A New Dimension to Data Warehousing: 2011 IOUG Data Warehousing Survey"; **p.259:** Forrester Consulting, "Delivering New Levels Of Personalization In Consumer Engagement," November 2013; **p.263:** Celebrus Technologies, Digital Marketing Insights report 2014; **p.265:** Nucleus Research June 2014—Report O128: "CRM pays back $8.71 for every dollar spent"; **p.267:** Symantec Internet Security Threat Report 2014, Vol. 19; **p.271:** World Bank via www.themanufacturer.com/uk-manufacturing-statistics; **p.273:** Hall, M., Jury, L., "I do … cost a lot: Weddings by the numbers," CNN.com, August 9, 2013; **p.275:** UK Agriculture and Horticulture Development Board 2014; **p.277:** International Organization of Motor Vehicle Manufacturers, www.worldometers.info/ cars; **p.279:** Scanlon, J., "How Mars Built a Business," businessweek.com, December 28, 2009; **p.281:** Paperchase; **p.284:** Intellectual Property report, Kilburn and Strode LLP; **p.287:** Statista, 2014; **p.289:** Toyota Motor Corporation; **p.291:** Dell Computers; **p.293:** Stratton, B., "How Disneyland Works," *Quality Progress*, Vol. 24, no. 7, 1991; **p.295:** Information Week; **p.297:** Denning, S., "Wikispeed: How a 100 mpg Car Was Developed in 3 Months," forbes.com, May 10, 2012; **p.298:** Bernard, J. M., *Business at the Speed of Now: Fire Up Your People, Thrill Your Customers, and Crush Your Competitors*, Wiley, 2011; **p.301:** Eurostat; **p.303:** Mintel; **p.307:** Artefact; **p.309:** "Singapore supermarket saves 4.5m Singaporean dollars a year with standards," iso.org, March 25, 2014; **p.310:** "The end of cheap China," economist.com, March 10, 2012; **p.313:** High Pay Centre; **p.315:** "Pegatron expanding China factory capacity for Apple iPhone 6 production," tech.firstpost.com, March 18, 2014; **p.317:**

Walmart; **p.319:** British Sandwich Association; **p.320:** "How Jack Welch Runs GE," businessweek.com, 1998; **p.321:** De Feo, J., Barnard, W., *Juran Institute's Six Sigma Breakthrough and Beyond: Quality Performance Breakthrough Methods*, Tata McGraw-Hill Publishing, 2003; **p.323:** Council of Supply Chain Management Professionals; **p.325:** A .T. Kearney, Internet Value Chain Economics report 2010; **p.327:** Corbett, M. F., *The Outsourcing Revolution*, Dearborn, 2004; **p.331:** "The Hidden Value in Reverse Logistics," Deloitte, January 2014; **p.333:** Global Benchmarking Network, "Global Survey on Business Improvement and Benchmarking," 2010; **p.334:** Pilot, S., "Companies are embracing corporate responsibility in their annual reports," *The Guardian*, September 29, 2011.